Psychoanalytic Perspectives on Women, Menstruation and Secondary Amenorrhea

"I can be a mother, a wife, a daughter, a sister and a woman without having periods." This book explores two of the oldest and most important symbols of all time: menstruation and secondary amenorrhea. Women of menstruating age commonly experience secondary amenorrhea – a cessation of periods – but most people have never heard of the term, nor do they realise what it represents. Danielle Redland's curiosity as to why this is posits that menstrual conditions need to be decoded, not just simply treated.

Surveying menstruation and Secondary Amenorrhea (SA) principally from a psychoanalytic perspective, with sociocultural, historical, political and religious angles also examined, *Psychoanalytic Perspectives on Women, Menstruation and Secondary Amenorrhea* draws secondary amenorrhea out of the shadows of its menstruating counterpart, and explores how narratives of womanhood and statehood dominate. Chapters on blood ideology and war amenorrhea, on Freud's treatment of Emma Eckstein and on the psycho-mythology of Pygmalion, present the reader with visions beyond patriarchy towards more thoughtful ideas on the feminine, challenging assumptions about gender, identity and what is deemed "good" for women. Rich in clinical examples, the book locates menses and their cessation at the heart of personal experience and examines psychosomatic phenomena, the link between psyche and body and the value of interpretation. From the author's own analysis to a variety of cases linked to hysteria, anorexia, stress, trauma, abuse, helplessness and hopelessness, individual stories and narratives are sensitively recovered and carefully revealed.

This refreshing example of multi-layered research and psychoanalytic enquiry by a new, female writer will be of great interest to psychologists, psychotherapists, healthcare and social work professionals and readers of gender studies, history, politics and literature.

Danielle Redland was awarded her PhD from the psychoanalytic studies department at Goldsmiths University of London in 2018. She works as a psychotherapist in private practice and as an assessor and intake counsellor in the charitable sector, as well as being clinical manager of a counselling referral service. Born and raised in Manchester, she now lives in London with her family.

"An extraordinarily compelling panorama of this still-taboo subject, with an original and innovative focus on secondary amenorrhea. Redland ranges from the social, cultural, historical and psychological role of blood in human experience to Freud's shameful encounter with it in the case of Emma Eckstein. The writing is scholarly and sensitive, and the book will find a warm reception on women's studies as well as psychoanalytic studies. As one who examined the work when it was still a PhD thesis, I can confirm that the transition to book form has been achieved to a superb degree."

Andrew Samuels, Former Professor of Analytical Psychology, University of Essex

"What does it mean when a woman of menstruating age stops bleeding and what does it matter to her or to us? Working through anthropology, myth and literature, Danielle Redland links the cessation of menses to unconscious registers suggesting that there is a communication of the psyche that looks to the body to find expression; she shows how these themes recur not only in cultural and historical narratives world-wide but also in examples she gives from the consulting room.

In this highly original and important text, Redland offers a psychoanalytic perspective on Ovid's *Metamorphosis* and George Bernard Shaw's *Pygmalion* while also examining the role of the male practitioner – analyst, doctor or both – in a study of Freud's failed treatment of Emma Eckstein. In a brand-new take on the dynamic between body and mind, Danielle Redland presses the question: is such an opposition still viable? The result is a ground-breaking analysis of what this means for women, symptoms and psychoanalysis itself."

Christopher Hauke, Jungian analyst, Senior Lecturer at Goldsmiths, University of London. Author of *Jung and the Postmodern: The Interpretation of Realities*

Psychoanalytic Perspectives on Women, Menstruation and Secondary Amenorrhea

Danielle Redland

Routledge
Taylor & Francis Group

LONDON AND NEW YORK

First published 2020
by Routledge
2 Park Square, Milton Park, Abingdon, Oxon OX14 4RN

and by Routledge
52 Vanderbilt Avenue, New York, NY 10017

Routledge is an imprint of the Taylor & Francis Group, an informa business

© 2020 Danielle Redland

British Library Cataloguing-in-Publication Data
A catalogue record for this book is available from the British Library

Library of Congress Cataloging-in-Publication Data
Names: Redland, Danielle, 1972- author.
Title: Psychoanalytic perspectives on women, menstruation, and secondary amenorrhea / Danielle Redland.
Description: Abingdon, Oxon ; New York, NY : Routledge, 2020. | Includes bibliographical references and index.
Identifiers: LCCN 2019058842 (print) | LCCN 2019058843 (ebook) | ISBN 9780367467005 (hbk) | ISBN 9780367466985 (pbk) | ISBN 9781003030478 (ebk)
Subjects: LCSH: Women and psychoanalysis. | Psychoanalysis and feminism. | Menstruation. | Amenorrhea.
Classification: LCC BF173 .R3668 2020 (print) | LCC BF173 (ebook) | DDC 150.19/5–dc23
LC record available at https://lccn.loc.gov/2019058842
LC ebook record available at https://lccn.loc.gov/2019058843

ISBN: 978-0-367-46700-5 (hbk)
ISBN: 978-0-367-46698-5 (pbk)
ISBN: 978-1-003-03047-8 (ebk)

Typeset in Bembo
by Swales & Willis, Exeter, Devon, UK

For Sarah, Evie, Jonathan and Benjamin

"It is curious (odd, unconsciously significant?) that the menses is rarely discussed not only in the literature, but actually in the 'course' of an analysis."

(Christopher Bollas, psychoanalyst and writer:
personal communication, 13 September 2016)

Contents

Acknowledgements

My psychoanalytic explorations have taken me to places beyond my wildest dreams, quite literally. My first analysis caused untold damage but is behind me now. I cannot overestimate the value of sublimating all of my angst and *tsuris* into writing my thesis and, in turn, this book. There were many people who were involved in this reparative process: They were around and about, in one way or another healing the wounds. This book is for all of them.

Change can be both a blessing and a curse and I would like to first thank my husband Adam. Despite unwittingly being caught up in a storm he was nevertheless able to trust in the potential that lay ahead. Our children too creatively furthered and enabled camaraderie and connections. They have been remarkable. To my parents, I am appreciative of their continued love, and to my brothers, thinking back to those days playing cricket in the garden always makes me smile.

This experience has been about building and rebuilding and my thanks go to Christopher Hauke, my PhD supervisor whose approach to psychoanalysis and his literary craftsmanship renders him a master builder. I could not have asked for a better mentor. To Professor Andrew Samuels who encouraged me to rework my thesis into a book, thank you for your suggestions and corrections borne out of my viva. Kate Hawes, Senior Publisher at Routledge seamlessly accepted my work for publication for which I am sincerely grateful and thank you to editorial assistant Hannah Wright and copy-editor Jeanne Brady.

I find projects like mine interesting in that you can never tell who will want to open their door to an enquiring stranger. Some perhaps did not hear the bell ring. Luckily, those that did made my search worthwhile. I boldly emailed Christopher Bollas with questions on menstruation and psychoanalysis. He replied almost immediately and I remember an equal exchange of thoughts and ideas. We covered a lot of ground in a short space of time. My fantasy is that he was at an airport in the United States of America, waiting for a domestic flight, scrolling through his emails to while away the time. And up popped my request. Riccardo Lombardi and Cynthia Rousso were also generous in their correspondence and easy to locate. So too, "Mary," "Belinda," "Rachel" and their families who gave me permission to share their stories for the first time in print, I am most grateful. Patients and their narratives are at the heart of this work.

I also want to mention Rabbi David Mason and Mr Demetrios Econo-mides, who represent markers of stability in my life. Tina Simmonds, who until recently supervised all of my clinical work, deserves a special mention for the way in which she held my practice. Experience counts.

In the spring of 2015, around Easter time, I telephoned psychoanalyst Francis Grier so as to put an end to my analysand wanderings in search of a safe house. We met three times as part of an assessment and he referred me to psychoanalyst (and former England cricket captain) Michael Brearley. That was the start of a new chapter. What luck. Indeed, what a blessed relief.

To old friends Sharon, Dani, Jessa, Yael and Carolyn thank you. Last but by no means least, to my canine companion Toby for all of our wonderful walks together in the woods and in the fields, often without a plan or course of action. We go around the houses and then … we come home.

Introduction

Red lines

Women and men continue their efforts to dismantle the menstrual taboo with conversations increasingly striking in their powerful socio-political, cultural and feminist lines of enquiry. Whilst some literary works focus on the anthropology and history of "the curse" with others designed to empower and seize the magic of menstruation, we have managed to reach a point where beliefs, superstitions and stories go hand in hand with evidence, facts and plain truths. Curiosity to explore and better understand the significance of puberty, menstruation, pregnancy and menopause, and the ways in which these events impact on us all, are increasingly allowed for. So too through better education and resources accessible to more women, young and old, and through a growing knowledge and a desire for that knowledge to explore the roots of the taboo, people feel less intimidated and more emboldened to articulate their thoughts and feelings on such matters. Importantly though, in certain quarters silence still prevails and the wish for dialogue is sublimated into research and observation focussing on cultures, religions and political systems which by their very design limit our engagement with these natural phenomenon and the women situated in them. For example a cross-sectional survey on menstrual patterns and disorders handed out by a team of researchers in Egypt to eight hundred secondary school teenagers resulted in an overall response rate of just 51.5%, considerably low compared to other studies. This was mainly due to girls and their mothers refusing to participate, the menstrual taboo defining it as shameful, dirty and a hygienic crisis that must not be spoken about (Adbelmoty et al., 2015).

Many similar studies both in developing and developed countries report a higher than expected prevalence of menstrual disorders, highlighting a need for further re-education by schools and health specialists. Whilst sex education in schools has been compulsory in England since 2017, only in 2020 is menstrual health included in the curriculum. Across the globe, an estimated 2 billion women bleed each month. In Third World and developing countries around 60% of girls miss school when they are menstruating due in part to stigma, but also because of practical issues such as lacking sanitary wear or easy access to toilets. Closer to home, in the UK, teenagers feel angst when menstruating at school because often they aren't allowed to go to the toilet during lesson time or take their bags to the toilet when sitting exams. An increasing number of girls from low-income families are truanting because they don't have sanitary wear. Many of them don't want to trouble their mothers or burden them with having to find the money to buy the essentials and so they keep quiet or they wrap socks or toilet roll around their knickers. The British Government in 2019 announced plans to develop a scheme to provide free sanitary products in secondary schools, colleges and universities. In January 2020, the Department of Education launched its free sanitary product scheme across all schools and colleges in England. Wales has a similar scheme as does Scotland which has extended its commitment to tackling period poverty by making products available in public places such as libraries and leisure centres. Some girls though are skipping school for a different reason – because they are unclear as to what is going on with their bodies. Recent studies still alarmingly show nearly half of all girls at menarche aren't really sure what's happening. Mothers are not preparing their daughters for their first menstrual bleed and they themselves might have their own complexes that prevent them from speaking openly about it. For psychoanalysts such as Mary Chadwick this is significant in that it has resulted in "sadistic manifestations of the woman in her treatment of the girl at her first menstrual period" (Chadwick, 1932: 34).

Chadwick's *The Psychological Problems in Menstruation* (1932) was one of the first psychoanalytic works on menstruation that explored unconscious as well as conscious motivators that organise our regard towards menstruation. Analysts that followed continued to paint menarche as an anxiety -provoking, dangerous and negative event that might attract maternal envy and revenge from the ageing mother as she sites her blossoming coming-of-age daughter. Menarche is the point at which everything changes. The adolescence's new acquisition brings with it her greatest task to date. It complicates the development of an identity, which Erikson skilfully describes as "a conscious sense of individual uniqueness … an unconscious striving for a continuity of experience, and … as a solidarity with the group's ideals" (Erikson, 1968: 208).

The need for support exists in all adolescent girls but is too often overlooked or unfulfilled. The anomalous, negative perceptions of menstruation are entrenched into our reality and clearly more work needs to be done to create a new version of reality that reflects our changed world.

Menstruation has always been the signifier of that which separates man from woman. It is the hallmark of the feminine position but, as we create a new pattern of discourse and if public perceptions change, we have to find room beyond the binary model to a more inclusive and open space, which includes the experiences of those in LGBT communities. It is trans men whose monthly periods put them particularly at risk from both external and internal world threats. Guys in the locker rooms are urinating whilst trans men are trying to change their tampons in secret. Many are targets of violence. Intra-psychically, they are at risk of self-harm and psychological damage, often undetected before it is too late. In the pursuit of defeminisation, many seek to biologically suppress their menses by losing a lot of weight. The few studies that exist show unquestionably the link between this group of people and anorexia and bulimia. For clinics such as the Gender Identity Development Service at the Tavistock and Portman NHS Trust in Britain, the difficulty in trying to help patients who come to pursue sex reassignment is to accurately assess if the gender dysphoria is real and sufficiently thought through or in early stages, in part fantasy. The clinic has come under heavy criticism, quite rightly so, for too readily accommodating the wishes of those who seek treatment, those who are too young to "know". Prescribing cross-sex hormones results in infertility. In 2016, approximately 1,1419 children were referred by their GP to the clinic. Of those who were pre-adolescent, around 80 per cent changed their mind and of those who were in adolescence, 80 per cent pursued treatment. Commentators strongly advocate that as a society we should be considering not that these girls want to become boys but that they do not want to become women. Importantly, an investigative look into their histories shows links to psychiatric comorbidity such as depression, anxiety, autism and self-harm, with many having experienced bullying at school that required intervention. This is extremely significant and we are slowly but surely coming to realise that the biological presentation of secondary amenorrhea (the interruption/cessation of menses) in women needs to be thought about as a marker in a wider picture made up of physiology and psychology. The narratives behind the presentation of secondary amenorrhea are often psychologically complex. Psychosexual immaturity, neurotic or psychotic disturbances, histories of trauma, abuse, neglect, conflict and confusion are some of the things that can ground amenorrhea *in situ*. Vitally, the very absence of menses can be the most visible sign indicating that a woman's physical and mental health need attention. This is the main reason for me wanting to write this book: to give full and proper attention to secondary amenorrhea that it so rightly deserves and to work out for myself, what my own amenorrhea was both revealing and hiding. I shall explain more on that shortly, but first the science bit.

Science and psyche

Put simply, Secondary Amenorrhea (SA) describes a cessation or an interruption in the menstrual cycle, sometimes prolonged, in women of menstruating and childbearing age. If not the healthy accompaniment to pregnancy or breastfeeding (the most common causes of amenorrhea which are ruled out before making a diagnostic evaluation), or if not linked to birth control medication, it is a condition that should be investigated but too often is not. The *British Medical Journal* classifies SA as a lack of menses in a non-pregnant female for at least three cycles of her previous interval or lack of menses for six months in a patient who was previously menstruating.

Prevalence of SA in women who have previously menstruated regularly is approximately 5–7% in the US and 3–4% in Britain. In developing countries, the frequency ranges from 5–9 per cent, similar to the figures from population-based surveys in Europe. The numbers are particularly over-represented in competitive endurance athletes (5–60%), ballet dancers (19–44%), enlistment (73% of women entering the US Military Academy), army recruits (25%) and women entering a religious order (16%). The higher prevalence in war and famine is unmistakable. In a groundbreaking publication, Dr Frances L. Drew (1961) collected together previously sourced data to examine the epidemiology of SA and its frequency rates. Drew gathered information from medical studies of endocrinology, psychiatric studies and concentration camp studies. The amenorrheic body was found to be entrenched in a system of intra-psychic vulnerability, neuroendocrine disturbances and external stress. Results ranged from 1.6% amongst gynaecological patients to 100% amongst female prisoners awaiting execution. Drew found the highest frequency rates were related to separation from home and family and to the extent of the threat associated with such separation. The figures were low during peacetime but rose to 16–51% following the bombings of Nagasaki and Hiroshima, highest amongst those closer to ground zero. Bear in mind that the standard rate at the time of Drew's publication was 4–6%. Different studies produce variable results from 0.3% amongst 734 women from Warsaw, Poland (Skierska et al., 1996) to 4.6% amongst 3,743 women in Copenhagen, Denmark (Munster et al., 1992 cited in Van De Walle & Renne, 2001). *Regulating Menstruation* (2001) highlights the ambiguity in the way in which data on secondary amenorrhea is collected and the differing benchmarks researchers refer to in indicating a return of menses. Historical texts that locate and describe "suppressed menses" are fascinating but lack numbers to formulate accurate data; still today "secondary amenorrhea continues to remain relatively undocumented, perhaps as a consequence of the discovery of the regulating properties of synthetic hormones that have reduced the need for greater understanding of menstrual irregularity" (Vane De Walle & Renne, 2001: 120).

Data on lactational and postpartum amenorrhea is also ambiguous. What constitutes a return to menses? Spotting or consecutive menstrual cycles? What is the context and what other factors (real and perceived) are necessary in analysing the amenorrheic event? Malnutrition, famine, disease, anaemia, abortion, stillbirth, supernatural spirits, the evil eye?

The epidemiology of secondary amenorrhea has been shifting focus onto psychological correlates: Stress and fear are seen as the primary psychological causes, their emotional content able to alter the sequence and patterning of hormonal release.

Whilst many cases of stress-induced amenorrhea are easily reversible, with menses resuming from between six to eighteen weeks, others are much more prolonged and persistent. These correlate to rooted psychological disruption and psychiatric disturbances, revealed to us notably through psychoanalytic literature. I have interspersed many of these cases throughout this book so that we might reach beyond the concreteness of the presenting problem. For the reader at the outset, central to an understanding of secondary amenorrhea is the composition of four important organ systems and the way in which they interrelate to one another. They are the central nervous system, the anterior lobe of the pituitary, the ovaries and the uterus. They are linked together on an axis and any disruption to this axis causes a schism resulting in amenorrhea: "Amenorrhea may be caused by an organic or functional defect in any one of these four interdependent links, the dysfunction of one being reflected in the structural or functional disturbances in one or more of the others" (Björo, 1966:70).

Discounting physiological amenorrhea such as before menarche (the first period), in pregnancy, in menopause, lactational (breastfeeding) or postoperative (for example, following a hysterectomy), and ruling out the use of oral contraceptives, amenorrhea can be categorised as either an organic or a non-organic condition. Examples of organic cases include anatomic defects in the genital tract, ovary insufficiency, chronic oligo-ovulation or anovulation and other associations to genetic patterns, endocrine systems and hormonal imbalances. A cessation of menses is often a significant precursory symptom of a serious medical illness which left undiagnosed could lead to osteoporosis, endometrial hyperplasia, or endometrial cancer. It might also be a symptom of endometrial tuberculosis or AIDS wasting, notably in developing countries. It can also be a side effect of some medication such as antipsychotic drugs, antidepressants and cancer chemotherapy. Lifestyle factors, such as low body weight and excessive exercise, will contribute to amenorrhea. As in cases of anorexia, secondary amenorrhea is linked to metabolic and psychogenic (of psychological origin) disorders. A psycho-endocrinological process triggers the amenorrhea and the malnutrition perpetuates it. In terms of non-organic diseases, there are early records such as Buchan's 1797 *Treatise on the Prevention and Cure of Diseases* of what is now commonly referred to as stress or emotional amenorrhea, formally classified as Psychogenic. Grief, sudden fright and anxiety can each "obstruct the menstrual flux" (Buchan, 1797: 368). Psychogenic amenorrhea is also frequently interwoven in the aetiology of neuroses and some psychotic states. In historical treatises, secondary amenorrhea and menstruation were written about extensively. Doctors desired to control and master each of them. Today amenorrhea is still widely viewed as an anomaly and an error that needs correcting with medical intervention but the debate as to what constitutes "normal" and what menstruation offers a woman is gaining traction.

Menstrual matrix

The dominant Hippocratic Tradition was that amenorrhea threatened a woman's "matrix". In The Middle Ages, lack of menses meant non-conception, without much understanding of the specific role menstrual fluid played in reproduction. Menses as a "visible red badge of femininity" (Dewhurst, 1972: 70) is an ancient concept. More recently, in the 1950s, menses was central to the invention of hormonal contraceptives. However, the contraceptive pill, which was first approved for use to alleviate menstrual disorders and is still prescribed to treat symptoms associated with menstruation, has long been criticised as a man-made imposition of recurrent "unnatural" bleeding prescribed by medics and pushed by pharmaceutical companies. The "pill" halts ovarian cycling and makes changes to the endometrial and cervical site required for fertility. It is marketed as giving women a "choice", but many argue that it propagates menstrual-related stigma. In her book *Issues of Blood: The Politics of Menstruation*, Sophie Laws (1990) quotes Dewhurst to make the point that too often women are "cheaply and conveniently" put on the pill. Laura Fingerson (2006) in *Girls in Power: Gender, Body and Menstruation in Adolescence* explains how the inventors of the contraceptive pill devised the three-week-off and one-week-on menstrual cycle not based on medical science but on the fact that women would feel reassured by a pill that replicates nature. The goal was to invent a successful and lucrative commodity. Thus, the contraceptive pill and its mimicking of monthly menstruation was believed to be more desirable and normal than amenorrhea. However as Alma Gottlieb and Thomas Buckley write in their seminal book *Blood Magic, The Anthropology of Menstruation*:

> the scientists who developed the contraceptive pill assumed both the normalcy and desirability of regular periods. Yet there is strong evidence that "normal" monthly periods are probably not that at all, historically and cross-culturally, but rather are most likely biologically anomalous products or particular cultural systems at specific historical conjunctions.
>
> (Buckley & Gottlieb, 1988: 44)

There has been a lot of research looking at the natural effects of breastfeeding and produced amenorrhea and the ways in which they are good for a woman's health, with menstrual periods viewed as disadvantageous. Indeed in tribal, religious and/or non-industrialised communities where women are often pregnant or breastfeeding, it is more common to have amenorrhea than menses. Brazilian gynaecologist Elsimar Courtinho argues that amenorrhea is more natural a state than menstruation. In *Is Menstruation Obsolete?* (1999), Courtinho along with endocrinologist Sheldon Segal writes that for preindustrial women "continuous menstrual cycling is not a natural attribute of human females" (Courtinho & Segal, 1999: 2). They cite the Mali tribe where women menstruate about a hundred times in their lives compared to western women who menstruate approximately 350–400 times. They suggest that regular repeated menstruation might be harmful to the health and well-being of a woman: "Recurrent menstruation ... is a needless loss of blood" (Courtinho & Segal, 1999: 159).

Other studies support this view and many women and physicians would prefer the choice of induced amenorrhea to monthly periods. The logic is that in waiting for and in getting their periods many experience premenstrual syndrome, stress, anxiety and pain, endometriosis, cramps, or anaemia. They might have to take time off from work/school which costs them economically, socially and personally. If bleeding is difficult and if there is no reason why women need to menstruate each month, tweaking the system with pharmacological amenorrhea is a practical option that offers them a resolution to their problems. They are reassured that this has no long-term negative health consequences while offering them more control and improved relief. The reality is that not many women do opt for an induced amenorrheic state because they believe that menstruation is a more natural condition associated with femaleness, fertility, health and youth. Similarly, many women who use oral contraceptives are uncomfortable staying on them long term. They feel the artificial bleeding is unnatural and coming off them reassures them of their womanhood (WHO, 1981).

Both menstruation and amenorrhea are regarded with intrinsic ambivalence but amenorrhea is perhaps considered far more elusive, enigmatic and outside the natural order of things. It hardly features in contemporary books on menstruation, and when it does it's hidden, rarely listed in the indices. It is unusual to see its formal title used except in medical literature and even though it is imbued in our everyday lives it doesn't have the euphemisms or slang words that menstruation has – "Aunt Flo," "have the painters in" for example. Research into menstrual issues is far from dry and I have found that people have rather a lot to say on the matter, many questioning their embryonic perceptions and projections as to what it all means. Presenting at conferences, men, notably middle-aged husbands and fathers, often come up to me invigorated by the idea that when they get home they will broach the subject of periods with their daughters. One female colleague was intrigued as to why her good friend in her early forties suddenly stopped menstruating soon after her mother had died even though she felt no psychological blockages with regards to this loss. One young anorexic woman described her newly found lean stature and amenorrheic state as that which separated her out and protected her from the "fat cows" who used to bully her at school.

My own amenorrhea linked me back to my childhood as the youngest of three, playing cricket with my two older brothers, happy to be one of the lads. I would field while my brothers played bat and ball. If the corky went over the neighbour's fence, I retrieved it. I didn't fight against the hierarchy, I didn't envy them having a penis and I didn't want them envying me having a womb. In some representational way, my secondary amenorrhea in adolescence meant I had both male and female attributes and not significantly lacking in either I could be the sister and the brother to my older male siblings. My alliance with patriarchy runs deep and the nature of relationships between fathers and daughters, sisters and brothers, between female patients and their male doctors, between female and male representations are picked up many times in this book and are central to our exploring the nature of menses and non menses. The role of the "father" is not always a threat to the sisterhood but can instead be an edifying and strengthening symbol in a woman's growth and development. It seems more so that the defiance of daughters is historically felt by fathers to be irrational and disordered. Secondary amenorrhea is a signifier in this defiance against patriarchy and we shall see the lengths that fathers referring their daughters to male doctors went to in order to stamp out this blight. Doctors were obsessed with treating menstrual irregularities resulting in calamitous consequences. So too Sigmund Freud and his colleagues in their investigations into hysteria and the associated menstrual irregularities were fixated on regulating menstruation at whatever cost to the patient. Chapter 6 will look in detail at Freud's failed treatment of his first analysand Emma Eckstein, a young woman presenting with hysteria and menstrual disorder. Interestingly, more than a hundred years on, studies of women who say they would like to be free from menstruation were put off by the idea that it would more likely be instigated by a male physician, with this act viewed as an intrusion into their female nature. The ambivalence that women have towards their periods has forever been a red rag to the bullish scientist/doctor who we can argue still views the matter through an androcentric lens, with women's bodies available and ready to be opened up for inspection, correction and regulation. Incidences of this will appear time and time again throughout this book. As we tunnel our way through patriarchy, different ideas on the feminine emerge and more women courting amenorrhea are located. I can be a mother, a wife, a daughter, a sister and a woman without ever wanting or having to menstruate.

Menstruation as a return to womanhood is for many questionable. Eugénie Lemoine-Luccioni explores this in her book *Partage des Femmes* (1982). Here, the Lacanian analyst writes about "Anne Marie", a patient who at age 18 begins to suffer from anorexia. For a couple of years she is amenorrheic, her periods stopping at exactly the same age as her mother's did. It is at the age of 23, that "Anne Marie" announces she is pregnant and wishes to leave the analysis. Charles Shepherdson picks the case up and explores it in his book *Vital Signs: Nature Culture, Psychoanalysis*:

> Faced with a client who stops eating, who stops bleeding, who stops dreaming, and who brings her pregnancy forward in order to stop analysis in this particular way, Lemoine-Luccioni can only regard these details as a chain, a symptomatic repetition. The pregnancy, she believes, is being used as a resistance. "Conceiving the child" is intended to *put a stop to the question* that has governed the entire analysis, namely: "If I do not have periods" (p.65) if I do not eat, *if I do not become a mother, am I nevertheless a woman?*
> (Shepherdson, 2000: 20; original emphasis)

There is often a power struggle in the room and the skill is to not match like with like but to offer room to think about what is being acted upon and resisted against by the patient. At the outset though, practitioners need to question the extent to which they even think about menses in an analysis, let alone allow for its discussion. Psychoanalyst Christopher Bollas reflects on patients who use the anorectic strategy to refuse the newly imposed body determined by biology (including menstruation): "the 'act' of interpretation in such a situation is not simply effective it is rather extraordinary" (Bollas, pers. comm. Sept. 2016).

Freud's earliest psychoanalytic imprints were marked because of the way in which he used the act of interpretation to read medical conditions as not just concrete biological, genetic and endocrinological facts but as that which can transcend beyond the parameters of medicine and the conscious thought applied to it. Knowledge need not be an obstacle to truth. The psyche and the unconscious phantasy life of patients who present with secondary amenorrhea can traverse space and time even though the physical being and the body, as science would have us understand them, appear to be telling a different story. Symptoms of a patient's illness are given a new meaning. Secondary amenorrhea is often located at the point of psychological disturbance. It can be interpreted as a condition deployed by the unconscious to keep the subject in an illusionary state of balance and order. This safeguards her from the dread of psychic fragmentation. For many women, secondary amenorrhea is a price worth paying for a sense of control and continuity. But what is at stake? What past experience or trauma and what future perceived threats are hidden in the narrative, as yet undisturbed and unexplored? This book will seek them out.

Me, myself and I

Psychoanalysis, amongst other things, endeavours to access people's internal worlds. It might spot or pick up that which medical doctors have overlooked. It can view menstruation and secondary amenorrhea as biological entities that exist in partnership with one another and importantly with complicated affairs of the heart and the mind. A disruption to the hypothalamic-pituitary ovarian axis that has shifted a menstruating body into a state of non-menses can be thought about as a representation of a disruption in the psyche of that same person's internal world. Narratives in the back-stories of many women with secondary amenorrhea often feature unresolved experiences of attachment, loss, trauma, fear, or neurosis. Palpable dis-connects are hard to bear and the internal world is sent off kilter. The schism is redrawn on the body, which adopts an amenorrheic state.

Contemporary research in psychosomatic gynaecology and obstetrics supports the hypothesis long held by Freudian psychoanalysis that many women who are infertile and who do not menstruate regularly might have in their history experience of trauma, abuse, neglect, or conflict. This new research is a significant and important development in our better understanding the ways in which the mind finds expression through the body and as a result of a collusive nature between the two is designed to spare the individual further damage from her realising the pains of reality. Secondary amenorrhea offers her a safe house. Like migration stories or conversion stories or rehabilitation stories, secondary amenorrhea is at the point of intersection; it's a halfway house. If life requires that we experience transformation, change, alienation, separation and loss but the individual feels unable to do this or refuses to surmount these developmental stages, she seeks resolution through a bodily condition such as secondary amenorrhea through which psychic conflict can be managed, even eradicated. Additionally, the menstrual flow and all the erraticism and mess that goes with that is staved off. The individual can on the one hand find refuge and solace, a temporary gap in proceedings, but on the other she might be shoring up and stifling that which needs to be thought about, talked about, expressed and felt. We shall see in the case studies of psychoanalytic treatment of women with secondary amenorrhea how the effects of the talking cure and the unravelling of that which is repressed can impact significantly to both good and bad effect.

Using a psychoanalytic lens in search for greater clarity on the matter is useful because the unravelling of information associated to a patient's experience might locate aspects of it in fantasy (known) or phantasy (unconscious). Whether it be real, imagined or what we term "as real", the psychic axis is no longer in a state of equilibrium just as the biological one is not. Nonmenses can represent and symbolise a vacuum in which emotions can be contained, and importantly repressed, as they are deemed too dangerous to see light of day. Over time, perhaps this state of secondary amenorrhea becomes a friend to the patient rather than a foe, as it defends against the complexity and mess that is normally associated with the bodily menstrual process and the mental maturational process. One of the difficulties in the treatment of these patients comes about when the body supposedly betrays the mind and the patient's menses suddenly returns. Cases studies in this book include women who have come to psychotherapy with secondary amenorrhea as a subsidiary feature to their presenting problem but who during the course of treatment "miraculously" start to menstruate and continue to have regular monthly periods. Some, who think themselves infertile, become pregnant without any medical intervention. The shift in the bodily mechanism is often mirrored by an internal shift in the psyche, but all this comes with its own health warning. Carefully managing the patient's metamorphosis, safeguarding the fragility and maintaining a psychic equilibrium are no mean tasks but they are imperative in ensuring the successful outcomes of these analytic encounters. If the patient experiences a rebirth, "shedding a skin" as one patient described it, what must be foregone?

It was the unearthing of these case studies in which my own seeds of curiosity took root but the driving force behind my doctorate research and my writing this book was from my own failed analysis, which I put down in part to the patient (me) and the psychoanalyst (him, his name will not appear in this book) not engaging or exploring my secondary amenorrhea and its abrupt U–turn. After a prolonged cessation of menses (during which I went through teenage, university, work and married life, IVF, motherhood and into adulthood), one day in my late thirties and about three years into my analysis the red came out of the blue so to speak. At the time, I was training to be a psychodynamic psychotherapist and my analysis was an integral part of the training. After this first period I had a monthly menstrual bleed and I still do, ten years or so on. In fact I am a woman whose body has perfected the art of the 28-day cycle. There is no one more regular than me, much to my total annoyance! How dare my body be so compliant to the whims of society that dictates that to be a woman one must menstruate? Where was my non–conforming, autonomous rebellion of a body, the body that more aptly reflected my ideas about myself? I wanted it back. I missed my amenor-rheic days. What constitutes being a "real" woman is discussed in later chapters as well as the contentious issue of menses being the red badge of femininity. My experience in my own analysis was that my womanhood was an integral aspect to the analytic coupling. Non-menstruating meant non-conception aligned to childhood and safe play. Menses meant I was a potential mother with my analyst a potential suitor and my unconscious life was rocked by his celebrating my return to menstruation. After all, he must have thought, was this not testimony to the power and magic of Freud's "talking cure"? Who, though, was the magician? There was definitely a struggle in my unconscious with regards to an omnipotent/impotent split. My own interpretation is that my analyst unconsciously believed that he had the power to "blow me the kiss of life" (his words) but he was deluded, fool-ishly. I was not a statue made of stone that he, like Pygmalion, could bring to life. If anything, I was to become Medusa with the power to turn *him* to stone. Many times I attempted to leave and he would call me back. My last exit I remember clearly. I felt naked, like damaged goods, half alive, half dead, like Ovid's Myrrha (who I write about in the Pygmalion chapter). My PhD was the child borne out of this broken analysis, a sublimatory act and a nod to the Life Force.

Just as many doctors treat secondary amenorrhea as an illness, an irregular-ity, an inconvenience, or an anomaly that interrupts and needs to be cured, by their mastery, so too in my analysis what was lacking were the conversa-tions and discussions and importantly the interpretations that create for an equally shared dialogue. The opportunity to think about that, which had become "lost", was lost to both of us. As things started to unravel in my ana-lysis, I felt as if I was a squawking hysteric resisting social conformity and desiring, demanding even, a master whom I could control. I imagined the terror of the child that believes she has so much power she renders her par-ents impotent. Their capacity to bear whatever comes their way is forever tested. As my analyst seemed to turn away, I was becoming increasingly unwell. In one session he told me that he had, on a cold dark winter's morn-ing, opened his car door and a female motorcyclist, coming at speed, had crashed straight into it. I told him he was admitting his careless lack of analytic holding that would, if left unchecked, cause me serious damage. I waited for him one day for a scheduled session and he did not turn up. He had gone swimming. He was not expecting me. The alarms bells in my unconscious began to ring, which I only realised much later on was a reminder of my own mother not "expecting" me. When she was five months pregnant, carrying me, she was mowing the lawn, ankles swollen, out of breath. She had no idea she was pregnant. The doctor confirmed it. She rushed straight to the telephone box and called my father, crying that she did not want this baby. He reassured her that I would be born and all would be well. My life could have been terminated abruptly. What must I have picked up from my mother's conscious and unconscious material during those perilous months in her waters? What distillations and contortions must my own unconscious have gone on to subsequently create? In terms of my analysis, whatever was being transferred it was seemingly smoke and mirrors. To ask a patient to collude with a secret with the words "don't tell anyone but …" was indicative of a special relationship gone wrong. I wanted to make it out of there alive. He seemed paralysed; meanwhile whilst the analysis had been losing shape, spinning off its axis into a dense fog of confusion, I felt myself to be on my own somehow managing to reconfigure a new-found sense of self with a new body boundary. So as to bring about a fresh start, by means of an end (just as in the menstrual cycle), a creation that can only emerge from destruction, I aborted the analysis and left. I wandered the psychoanalytic land, in self-imposed exile, and I felt enough peace to try and reflect on and process my experience. Exile is a form of silencing but paradoxically it is the space that provides the freedom and safety to speak out. "Cursed" perhaps (like so many young girls feel at menarche and so many women declare in their struggles with menstruation), but nevertheless the job had been done. The analytic cord had been cut. Oh, and I survived.

From my trying to work out psychoanalytically what had happened, I discovered very important patterns that made a lot of sense when thinking about patients for whom issues of symbiosis and individuation, separation and loss are tantamount; no more so than with acute cases of anorexia, hysteria, narcissism, trauma, abuse, neglect and deprivation, all of which have important links to secondary amenorrhea and will be carefully examined in this book.

I had not intended to refer to my own analytic experience, nor indeed my border crossing from amenorrhea to menses, but having consulted with several colleagues it made sense to "testify". This of course comes with its own set of challenges – does this confuse the issue more than it clarifies it? What amount of disclosure is the right amount? What is the purpose and relevance of my declaring and am I able to discern my own motivation and my own subjective view within a wider objective stance that can help this study along? To not have mentioned it would have allowed for my continuing anonymity but the further I advanced in my research the more I thought it would be more truthful and helpful to state my own position as writer/

researcher. Also, if truth be told, I want to speak out so that others might too. I try to recall it as if with a third eye (that which was lacking in my own analysis) and I am cautious to remain in the analytic stance. On a personal level, this book bears testimony to my own early struggles as an analysand, the experiences of which are an increasingly distant memory, the scars from which still sometimes sting. Experiences are often both a blessing and a curse and I think this ambivalence is analogous to the way in which menstruation and secondary amenorrhea are often thought of and felt. I hope this book, in its exploration of such powerful symbols, will reveal and illustrate the depth of such thought and feeling.

Chapter summaries

Psychoanalysis can help us to think about why communities and groups and individuals turn to the symbols of menstruation and secondary amenorrhea to find a second structure, a second line of narrative beyond conscious thought. Through encounter and interpretation, a dynamic system and other realities that are characterised by a series of processes operating under different rules to consciousness can emerge. As French psychoanalyst Serge Leclaire beautifully describes in *La Réalité du Désir*:

> The unconscious is not the ground which has been prepared to give more sparkle and depth to the painted composition: it is the earlier sketch which has been covered over before the canvas is used for another picture. If we use a comparison of a musical order, the unconscious is not the counterpoint of a fugue or the harmonics of a melodic line: it is the jazz one hears despite oneself behind the Haydn quartet when the radio is badly tuned or not sufficiently selective. The unconscious is not the message, not even the strange or coded message one strives to read on an old parchment: it is another text written underneath and which must be read by illuminating it from behind or with the help of a developer.
>
> (Leclaire cited in Lemaire, 1977: 137–138)

With my psychoanalytic thinking cap on, I have endeavoured to write a book that will show the ways in which menstruation and secondary amenorrhea feature in the realms of medicine, religion, history, anthropology, politics and literature. Chapter 1 will seek to give an overview of how secondary amenorrhea and menstruation are used as symbols and understood by humankind. In societies and cultures, they are often polarised at either end of the spectrum and they are tools employed in the wars for and against gender, economic and social division. They can each symbolise omnipotence or impotence, inclusion or exclusion; secondary amenorrhea in its own right deserves to come out of the shadows of its menstruating counterpart, freed from stigma and taboo to reveal itself as that which is rich in symbolism with a multiplicity of narratives and identities. On a national level, it can be viewed as a source of good and/or evil that has the power to restore, save, or destroy. Psychoanalysis enables our exploration into what it means to be "the other". Chapter 2 will look at the symbolism of menstrual blood during Nazism, with the blood of Jewish women politicised as the biggest threat and pollutant to the Aryan race. We shall explore War Amenorrhea and reflect on the impact a cessation of menses had on female camp inmates and the legacy it left with those who survived.

Chapters 3 and 4 will focus on the clinically orientated and the socio-psycho-biological significance of amenorrhea. The many ways in which amenorrhea is linked to psychological unrest will be presented. SA is linked to trauma, stress, abuse, neglect, psychogenic disturbances, hysteria, insanity, eating disorders, anorexia and pseudocyesis (when the body mimics the state of pregnancy). An in-depth look into anorexia and eating disorders will question the degree to which menses and non-menses are useful indicators of a patient's mental health and the role that psychotherapy can have in supporting recovery. The boundaries that separate "in" from "out" and "I" from "you" are considered continually. We shall see how transitions are resisted and how the unconscious seeks to preserve the status quo at whatever cost.

Change and the resistance to change are explored in the context of one man's view of his alien surroundings – Pygmalion – and in Chapter 5 we focus on his story, both Ovid's version in *Metamorphosis* and George Bernard Shaw's retelling of the tale in his play *Pygmalion*. Ovid and Shaw were revolutionaries whose works were designed to disrupt the reader's assumptions about certain beliefs, asking that they rethink how they view the world. Ovid's work can be seen to represent the pre-Oedipal, pre-verbal world in which the ambiguity between what is illusory and what is real is at its most heightened. Unconscious phantasy is communicated and defended against through the body and through the gaze. The creation of his mute statue in some ways enables Pygmalion to live in a society that he does not feel part of. So too Eliza Doolittle in Shaw's play feels alienated but, in stark contrast to Pygmalion, she enters into a linguistic process that reaches out to some sort of resolution. As we go through the texts, we shall make links with the bodily text of secondary amenorrhea through clinical material. There will be many references to Freudian theory and other significant psychoanalytic concepts that will hopefully engage both those who are familiar and those who are new to the work.

With an understanding of psychoanalytic approach and technique established by the time we reach the final chapters, we end with a detailed account and review of Freud's treatment of Emma Eckstein. Eckstein presented with hysterical symptoms and irregular menstrual bleeds but Freud's incessant focus on the methodology of his co-doctor Wilhelm Fliess caused Eckstein to haemorrhage through the nose and she nearly bled to death. Freud had a white-out, too afraid to confront the part he played in her mistreatment. He overlooked many aspects of the analysis, notably that she had embodied his desires and that she was tied to her creator just as Eliza was with Higgins and Galatea with Pygmalion. Ties are formed in such a way that they can never be truly severed. The treatment is never truly terminated.

Freud asked what are the forces "impelling" the patient i.e. "to do work and make changes?" (Freud, 1915a: 164–165). In the concluding chapter, we shall evaluate Freudian psychoanalysis for those women whose secondary amenorrhea, either as a silent witness, a cry for help or a defiant protest, appears too entrenched to forgo. How can Freud's theory, steeped in patriarchy, successfully challenge this position? What are these women seeking? What lack in the psyche is lack of menses filling? If we are to truly make progress in our understanding of womanhood, motherhood, sisterhood, daughterhood and the feminine, then we must realise that what is present in the absence and absent in the presence, elucidated in the symbols of amenorrhea and menstruation, must be realised.

Bibliography

Adbelmoty, H.I., Youssef, M.A., Abdallah, S., Abdel-Malak, K., Hashish, N.M., Samir, D., Abdelbar, M., Naguib Hosni, A., Abd-El Ghafar, M., Khamis, Y. & Seleem, M. (2015) "Menstrual Patterns and Disorders among Secondary School Adolescents in Egypt. A Cross-Sectional Survey", *BMC Women's Health*, 15: 70–76.

Behar, R. (1997) *The Vulnerable Observer – Anthropology That Breaks Your Heart*. Boston, MA: Beacon Press.

Björo, K. (1966) "Amenorrhea: A Study with Particular Attention to the Problems of Ovarian Failure", *Acta Obstetricia et Gynecologica Scandinavica*, 45(S1): 68–124.

Buchan, W. (1797) *Domestic Medicine or a Treatise on the Prevention and Cure of Diseases by Regimen and Simple Medicines*. 20th edn. New York: James Lyon & Co.

Buckley, T. & Gottlieb, A. (eds.), (1988) *Blood Magic, The Anthropology of Menstruation*. Berkeley, Los Angeles & London: University of California Press.

Chadwick, M. (1932) *The Psychological Effects of Menstruation*. New York: Nervous and Mental Disease Publishing Company.

Courtinho, E. & Segal, S. (1999) *Is Menstruation Obsolete? How Suppressing Menstruation Can Help Women Who Suffer from Anaemia, Endometriosis or PMS*. New York & Oxford: Oxford University Press.

Dewhurst, J. (1972) *Dewhurst's Textbook of Obstetrics & Gynaecology*. ed. D.K. Edmonds. Oxford: Blackwell Publishing Ltd.

Drew, F.L. (1961) "The Epidemiology of Secondary Amenorrhea", *Journal of Chronic Diseases*, 14(4): 396–407.

Hippocrates, "Epidemics", VI.8.32, trans. W.D. Smith (1994) *Epidemics II, IV–VII*. Cambridge, MA: Harvard University Press.

Erikson, E.H. (1968) *Identity, Youth and Crisis*. New York: W.W. Norton & Company Inc.

Fingerson, L. (2006) *Girls in Power: Gender, Body and Menstruation in Adolescence*. New York: State University of New York Press.

Freud, S. (1915a) *Instincts and Their Vicissitudes*. SE, XIV: 109–140. London: Hogarth Press.

Freud, S. (1915b) *The Unconscious*. SE, XIV: 159–215. London: Hogarth Press.

Langer, M. (1951) *Motherhood and Sexuality*. trans. N. Hollander (2000). New York: Other Press.

Laws, S. (1990) *Issues of Blood: The Politics of Menstruation*. Hampshire & London: The Macmillan Press Ltd.

Lemaire, A. (1977) *Jacques Lacan*. trans. D. Macey (1970). East Sussex: Routledge & Kegan Paul Ltd.

Lemoine-Luccioni, E. (1982) *Partage Des Femmes*. Paris: Seuil.

Munster, K., Helm, P. & Schmidt, L. (1992) "Secondary Amenorrhea: Prevalence and Medical Contact – A Cross Sectional Study from A Danish County", *British Journal of Obstetrics & Gynaecology*, 99: 430–433.

Ovid. (1986) *Metamorphosis*. trans. A.D. Melville. Oxford: Oxford University Press.

Romanyshyn, R.D. (2013) *The Wounded Researcher – Research with Soul in Mind*. New Orleans, LA: Spring Journal.

Santoro, N.F. & Neal-Perry, G. (eds.), (2010) *Amenorrhea: A Case-Based Clinical Guide*. New York: Springer.

Shaw, G.B. (1916) *Pygmalion*. reprint D.H. Laurence (ed.), (2003). London: Penguin Books Ltd.

Shepherdson, C. (2000) *Vital Signs: Nature, Culture, Psychoanalysis*. New York & London: Routledge.

Skierska, E.J., Leszczynska-Bystrzanowska, J. & Gajewski, A.K. (1996) "Risk Analysis of Menstrual Disorders in Young Women from Urban Population", *Przeglad Epidemiologiczny*, 50: 467–474.

Van De Walle, E. & Renne, E.P. (eds.), (2001) *Regulating Menstruation – Beliefs, Practices, Interpretations*. Chicago, IL & London: University of Chicago Press.

World Health Organization. (1981) "A Cross-cultural Study of Menstruation: Implications for Contraceptive Development and Use", *Studies in Family Planning* 12: 3–16.

1 Currencies of blood and laws of the land

This chapter will outline the main ways in which the amenorrheic woman and the menstruating woman are viewed and used by societies and groups. We shall see them in political, cultural, medical, anthropological, religious, literary and historical contexts. The chapter will set about to fill in the gaps in our understanding of amenorrhea and menstruation and will question how and why amenorrhea is experienced as being outside the "natural" order of things. If we look at amenorrhea and menstruation as signifiers in the wider socio-cultural context, both the amenorrheic and the menstruating woman can be construed as possessing both positive and negative forces. They appear in composite guises depending on what is needed of them at any given moment. For example, the menstruating woman is aligned with the very existence and continuation of the whole of the human race. Her monthly menstrual cycles provide the arena in which a procreative act can ensue. She is a force of nature and the survival of the species depends on her. Meanwhile, this very same menstruating woman has been cast aside as inferior and polluting. She has been vilified as insane and a danger to the healthy organisation and progression of the collective. As for the woman with amenorrhea, she can be seen as a saviour, a survivor and a martyr in times of economic hardship, political strife and religious awakenings. Anomalous to the natural order, she represents other worldly qualities on this earth either in light or in shade. During medieval times, she was a sorcerer and a witch. In stark contrast, in biblical times she was revered as being close to the Divine. Our exploration into the way in which menses and non-menses are used as powerful symbols will highlight the need and dependency that "man's" attachment with them ensues.

Menstrual taboos, rituals and segregation

> Wherever primitive man has set up a taboo he fears some danger and it cannot be disputed that a generalised dread of women is expressed in all these rules of avoidance. Perhaps the dread is based on the fact that woman is different from man, forever incomprehensible and mysterious, strange and therefore apparently hostile.
>
> (Freud, 1918 *SE* XI: 198)

Menstruation has long been a point of power that can cause things to happen, to interrupt or to terminate. In Swazi culture, a menstruating woman who goes near a pregnant cow will cause it to miscarry. If she picks vegetables, they will wilt. But it is also regarded as a life symbol that can purify as well as pollute. It cleanses a woman after she has given birth and only then can her husband cohabit with her (Kuper, 1947: 107). Similarly, menstruation has a dual role in Judaism. In one way "As yeast is good for dough, so is menstruation good for women" (Vosselmann, 1935: 121). At the same time according to Jewish Karaite tradition, if a menstruating woman moves towards and looks at a lactating woman, it is believed that the mother's milk will stop flowing. To break the spell, the lactating woman urinates over the urine of the menstruating woman. Urine has no link to reproduction and is not a symbol of power of strength (Tsoffar, 2004).

In the early stages of civilisation, menstruation symbolised reverence and sacredness rather than a pollutant and women, who were socially prominent and responsible for social organisation, designed the menstrual taboo to create separateness between themselves and men. As Erich Neumann writes in *The Great Mother: An Analysis of The Archetype* (1955):

> The matriarchal epoch was the source of totemism, and exogamy and taboo as well as the principle of initiation seem to have belonged originally to the central institutions of the female group. One indication of this is that many female mysteries were taken over by the men and that in some the men still wore the more primordial woman's dress. We even have traditions – among the primitive aborigines of Tierra del Fuego, for example – to the effect that the earliest mysteries of the moon goddess, against which the men rebelled under the leadership of the sun, slaying all grown women and only permitting ignorant and uninitiated little girls to survive.
>
> (Neumann, 1955: 290)

In *The Metamorphosis of Baubo* (1994), Winifred Lubell explains how the Paleolithic symbols of female power including the vulva and menstrual fluid signified the way in which female energy was aligned with the earth's sacred energy. Earlier images dating back to 30,000 BCE show rituals in which chosen women would squat over fields and their "moon blood" would fall onto the newly ploughed fields. The "magical" regenerative qualities of the menstruating vulva were just as much about religion and cosmology as they were about biology. In tribal communities today such as in the Ebrié tribe of the Ivory Coast, menses is, like the erection, "associated with fertility, not pollution; desirable, and traumatic to lose" (Niangoran-Bouah, 1964: 54). In contrast, the amenorrheic state is the cursed and polluted state, the worst form of punishment that can befall a woman. If a woman picks fruit from a tree, which is mystically protected by its owner, she will become amenorrheic. A man can be inflicted with impotence if he too takes fruit from this tree. Both states are reversible when the crime is confessed. Amenorrhea symbolises lack of potency. The desired state is one imbued with the life force of menstruation and some men will go to extreme lengths to grasp it. Tribal men of New Guinea perform periodic ritual bloodlettings in what anthropologists call "male menstruation" or "imitative menstruation". Gilmore writes in *Misogyny: The Male Malady* (2001)

> the men believe they can capture not only the potency but also the fertility that nature bestows upon women. The men want this sexual transfiguration desperately because they feel that men are weak and need woman's attributes to thrive.
>
> (Gilmore, 2001: 184)

Across Melanesia, there are accounts of male nose bloodletting as a way to initiate and imitate female menstruation. Less common is the practice amongst Wogeo men who incise the tongue of young boys to access menstrual agency. Older youths and men make an incision in their penis, as described in Ian Hogbin's *The Island of Menstruating Men* (1996).

The felt experience of menstrual blood as a sacred energy has in many societies disappeared. With the development of civilisation driven by aggression, hierarchy and power, wise blood was supplanted by the obscene and polluting. Anthropologist Mary Douglas in her book *Purity and Danger: An Analysis of Concepts of Pollution and Taboo* (1966) writes about the Mae Enga who believe that to come into contact with a menstruating woman will cause a man to become sick, causing him to vomit, turning his blood black. If there is no counter-magic, he will eventually die. Referring to the 1963 study of the Mae Enga of Papua, New Guinea by Dr Meggitt, Douglas writes: "it is argued that this reflects the strain bought about by inter-clan marriages and exogamy – 'we marry the people we fight.' – this Delilah complex is that women weaken or betray" (Douglas, 1966: 148).

Anthropologist René Girard explains in *Violence and the Sacred* (1979) that the violence implied by menstrual blood is far greater than blood connected to wounds or aggressive acts. This is because of its connection to sexuality and the generative process. It can lead to rivalry and incest inside a community. The threat of menstruation is at its most heightened at menarche, when a prepubescent girl gets her first period. Simone de Beauvoir famously commented on the universal feature of this developmental stage. She wrote that a pre-pubescent "carries no menace, she is under no taboo and has no sacred character … But on the day she can reproduce, woman becomes impure" (de Beauvoir, 1949 [1952]: 180).

This holds true today in many parts of the world. In some communities, stringent rituals that demonstrate people's affiliation to this belief are steeped in traditions of sacredness but are now viewed as sacrilegious. In some remote parts of Malawi such as in the village of Nsanje, girls as young as 12 and 13 are made to have sex with a male paid sex worker, a "hyena", once they reach puberty. The ritual "cleansing" takes place over three days after their first menstrual bleed and marks the passage from childhood into the "heat" of womanhood. The girls believe that if they refuse, their family members will be cursed with disease or death. What is significant is that the custodians of this initiation are the elder stateswomen who tell the girls what their duties are as wives and sexual partners. The "hyenas" are often HIV positive and do not use condoms but on the whole the elder women are defiant that the practice must continue. Historically, pubescent girls around the age of 15 were chosen as wives and it was their new husbands who would carry out the ritual. Now though the girls reach the age of menarche much younger and their age is irrelevant when it comes to the initiation act they are forced into with the male "sex workers".

This story caught the media's attention across the globe and the government of Malawi knows it must be seen to be investigating this sexual initiation practice. But it is a long-held belief that change can only come when the younger generations are enabled to let go of the cultural and traditional practises that define their older relatives and ancestral forebears. This is the most complex of challenges. Dismantling the menstrual taboo brings with it the threat of dismantling a whole community, society, organisation, civilisation, even. The taboo keeps the abject body at a distance, the pollutant away from the symbolic order. In the case of the ancient Greeks, it was ingeniously played out in the annual autumn festival called Thesmophoria.

Thesmophoria was specifically designed to "celebrate" puberty and menstruation. Suspecting that their womenfolk had the potential to revolt, borne out of their frustration at being so markedly segregated from public view, locked indoors for most of their lives, these women were given their own festival. It is from Aristophanes' satire *Thesmophorizaousae* (411 BC) (2015) that we glean much of this cult status. Archaeologists have located Thesmophorion sanctuaries or epigraphic evidence in over fifty sites in Greece and its surrounding areas, with some dating back to the second millennium BC. At the start of this festival, free adult women would leave their homes and congregate in makeshift tents for three days. In Athens, they would meet on the Acropolis and carry out sacred rituals, led by women for women. Men were completely excluded. Importantly though many scholars agree that this was not a shining example of mankind celebrating the totality of women. It was more a case of "nothing else but the periods of the Greek women elevated to an annual festival accommodated with this name in the sphere of Demeter Thesmophoros" (Kerenyi, 1975: 157). It was perhaps a vehicle designed by male citizens to allow the women to let off steam. Men were merely placating their women. Barbara Goff explains it well in her paper "The Priestess of Athena Grows a Beard: Latent Citizenship in Ancient Greek Women's Ritual Practice" (2007). Goff writes:

women's latent citizenship emerges and becomes prominent in ritual...To the women, who perform it, the Thesmophoria offers the contours of a kind of citizenship, although it can also be read to construct its female participants as the outsiders who define male citizenship by contrast.

(Goff cited in Pollock & Turvey Sauron, 2007: 51)

That the menstrual taboo is engrained in civilisations is well illustrated in "Reconsidering the Menstrual Taboo: A Portuguese Case" (Lawrence, 1982). The observations recorded by anthropologist Denise Lawrence show the extent to which a town in Southern Portugal adhered to strict taboos relating to the curing of pork and the preparation of pork sausages. The fixed gaze of the menstruating woman on the pork would cause it to spoil. Her contaminated body could contaminate the meat. When a woman arrives at the site of meat preparation, she is asked if she is able to see and she can only enter if she replies, "I can see." One can wonder whether a woman can ever be completely sure she is "clean" in which case is she intentionally or unintentionally being deceitful? In "Menstrual Politics: Women and Pigs in Rural Portugal", Lawrence explains that these women maintain prohibitions in their own interest and that

women's behaviour can be explained not in reference to assumptions of male dominance over women but to women's conscious choice of modes of behaviour reflecting strategic goals important to their own perceived self-interest. Women are the principle actors in maintaining the menstrual taboo because it allows them to control certain social interactions within and outside the household and affords them a rationale for protecting economic privacy of their homes, for which they hold primary responsibility.

(Lawrence, 1988 cited in Buckley & Gottlieb, 1988: 117)

It might be that all of this props up and colludes with the punishing menstrual taboos and rituals that are principally driven by a man's envy of woman and his desire to dominate her. But at least Lawrence's understanding of these women challenges us to question this assumption. If men do feel undermined then perhaps the concentration and focus on a task as important as food preparation can dissolve the tension. As Douglas explains, "when moral principles come into conflict, a pollution rule can reduce confusion by giving a simple focus for concern" (Douglas, 1966: 133). In this way, the clear, open and easily understood practical rules contain the more mystical and spiritual aspects enveloped in the rituals and the taboo. It is all re-branded as a positive movement to bring a sought after order to the group. What is being protected is

perceived creative, spirituality of monstrous women from the influence of others in a more neutral state, as well as protecting the latter in turn from the potent, positive spiritual force ascribed by such women. In other cultures menstrual customs, rather than subordinating women to men fearful of them provide women with the means of ensuring their own autonomy, influence and social control.

(Buckley & Gottlieb, 1988: 7)

Women of the Mogmog Island in the Pacific atoll of Ulithi enjoy being separated out into shelters and huts during their time of menstruation. They talk and weave, taking a break from routine labour. The idea that women self-select their segregation makes me think of primatology studies of baboons in Kenya; these found that in the days leading up to menstruation, the females would seek out a quiet place and reduce contact with group members, spending around 30% of their time up in the trees. Analysis of the data found that premenstrual and perimenstrual behaviour changed amongst female yellow baboons. This shows "some intriguing similarities to several commonly reported behavioural symptoms of premenstrual syndrome" (Hausfater & Skoblick, 1985: 165).

Choosing to separate themselves out from the social group, human females have similar hormonal systems to the baboon in their seeking out "menstrual quietude" (Hood, 1992). The system of segregation is interesting when it comes to groups migrating and relocating. In Ethiopia, Jewish women observed the purity laws according to their literal reading of the biblical text and this was significant in distinguishing them from their Christian neighbours. Women who were menstruating or who had recently given birth lived in their community's menstruating hut (*yamargam gogo*), which was often placed centre stage in the middle of the village. Here they were separated from the family home and from the domestic routine. Together, these women shared news and information. When they resettled in Israel in the 1980s and 1990s, many resisted Western persuasion to give up their rituals even though they were not in line with rabbinic law and customs of Jews in Israel and elsewhere. They were housed in small government-owned apartment blocks, where the lack of space and the basic structure could not allow for the complete separateness that the women were used to. Some women slept in cupboards or on balconies in an attempt to improvise. Others slept together in the corridors of apartments or hotels, giving a semblance of segregation at a community level. They felt ashamed and guilty and longed for their homes and the purity rites, which had provided them with feelings of cleanliness and surety in their identity.

More recently, there is an increasing amount of concern over the use of menstrual huts that have been found to be lacking in basic standards of hygiene. They are instead hubs for disease and infection and their flimsy infrastructure makes them unsafe. As recent as 2019, a mother and her two sons were found dead in a windowless cowshed in Nepal. Observing the Hindu purity laws of "*chhaupadi*", she had isolated herself in the makeshift menstrual hut. She had lit a fire for them all to keep warm but they are believed to have died of suffocation. The ritual was banned in 2015 but many women still believe that non-compliance will invoke bad luck and suffering: Tradition and superstition are strong. We are far from the prototype of the hut, which was originally designed to give women a safe space and to protect the potency of their menstruation, whose powers not pollutants had the capacity to affect a hunter's luck. Menstruating women of Northwest California's Yurok Indians would communally bathe in a "sacred Moontime pond" in the mountains and meditate whilst on menstrual leave. The "seclusion" and "protection" of women is not the same as the "banishment" of women. There is a difference between asking what women need as opposed to what's wrong with women. To what degree has the introduction and implementation of the huts been reconstructed by patriarchy to undermine women's rights and freedoms?

Blood lines

During the 1970s, when menstrual activism was gathering momentum, many female artists created works to reclaim the positive images of menstruation and menstrual seclusion. In a performance "Menstruation II" (1979), artist Cate Elwes enclosed herself in a white box, which had a glass panel on one of its sides through which she could be watched. Viewers could pass questions to her and she would write her answers on the walls inside the box. The performance took place while she was menstruating. Dressed in white, her menses bled freely. Elwes commented that her menstruation work "confronted forcible eradication of women's biology from culture". In "Menstruation I" (1979), Elwes was dressed in white and sat on a round sheet drawing and writing as she bled. As well as reforming the narrative on menstruation, these pieces exemplified how an event of the body

> is not reducible to biological essentialism, a facet of patriarchal ideology which supposed a primordial difference between the sexes determined by anatomical and specifically genital structures. How the body is lived and experienced is implicated at all levels in social and societally determined psychic processes.
>
> (Parker & Pollock, 1987: 29, cited in Samuels, 2015: 106)

Judy Chicago created "Menstruation Bathroom" (1972) which was a bin filled with used tampons and "Red Flag" (1971) a lithograph of a bloody tampon being pulled out from between a woman's legs. Carolee Schneemann performing "Interior Scroll" read from a long piece of paper as she slowly pulled it out of her vagina (1975). These works amongst others reclaimed the rights of women to view their bodies through their own eyes. The procreating qualities of women were expressed in Romanian artist Timea Páll's work "The Diary of My Period". Páll collected her menstrual blood and used it to paint nine squares of one large canvas to make a picture of a baby in the womb. Páll (2017) said of her work: "The periodic elimination of my ovum with my menstrual flow inspired me to give birth to something which has a biological end, and to create the start of the end."

In 2017, artist Marisa Carnesky bought "Dr Carnesky's Incredible Bleeding Woman" to the stage. The play, inspired by her own doctoral research project, was about the associations and taboos of menstruation: Jesus' blood on the cross being the menstrual magic ritual appropriated by patriarchy and the disregard for our bodily cycles reflecting our ambivalence to the cycles of the planet were just two of the many ideas. Earlier, in 2013 Chilean artist Carina Úbeda had exhibited what was a collection of five years worth of her used sanitary rags embroidered with words such as "destroyed" and "production". Her work was displayed at the Centre of Culture and Health in Quilotta, Chile. I am reminded of Germaine Greer's words in her book *The Female Eunuch* (1971 [1993]: 57): "if you think you are emancipated you might consider the idea of tasking your own menstrual blood – if it makes you sick, you've a long way to go, baby."

This is a far cry from the clean lines and unblemished skin that dominated figures of idealised beauty of the late twentieth and early twenty-first century. No marks, no flaws and often no pubic hair but rather "lean, taut, smooth and hairless, something like a mobile, androgynous statue" (Sceats, 2004: 66). This fits the image of Pygmalion's statue Galatea from Ovid's *Metamorphosis* (1986), which we shall study in detail in Chapter 5. The Pygmalion verse describes the way in which one man relates to his "model" statue. The sculptor's perfect statue represents his idealised version of life. His model represents the model of the mind, organised and composed of clean lines and clearly identifiable separate parts. For many feminists, this commodification of the body is abhorrent as it suggests that mess (for example, menstrual mess) is done away with, assigned to the artist's wastepaper bin.

To find a time before portraiture of women had been hijacked and held hostage by the might of man's patriarchal (phallic) pen, we can go all the way back to the Old Stone Age where it is believed that women, using basic stone tools, drew pictures of themselves into the rock face. "The Woman of Le Gabillou" was discovered in 1940 and dates back to 15,000 BCE. It is a drawing of the simple outline of a woman's body, Matisse like. It shows the curve of the belly, breast, one leg bent and a bend in the line to locate the vulva. Like so many Paleolithic vulva images of its time, be it in drawings or on objects, it tells a story of womanhood

> sometimes associated with the mother goddess or presented as a symbol and aspect of her story, sometimes in graves, sometimes associated with other symbols. These uses and variations increase our understanding of the complex, interrelated nature of the story and take it out of the realm of mere sexuality. It is not the anatomic "sexual" organ that is being symbolised, but the stories, characters and processes with which the symbol had become associated.
>
> (Marshack, 1972: 279)

Interestingly the famous vulva painting by Gustave Courbet, "L'Origine du Monde" is censored on social media. The 1866 work is of a reclining woman's naked torso, legs open and vulva exposed. It is regarded as a major work of art but by many is branded pornographic. It is said to have inspired Lucian Freud's "Naked Girl Asleep" (1968). Do these artworks, like the Paleolithic images, paint a reality and not an ideal or a stereotype, a projection or perception? Lucian Freud's paintings can be viewed as both life studies and portraits, revealing the biology and the psychology, stories and the gaps in those stories of his sitters. The naked portraits are far from romanticised or idealised: Freud would say they exist as accurate representations of what he has seen before him, open to scrutiny. Freud argued that his paintings were to be "truthfulness as revealing and intrusive, rather than rhyming and soothing". "Standing by the Rags" (1988–89) is a large oil painting of a nude woman on a heap of white rags. The rags are painted in as much detail as the woman. Freud would use the cloth to wipe his brushes, making his presence in the picture known. The smeared paint on the sheets might represent blood and other bodily secretions. So he gets in on the act in more ways than one, perhaps in omnipotence trying to surmount his own unconscious fears of being left out or worse, castrated. Does this suggest that the female model is a threat? Is he challenging her perceived potential as a pollutant with his own secretions to signify the difference between what is within and without female and male? Is he just yet another man who is unable to be "natural" around menstrual symbols? Just over one hundred years earlier, Edvard Munch painted "Puberty". Central to the painting is a young girl around the age of puberty, naked and sitting on the edge of a bed. Her legs are closed and her hands rest on her lap. Many interpret this as a work on sexual repression, both of the sitter and the artist. A large shadow is cast behind her possibly representing either male or female genitalia and a foreboding of the process of puberty. Dark and phagocyte, it can be seen as engulfing and threatening the sitter's small and fragile frame. Phallic in shape, it can represent the looming days of patriarchy that will domesticate this child and prepare her for marriage and motherhood, robbing her of play. The transitional process of puberty signifies the shift from childhood to womanhood and those long-yearned-for days of youth are cast aside as memories, lurking in the shadows of a new dawn. The shadow in the painting is a warning sign of the trauma and the loss that is to befall this young girl. At the time of Munch's painting, it was widely believed that a girl getting her period might lead her into adolescent insanity. The onset of sexuality has often been drawn as preternatural. In the story of "Sleeping Beauty", a tale of menstruation, the girl is prevented at all costs from the experience of bleeding. It is the king that takes action to spare the princess from the angry fairy's curse. As far as he is concerned, his whole kingdom is at risk. The innate need to split off impurity and spin it into a threat is reminiscent of the biblical story in Genesis: "And G-d created man in His image, in the image of

G-d He created him; male and female He created them" (Genesis 1:27 cited in JPS, 2000: 2).

This is widely interpreted as Adam being created as one being, originally designed to be able to live on his own. What happens next is that Adam is first "coupled" with Lilith. According to Ragnheidarottir in her book *Quest for the Mead of Poetry – Menstrual Symbolism in Icelandic Folk and Fairy Tales*: "Adam is said to have favoured the missionary position in sex, but Lilith pointed out that she was his equal and refused to lie beneath him" (Ragnheidarottir, 2016: 127). Pamela Norris in *Eve: A Biography* (1990) writes: "when Adam threatened to overpower Lilith by force, she uttered the magic name of G-d and flew away to the Red Sea ... where she lived with an order of lascivious demons and became renowned for her promiscuity" (Norris, 1990: 278).

The Red Sea is likely to represent menstruation and whilst Lilith was replaced by Eve, we have from the very start the picture of Adam vulnerable and at risk from the cursed, menstruating, scheming woman. But the two women might also represent the split between the first age of woman, pre-menarche, naïve and impressionable, and the lustful, sinful, lewd age post-menarche. Without a firm hand both are a threat, their impulses and drives easily stoked by temptation and intrigue:

> The margins of the body, in particular, the markers of fecundity – menstruation, pregnancy, the menopause – stand as signifiers of the difference between within and without the male and female, necessitating containment through taboo and ritual, in order to keep the abject body at a safe, non polluting distance from the symbolic order.
>
> (Ussher, 2006: 5)

Eve is a great example of how a repeated image creates an identity, a theme explained by Judith Butler in her book *Gender Trouble: Feminism and the Subversion of Identity* (1990). Butler explains how if we start at the beginning and take gender itself, it is not something that is and that causes things to happen but rather, it is a

> performance discursively constituted, something one does rather than what one is: Gender is the repeated stylization of the body, a set of repeated acts within a highly rigid regulatory framework that congeal over time to produce the appearance of a substance, of a natural sort of being.
>
> (Butler, 1990: 33)

Menstrual matter is arguably the first blot on the gender landscape that separates woman out from man. It will not wash away. Many will play on mankind's fear of the powerful menstrual bleed and man's ability to control and correct it as a way to demonstrate man's ability to restore social, religious and political order. But in times of desperate need, when a decaying landscape appears beyond redemption, man turns to a different symbol – amenorrhea.

Amenorrhea – a narrative of epic proportions

The amenorrheic woman is beyond the simple tale of man's management of the feminine problem. Her narrative is one of epic proportions. This is a woman who is immune to and beyond the waxing and waning of earthly existence, represented by menstrual cycles and procreation. She is beyond representation of the body "associated with notions of corporeality" (Buckley & Gottlieb, 1988: 76–77). In fact, she is much more a symbol of order itself. She is closely aligned to the goddesses, saints and Amazonians than she is to womankind, with a more superior status and narratives of redemption, salvation and survival. After all, have you ever heard of a Greek goddess troubled by her periods, her acts of heroism compromised by stomach cramps and menstrual mess? Amenorrhea represents longevity and immortality not through procreation, reproduction and childbirth like menstruation, but rather through salvation. However, when the symbolism of saviour, warrior, or leader turns sour, the very nature and constitution of womanhood spins her status off the trajectory of a superior reality into that of delusional fantasy. She is alas, just a woman, nothing more. We shall see how the regard for the amenorrheic woman rests on a pendulum so big that it can swing from one end, from the place of majesty, awe and the sublime to the other, where disgust, loathing and the inhumane reside.

Let us start with the famous case of Joan of Arc (1412–31) whose amenorrhea elevated her to sainthood. Non-menses of the amenorrheic and a young virgin's pure mind, pre sexual knowledge, were gold dust to medieval man. The amenorrhea of Joan of Arc symbolised a power and purity that could somehow conquer the enemy and rid the world of evil. She represented the coming together of a disembodied State. She would save and restore France. Living in the early 1400s, she was a figure of chastity and of angelic cleanliness, which was mirrored by her absence of menses. Amenorrhea although thought of as a failure, was in medieval times linked with outstanding strength, as this extract from a medieval medical text shows:

> Such a failing of the menses happens on account of the power and quality of strength, which digests well and converts the nourishment from the limbs until no superfluities remain, as it so happens amongst strong, mannish women who are called viragoes.
>
> (cited in Warner, 1981: 11)

Unencumbered, Joan of Arc became the ultimate warrior. However, despite her presenting like a man, including the way in which she dressed, the blood she shed in warfare was not considered as important as that of a man who bled masculine blood (McCracken, 2003). Given a bespoke suit of armour, a banner and a sword by the Dauphin, she marched with her army to Orléans and in four days took back the town from the English. The Dauphin was crowned King Charles VII and all was at last well. But on her way to liberate

Paris, the young "maid" was captured. It was a simple script from the outset. If she wins she truly is God's messenger, if she loses she is the maid tempted and corrupted by the Devil. In 1431 she was burned at the stake for heresy. Jean Toutmouille is said to have heard her crying in prison on the morning of her execution: "Alas! That my body, clean and whole, never be corrupted, today must be consumed and burnt to the ashes!" (Douglas Murray, 1902). It is now her corporeal body that defines her purity. To underplay her spiritual, transcending status as God's interlocutor, her amenorrhea was described not as a holy signifier but as a biological consequence of fasting (albeit religious) and athleticism.

The wasting-away of the body, termed "consumption" in the fourteenth century, was a condition discussed as early as at the time of Hippocrates. If the cure for this wasting-away and its associated amenorrhea was not to be found in a covenant with God, then according to the medical literature the best thing for it was marriage and motherhood:

> My prescription is that when virgins experience this trouble, they should cohabit with a man as quickly as possible. If they become pregnant, they will be cured. If they don't do this, either they will succumb at the onset of puberty, or a little later, unless they catch another disease. Among married women, those who are sterile are more likely to suffer what I have described.
>
> (Hippocrates, ca. fourth century BCE cited in Eghigian, 2010: 36)

In *Case Reports in Psychiatry*: "A Case Study of Anorexia Nervosa Driven by Religious Sacrifice" (Davis & Nguyen, 2014), the reader is presented with a 66-year-old patient who first started restricting her food intake at age 13, when studying to be a nun at a Catholic convent. She had her first period around the age of 12 and when she was 13, her periods stopped. She says she was not trying to be thin or attractive, but through self-starvation she was hoping to be closer to God and would one day become a saint through asceticism. Davis and Nguyen's review of the literature shows that in Christianity, fasting was common amongst religious girls, some to the point of death. Along with flagellations and lifelong virginity, these girls were termed "anorexia mirabilis", which was not a disease nor was it associated with the modern-day anorexia nervosa which is related to the idealisation of thinness and perceptions of body image. Davis and Nguyen write about a girl (St Wilgefortis) who was made a saint between 700 and 900 CE. Her father, the King of Portugal, had found her a suitor but she had already vowed to serve God. She starved herself and the suitor withdrew. By way of punishment, her father had her crucified. Representing freedom from physical and social burdens of womanhood, she was eventually sainted. Many of these cases of holy fasting show abstinence to the point of death. Whilst they aimed to reach God, the transformation that these women were pursuing took them further away (perhaps unconsciously driven) from marriage, childbirth and mother-hood – that which was expected of the ordinary girl.

So, Joan of Arc whilst displaying a strength and defiance in the face of the enemy (England), was also displaying non-conformity against an enemy much closer to home – the triad of men, marriage and motherhood. And whilst she has become a symbol of victory against foreign invasion on the political stage (controversially she is used by *Le Front National* as an emblem of national sov-ereignty and independence), she is also a poster girl for the outsider, the pro-testor who votes against mainstream ideologies.

In the Old Testament, we find amenorrhea as a key component in the story of matriarchy. Although forewarning infertility, it paradoxically secures the future of the Jewish people. The matriarchs who struggled to conceive defied nature and talked to G-d. They were women of valour, power, influ-ence and purpose. Their amenorrhea set them apart from the rest and so too their offspring. Sarah, the first matriarch, is an interesting case. At the start of Chapter 4 of the Torah, "Vayeira", which translates as "and He appeared", Abraham asks his wife Sarah to "knead and make cakes" for their new visitors (angels). But he does not serve them. One interpretation is that Sarah, whilst preparing the dough, starts to menstruate rendering the food impure. "Where is your wife, Sarah?" the visitors ask. "There in the tent" Abraham replies. Has Sarah segregated herself in menstrual quietude? The other reference to a menstrual hut is several chapters on when Rachel says to her father Laban "Let not my lord take it amiss that I cannot rise before you, for the period of women is upon me"" (Genesis 31: 35 in JPS, 2000: 65).

So, Sarah starts to menstruate but let us not overlook the fact that she is now 90 years old. From inside the tent, she hears the visitors saying she will give birth to a child in a year's time (Genesis 18:9–16 in JPS, 2000: 31). It is significant that she hears this from the angels and not from her husband, because it signifies she is on a higher prophetic level than her husband. She laughs. In ancient Arabic poetry the verb "to laugh" can also translate as "to menstruate". But many scholars read more into the meaning of Sarah's laugh-ter. Some suggests it reveals her scepticism and lack of faith. I understand it as a communication of Sarah's fury at God's decision to interrupt and change the course of events. Understandably, she is ambivalent about menstruation and the associated tasks of pregnancy and birth. This is the job of women but surely she is beyond this? Menstruation represents physicality and mortality but Rambam, the influential Torah scholar and philosopher from the twelfth century, writes that a prophet must develop fully as a human being before obtaining the power of transcendental prophecy. But there is something about Sarah now being like ordinary womanfolk that I think she would rather reject. The Midrash (rabbinical interpretation and further investigation) says that Sarah asks if now withered and old she is to represent renewal with menstrual periods and she goes on to say "God has bought me laughter, everyone who hears will laugh with me." Menstruation and childbirth con-signs women to the earthly realms. In contrast, amenorrhea correlates to prophecy within which a woman's relationship with God, not her body, is used as an agency for change.

Another useful example from the Old Testament is Hannah from the Book of Samuel I, who in her barren and presumably amenorrheic state ("for the Lord had closed her womb"), prays to her G-d and is blessed with a child (Samuel 1:1–2:22 in JPS, 2000: 571–575). Like Sarah, Rebecca and Rachel, and indeed the Virgin Mary of the New Testament, she is immortalised as a woman who is closely connected to G-d and whose offspring plays a pivotal role in a people's future. Samuel grows up to become a prophet and anoints Saul as the first King of Israel and after him, King David. Hannah had prayed religiously and devoutly to G-d for a son, promising that she would give him up to serve G-d if her prayers were answered. Her communications with G-d were of the highest order. And in her years of barrenness (estimated to be 19 years) she spent her time talking, discussing, praying to G-d, in such a way that the rabbi thought she was drunk. Once pregnant, her attachment to G-d through prayer was interrupted and having previously felt in the realm of the Divine, her pregnancy was sobering. What she manages to do is to accept that she is not like the angels but is instead human. However the part she plays in humankind changes destinies. In her prayer she uses the term "Lord of Hosts" (v.11) and the rabbis assert she is the first person to do so:

> Master of the Universe! There is a heavenly host and an earthly one. The heavenly host neither eat nor drink, are not fruitful and don't multiply, and do not die, but live forever. The earthly host eat and drink, are fruitful and multiply and die. I do not know to which host I belong, whether to the heavenly host or the earthly one. If I am of the heavenly host, for I do not give birth, then I do not eat of drink and I shall not die, but live forever. But if I am of the earthly host, let me then eat and drink, give birth and die.
>
> (Friedmann, 1890: 43)

The strength and resilience of women like Hannah transcend the sexual powers of their menstruating counterparts – the Delilahs of these texts whose sexuality is linked to treachery and betrayal. The Virgin Mary from the New Testament symbolises a more expansive depth in that her conception is an immaculate one. She really is incandescence personified. Not a drop of menstrual blood or semen in sight. In her not experiencing sex or death, the Virgin Mary is construed by the Catholic Church as beyond human. She is described in the Gospel of Luke as "the handmaiden of the Lord": "And Mary said, "Behold, I am the handmaid of the Lord; let it be to me according to your word." And the angel departed from her" (Luke 1:38, RSVCE, 1965, 1966). With the angel Gabriel's departure, she learns she is to be the mother of God. She has already asked, "How shall this be, since I have no husband?" (Luke 1:34, RSVCE, 1965, 1966), but despite her pregnancy, her giving birth, motherhood and her breastfeeding, the cult of the Virgin Mary makes her not a woman at all. During and following the birth of Jesus, there were no marks to suggest her status as a virgin had been broken. Her body is the site of power, but she is a conduit, a vessel of future power and the piecing together of her genealogy has a male bias. We are in the realm of the transcendental, the inexplicable, that of which man is in awe, afraid and wary. Achieving an accurate balance between power and passivity is nigh on impossible but if achieved, what emerges is quite spectacular.

One of the most extraordinary examples of the way in which a woman created a story for herself using the image of the Virgin Mary was the English Queen Elizabeth I (1533–1603). She propelled herself out of the patriarchal imprint of a transparent, passive woman who belonged to man, into an active self-agent powerful in political and public life. She had to get the balance right so that she would inspire her subjects who would both revere and fear her, but at the same time she had to ensure her unique and foreign status did not threaten or alienate her from them. This queen, the creator and commander of a Golden Reign, presented herself as someone of dual sex. She modelled herself on the philosophy of the King's Two Bodies from the Middle Ages. As described by lawyer Sir Edmund Plowden (1518–85) in a collection of French legal cases, *Les Commentaries ou Reports de Edmund Plowden* (1571), one body of the king signifies his physical body and the other is an abstract concept of the king and his relationship with his subjects. His physical being is that of a man of nature who lives and dies but it is tied to an immortal political ruling power whose position is a divine investiture. Thus the king is both God and Man, just like Jesus. The Body Politic was considered the "mystic body" (Kantorowicz, 1957: 15–16), representing the mutual responsibility of the subjects to their king and the king to his subjects. Whilst Elizabeth's outward corporeal body of a woman might have been associated with weakness of nature, her metaphysical body, the body politic, was that of a monarch. Internally was the place where the secrets of the state were kept. Her royal consciousness and her power were that of a male ruler, privy to no one. Hence she was not the transparent woman in man's image. And even biologically speaking she was not a woman in a man's world, for it was widely believed that she was amenorrheic. Christopher Hibbert writes in *The Virgin Queen* "when she reached the age of menstruation, her periods were highly irregular or, as some reported, non existent, as in the case of amenorrhea" (Hibbert, 1990: 31).

Elizabeth I was referred to as Your Majesty or Your Highness, which are gender-neutral terms and sometimes she used language and symbolism to equate the womanhood of the Queen to that of the Virgin Mary. In this sense, she is not akin to the menstruating women whose very menses defines all things corporeal for both women and men – waste, decay, death. Her blood was not that of a woman, it was that of a monarch, a leader and a warrior. She was to show her subjects that she could walk amongst men as one of them yet also as one above them. She declared to her troops in her famous 1588 Tilbury Speech, just as the Spanish were about to invade: "I may have the body of a weak and feeble woman, but I have the heart and stomach of a king, and a king of England too!" In other words, the mind and intellect are more important than the body. She might have the body of a feeble woman but she *is* King.

Let us put this powerful holy Protestant Spirit against her nemesis, Mary I, the first Queen of England, a staunch Catholic: Elizabeth the Virgin Queen versus Mary, the perceived blood-haemorrhaging, crazed and paranoid Queen. Mary was known as "Bloody Mary" for her persecution of Protestants in her attempt to restore the Catholic faith. As queen, she would believe herself to be pregnant even though she had not had intercourse. Her stomach became swollen and her menses stopped but although her amenorrheic state replicated that of pregnancy, she was indeed without child. If we consider this further, perhaps her pathology was an unconscious defence and repression against feelings of rage in the face of a narcissistic father (Henry VIII), who had denied her legitimacy. The blood that was shed in the name of religion and restoration might have been an attempt to restore her own psychic equilibrium by killing off what the unconscious perceived as the psychic enemy. Some say that Queen Mary got her nickname Bloody Mary from her violent reaction to her discovering that she was not pregnant. Following Mary's death, in 1558 Elizabeth succeeded her childless, older half-sister to the throne but many Catholics in England and abroad viewed her as illegitimate, calling Mary Stuart queen of Scotland the rightful queen of England. Interestingly, it was Elizabeth's execution of Mary Queen of Scots for treason that led to an attack on the image of her Golden Reign as being beyond the realms of contamination; an image that Elizabeth had up till this point so brilliantly executed herself. In "From Hillary Clinton to Lady Macbeth: Or, Historicizing Gender, Law, and Power Through Shakespeare's Scottish Play" (2008) lawyer Carla Spivack quotes Robert Naunton, secretary of state to James I, as describing this act as the "one staine or taint" (Spivack, 2008: 67). Now, Elizabeth had royal blood on her hands and on her soul. Her morality was questioned and she became no longer immune to the judgements made in God's court, the "court of conscience". Those that question this blight on her reign argue that not once did Elizabeth reveal her innermost thoughts: "Thus, the royal conscience remained undefiled because its working remained hidden" (Spivack, 2008: 71).

Spivack compares this hidden conscience with the conscience of Lady Macbeth. The more Lady Macbeth exposes her conscience, the greater the collateral damage. Shakespeare's play *Macbeth* shows us a female monarch losing her crown (and her sanity). Spivack suggests that female rule, atypical in history until Elizabeth's reign, suffered a torrent of post-rule resistance and protest, wielded in literary works. *Macbeth* was written 15 years after the queen's speech at Tilbury and was probably performed in front of King James I as a celebration of his accession to the throne. James I was preoccupied with hunting down witches and crazed amenorrheic women (characterised by several female characters in *Macbeth* who represented the curse of barrenness, and harked back to Elizabeth's curse of childlessness). Whereas Elizabeth revealed nothing of her inner thoughts to her subjects to the extent that many saw her as a Medusa-like figure dangerous to gaze upon (this might also reflect the lengths to which she had to go, later on in her reign, to secure her throne), Lady Macbeth was available for all to look at. Her body and mind were open to investigation and interpretation. Lady Macbeth was a warning of what can happen when you put a woman on the throne:

> In Lady Macbeth, then, the female body is no longer imaginable as a locus for the secrets of the state; it is now transparent, accessible to the moral judgements of all, and deprived of the opacity necessary for the exercise of political power. This rewriting was achieved through the reworking of Queen Elizabeth's iconography; in Macbeth the symbols that helped legitimise a female sovereign were given new meanings that undermined the idea of female rule.
>
> (Spivack, 2008: 78)

It is interesting that whilst we might regard Lady Macbeth as having a conscience, in many interpretations of Verdi's 1847 Italian opera *Macbeth*, she is cast as an omnipotent narcissist and all the feelings historically associated with women such as guilt, remorse and sensitivity are lacking. She is portrayed as malevolent, sultry, a siren, bare bones in physique yet punching well above her weight. In contrast, Macbeth is not necessarily weak; he has a conscience and this is what brings about the couple's undoing. Sigmund Freud wrote that Macbeth and Lady Macbeth were to be viewed as two aspects of the same person. Fear, hallucinations and sleeplessness originate in Macbeth but it is Lady Macbeth who embodies them becoming increasingly unstable, talking in her sleep, remorseful, lamentable and broken. In "Some Character-Types Met Within Psychoanalytic Work" (1916) Freud interprets their first murder, the killing of King Duncan, as parricide: the mother (Lady Macbeth) incites the son (Macbeth) to kill his father and once he is murdered, the chaos of a destructive mother is unleashed. For a different interpretation, Shakespearean scholar Janet Adelman suggests in her paper "Born of Woman: Fantasies of Maternal Power in Macbeth" (1985) that King Duncan is murdered for his female vulnerability and for his lacking effective power. This endows Macbeth and Lady Macbeth with a new power, in the maternal image. Whilst many think of Lady Macbeth as anti-feminine in her plea to be unsexed – she is attractive to her husband and magnetically intriguing to us – the two of them are symbiotically tied. It appears that the more their actions and their thinking becomes out of kilter, the more hysterical she becomes. The loss of attunement affects her. Perhaps the deaths, the killings, symbolise the Macbeth children; acts of creativity that they perform together? As a couple they are childless, their generational line is to be empty of offspring. Their success breeds failure. Some retell the story as beginning with the couple mourning the loss of a child. In the 2015 widely acclaimed film *Macbeth*, directed by Justin Kurzel, the opening scene shows the couple watching over the burial of a young infant. This certainly makes what follows easier to digest and is reminiscent of earlier interpretations. The idea is that Lady Macbeth's procreative, fertile potential is to be murdered. Her future ambition is "a sublimation of a repressed sexual impulse, the desire for a child based upon the memory of a child long since dead" (Coriat, 1912: 28–29).

I wonder what Coriat meant by "memory" in his book *Hysteria of Lady Macbeth* (1912). In my reading of it, the memory is not of an actual child but of the wish and fantasy and imaginations of a state with child that eventually overwhelms Lady Macbeth and all that energy and commitment regenerates itself into an impulse and drive redirected to kill. To underscore the complex mind of Lady Macbeth, Coriat makes a useful distinction between Shakespeare's character and the ancient Greek writer Aeschylus' Clytemnestra. Clytemnestra is often seen as Lady Macbeth's archetype; her sexual deviancy, cunning and lack of remorse determine the plan and execution of the murder of her husband King Agamemnon. But Coriat usefully points out:

> Clytemnestra is essentially and fundamentally criminal, deceitful, voluptu-
> ous, coldly calculating in her motives and shows none of the symptoms
> which make Lady Macbeth the irresponsible victim of a definite psycho-
> neurosis. Lady Macbeth reacts only as her unconscious complexes make
> her react, Clytemnestra is the willing slave of her conscious will; one is
> a flawless and consistent type of hysterical dissociation, the other, the
> incarnation of criminal tendencies.
>
> (Coriat, 1912: 34)

That hysteria dissociation is "the result of unconscious conflicts of complexes" allows for the hypothesis that amenorrhea is a result of an internal displacement of something intra-psychically persecutory onto the body and with the removal of the menstrual flow there is a removal of that which is persecutory. Externally, Lady Macbeth can identify and locate the enemy by aligning herself with the Weird Sisters. They can call on the spirits to change the course of events. The Witches use their powers to influence the way the State operates and Lady Macbeth urges that the operatives, the working of her female bodily state, be altered. All these women are described as defeminised. If Lady Macbeth is to bring about a change in her personality, a psychological remodelling requires also a physiological one. An unsexing of both her biological and mental make-up is the only way to ensure she has a spirit capable of murder. But she is not up to the task. Her manic need to clean the blood spots off her hands reveals the non-rationale and acts as a stalemate that expresses her inability to make a choice to push on through or to hold out. This compulsive act needs to be interpreted as being more than an attempt to alleviate guilt. As psychoanalyst Ronald Fairbairn interprets (1952), obsessional behaviour is a conflict between separateness and identification with an internal dilemma of whether to hold on to the exciting aspects or to evacuate the rejecting ones in the internal world of object relating. An inability to resolve this question is expressed in the rituals of the person who is obsessive compulsive. Consciously, Lady Macbeth wants to remove the stains but unconsciously she wants to hold onto the feelings that are familiar to her which is why, despite her continual hand washing, her hands remain blood-stained. The ritual of hand washing does not offer relief, as you cannot wash away feelings that you don't actually want to let go of. Lady Macbeth's unconscious does not want to let go of the internal conflict for fear of where that might lead. Her unconscious is aligned to the status quo. In its simplest form, what we have here is Elizabethan physiological psychology in that a woman believes that unsexing her biology will bring about a mental defeminisation. It is suppressed menstruation that will be the most effective way of shoring up qualities associated with women. But as Jenijoy La Belle writes in "'A Strange Infirmity' Lady Macbeth's Amenorrhea":

> She abjured her womanhood in order to be impregnated with cruelty, but the amenorrhea has further results which she had not considered. Indeed, Shakespeare attributes to her those very symptoms that contemporary and near-contemporary medical books claim will occur when a woman's natural visitings cease.
>
> (La Belle, 1980: 383)

In other words, the amenorrhea replaces the old set of troubles with new ones. The symptoms of amenorrhea written in the manuals such as John Sadler's *The sicke vvomans private looking-glasse wherein methodically are handled all uterine affects, or diseases arising from the wombe; enabling women to informe the physician about the cause of their griefe* (1636) include faintings, "swoonings", "melancholy passions" and "fearfullness" (Sadler, 1636: 20–21). Similarly, *The Anatomy of Melancholy* (Burton, 1652) presents amenorrheic melancholy, this time accompanied by "troublesome sleep" with "terrible dreams in the night, dejection of the mind, much discontent" (Burton, 1652: 478 cited in La Belle, 1980: 383). These are the things that haunt Lady Macbeth.

In "Macbeth: The Prisoner of Gender" (1983), Robert Kinbrough explains how the play can be interpreted as one that is about gender and not about sex or unsexing. Rather it is an "essay towards androgyny". Kinbrough quotes philosopher, poet and a founder of the Romantic movement in England Samuel Taylor Coleridge (1832): "The truth is, a great mind must be androgynous." This is in turn referenced alongside Virginia Woolf's analysis of Coleridge in *A Room of One's Own* (1929), which is followed by Woolf's ideas about androgyny in Shakespeare as being "the type of the androgynous, of the man-womanly mind ... one of the tokens of the fully developed mind that it does not think specially or separately of sex" (Woolf, 1929).

Woolf is an interesting case of a woman seeking unity of mind and fulfilment from an androgynous state rather than from the experience of motherhood, the regarded route to good health. It is widely recognised that Woolf
suffered from bipolar disorder or a borderline personality disorder of which
chronic suicidality featured. Her husband Leonard kept a record of her menstrual activity for ten years after a suicide attempt. As Pankren writes in *Virginia Woolf and the "Lust of Creation:" A Psychoanalytic Exploration* (1987):

> Closely scrutinizing Virginia's menstruation pattern, Leonard kept records,
> noting she had no periods from August to November 1913, when her
> weight was at its lowest. During this time, she was acutely disturbed, and
> had four nurses in attendance. The inner struggle with Leonard over the
> issue of having children was at its height at the time she was starving herself
> and not menstruating.
>
> (Pankren, 1987: 69)

Woolf's search for an androgynous ideal in her writings appeased her own personal frustrations. She sought to move beyond the confines of gender towards
realizing a form of humanity based on a creative and procreative being through
a fusion of the male within the female within her. Woolf was all too aware that
in concrete terms, non-procreators were seen as non-contributors who added
little to the society in which they lived. Her world was dominated by the views
of physicians such as Dr Henry Maudsley in Britain who discouraged women
from seeking out an education in favour of concerning themselves with domestic
matters (Maudsley, 1894). Similarly, R.W. Parsons in the US regarded physiological destiny and intellect as mutually exclusive: "Nature has ordained that the
vast majority of women shall become wives and mothers, and if they are
exhausted mentally as well as physically, how is it possible to keep the race
strong, and healthy?" (Parsons, 1907: 116).

If a woman's energy was being used up in mental activity, her reproductive capabilities were compromised. Men were of the mind, women of the body. Gynae-
cologists such as Lawson Tait were adamant that "young girls should not play
music or read serious books because it makes much mischief with their menstrual
cycle and the intellect" (Tait, 1880: 813–814 cited in Studd, 2006: 411).

Even though contemporary women doctors such as Mary Puttman Jacobi and
Elizabeth Garrett Anderson refuted such views, they counted and they carried
weight because they resonated on a different register to that of pure medicine.
These male prescriptions healed the ills scored out of gender divisions and as
a result, creativity and intellect amongst women were lost to the world. In
A Room of One's Own, Woolf (1929) refers to Shakespeare's time of writing
when "any woman born with a great gift in the sixteenth century would certainly have gone crazed, shot herself, or ended her days in some lonely cottage
outside the village, half witch, half wizard, feared and mocked at."

In these times, women who were short of husband and children were viewed
suspiciously as anti-state conspirators, potentially threatening and destabilising. If

they were talented or wild of spirit they were on the margins, their dreams real-ised in another world, that of sorcery and witchcraft. The fortunate went mad, the less fortunate burned at the stake. The three witches in *Macbeth* represent gender ambiguity, a threat to a state of equilibrium. They appear immune to change beyond the confines of humans being human. The silent amenorrhea speaks volumes of their capacity to be outside of society. The visible features like their beards (I.iii.46) refer more specifically to a defeminisation of their sex. It was viewed as early on in the time of Aristotle and Hippocrates that when a woman's menses stopped, she might resemble a man with facial hair. The phys-ician John Bannister in his publication *The Historie of Man* (1598) wrote about women with beards and referred to the story in Hippocrates' *Epidemics* (VI.8.32) (1994). In the story, Phaetousa, the wife of Pytheas and a mother to their chil-dren, stopped menstruating and grew a beard when her husband was exiled from their home: "her body was masculinized and grew hairy all over." The doctors treating her agreed that the "one hope of feminizing her" was "if normal men-struation occurred" (Hippocrates cited in Hirsch, 2008: 66–67). In *Werewolves and Women with Whiskers: Figures of Estrangement in Early Modern English Drama and Culture* (2008), doctorate candidate Brett Hirsch explains that the body was often described like an oven:

> In male bodies, hairiness is evidence of the "superior" male capacity to refine and purge superfluities through pores as sweat or as hair. Female bodies, on the other hand, apparently lack these mechanisms for expelling waste, and rely instead on menstruation to do the job. Thus cases of bearded women, such as those reported by Hippocrates or captured on canvas by Ribera, were interpreted as being the result of the female body lacking the ability to properly purge itself by menstruation.
>
> (Hirsch, 2008: 69)

Hirsch quotes from a 1605 translation of Le Loyer's *A Treatise of Specters or Straunge Sights, Visions and Apparitions* in which amenorrhea is described as that which "troubleth the braine" with "idle fancies and fond conceipts", "diverse imaginations of horrible spectres" and "fearful sights". Some sufferers were known to have "cast themselves into wells or pittes" or to "destroy themselves by hanging, or some such miserable end". Women with amenorrhea were sus-ceptible to melancholy, delusions and insanity, their suffering intensified by the lack of a strong man in their lives. Left, they develop an unyielding will of their own.

In an exhibition at the British Museum in London called "Witches and Wicked Bodies" (Sept. 2014–Jan. 2015), curator Deanna Petherbridge presented an array of images of witchcraft from Graeco-Roman pottery to Renaissance and nine-teenth-century artworks to pieces from the turn of the twentieth century. The femme fatales included Lilith and the Nordic Valkyries and Giovanni Battista Cas-tiglione's etching of Circe, the infamous beauty who turned Odysseus' men into beasts in Homer's classic tale. Alongside the beautiful sirens and seductresses hung pictures of the monstrous: Fuseli's masculine Weird Sisters from *Macbeth* and Goya's malevolent witches, greedy and corrupt. Goya used the imagery of witches to attack the divisive social, religious and political ills of his day. Their symbolism was powerful and threatening. It was in 1484 that Pope Innocent VIII drew up a text on how to root out and kill witches for their consorting with the devil, lustful and carnal. *Malleus Maleficarum*, written by Dominican friars Heinrich Kramer and Jakob Sprenger (1484 [1971]), was followed for at least three centuries and many writers describe the witch-hunts as genocide. Anyone who did not fit with the image of the pious Christian was killed in accordance with the papal bull. The one constant theme throughout is that of misogyny. Amenorrhea was its accomplice. The witch who does not bleed menses and who when pricked with a needle "the absence of blood was an infallible sign" of her guilt is as obscene and dangerous as the bloody Medusa, the embodiment of the Devil, whose menstruating blood dripping from her snake hair is fatal. No longer women, these figures are monsters that must be hunted down. It was James I who came up with the most cunning plan to get rid of the danger of gender ambiguity represented by the witches. He declared that by determining the gender of a witch you do away with the threat and more specifically, by revealing her as the woman, her perceived power is taken away from her. The king would literally lift up the skirts of women who claimed to be demonised to reveal their female genitals. This gender "performance" was dismantled and now that the witch was seen as a woman, the truth of the matter was that her witchcraft had been a sham. And then her narrative, having dropped a stitch, was knitted back into that of a lustful, vain, transparent woman who needed firm management by man. She does not possess power. Her energy is unhinged madness. Her body proves it so.

A good example in the literature of such a woman is Bertha Mason in Charlotte Brontë's 1847 novel *Jane Eyre* (1847 [2010]). Diagnosed as insane, she was locked up in the attic, hidden from view by her husband Lord Rochester. The doctors described her as possessing a hysterical madness and they linked her mental illness with her menstrual irregularities. Brontë will have referred to the medical encyclopaedias to formulate Bertha's character, whose worst attacks came when the moon was blood red. Her madness, morality and sex drive were all linked to the periodicity of the menstrual cycle. She went by the moon. Bertha is described as a "clothed hyena" and scholars have noted how this portrays her as subordinate and denigrated. Interestingly, however, the female spotted hyena is in fact far superior to her submissive male counterpart. She has no external vagina; instead her clitoris is larger than the male's penis, and she urinates and mates through it. During pregnancy, she pumps her babies with extra amounts of androgen, the hormone associated with masculine aggression, so that she might bear male offspring capable of matching and mating with the formidable females. In the Arabic collection of poems *The Hamāsa of Abū Tammām* (804–845), the Arabic verb "*tadhaku al-dabcu*" used in the text in reference to laughing hyenas can controversially be taken to mean both to laugh and also to menstruate (Pinckney Stetkevych, 1993: 66). Bertha Mason of "dark" hair and "black" face is heard to laugh from the attic of Thornfield Hall. She is the mystical "other" to her polar opposite, the white, pure, reserved Jane Eyre. Elaine Showalter usefully writes

> To contemporary feminist critics, Bertha Mason has become a paradigmatic figure ... the dark double who stands for the heroine's anger and desire, as well as for all the repressed creative anxiety of the nineteenth-century woman writer. They point out that Bertha not only acts for Jane in expressing her rage towards Rochester's mastery but also acts like her, paralleling Jane's childhood outburst of violent rebellion against injustice and confinement. What is most notable about Brontë's first representation of female insanity, however, is that Jane, unlike contemporary feminist critics who have interpreted the novel, never sees her kinship with the confined and monstrous double, and that Brontë has no sympathy for her mad creature. Before Jane Eyre can reach a happy ending, the madwoman must be purged from the plot, and passion must be purged from Jane herself.
>
> (Showalter, 1987: 68–69)

Madness and hysteria must be split off and denied in oneself. It must be projected elsewhere. Furthermore, three's a crowd and Bertha shall be confined to the patriarchal wastelands like all other madwomen. Paradoxically, the further these women roam the more men become fascinated in them. It didn't have to take a diagnosis of insanity or hysteria to attract the attention of the investigative researcher. All that was needed was a woman, her body and the age-old question of her femininity. The starting point for research and analysis was menarche and from then on a woman's menstrual bleeds provided the matter through which man could monitor and track her state of health and well-being and, by proxy, his too and that of the world at large. The symbolic power of the menstrual bleed and the issue of its containment we shall now open up.

Policing, patrolling and politicising menstruation

Our journey here starts in Freud's time, in the political arena of nineteenth-century industrial capitalism of Northern Europe, during a time of social division in labour. Men were seen as autonomous, rational contributors who were in control of their own fate. At the same time, they were tiny parts in bigger economic production lines. Not taking to this lightly, they found relief from this contradiction through the act of displacement onto the body. The consensus was that men could cure themselves of illness and perversion if they willed it so, being rational gatekeepers of good health and reliable common sense (thus mirroring their economic prowess). By comparison, a woman lacked any such sophistication and her character and disposition were at the mercy of her body. As described by Moscucci in *The Science of Women* (1990) a woman's body was seen and treated as "a closed system in which organs and mental faculties competed for a finite supply of physical or mental energy; thus depletion in one organ resulted in exhaustion or excitation in another part of the body" (Moscucci, 1990: 104).

Women were viewed as a liability and, prone to erraticism and instability, their bodies represented an alternative stark "economic" reality that needed to be monitored and regulated by men. Menstruation, "the moral and physical barometer of the female constitution" (Burrows, 1828: 146), haunted men. In most cases relating to menstrual dysfunction, doctors and, later, psychoanalysts believed that at the root of the problem lay sexual stimuli, either repressed or excessive. It was notably an excess of masturbatory activity that needed attending to. A man not only had the power to control himself, but was the man for the job when it came to curing wanton women.

In *Discourses of Menstruation: Girls, Menarche and Psychology* (1995), feminist Kathryn Lovering writes in her Goldsmith's thesis that historically all ideas about menstruation and the female body are

> construed by power relations. They are an aspect of the late 19th and early 20th century creation of two specific, gendered human subjects, the dominant, active male and the subordinate, passive female, who have separate spheres of activity, the one public and the other domestic.
>
> (Lovering, 1995)

As Delaney, Lupton and Toth describe in their book *The Curse: A Cultural History of Menstruation* (1976 [1988]), a woman's menstrual cycle and her achievements are inextricably linked: the greatest achievement being procreation. This in a way sidelines the importance given to increased productivity achieved through greater "cycle awareness" because at the end of the day it is not production but rather reproduction that is central to the continued existence of all species. The baby as a reproductive commodity, a human resource, will save the world. For humans, in economic terms production depends on reproduction. Therefore a woman in childbirth is extremely valuable. Paula Treichler explains in her paper "Feminism, Medicine and the Meaning of Childbirth" (1990):

> Certainly productivity in childbearing was linked to the labor-intensive needs of both colonialism and capitalism, interests that have at once placed childbirth within the realm of the public interest and given the state certain oversight responsibilities. In turn, the health of childbearing becomes a signal of the health of the state: mortality and morbidity statistics for women and infants, for example, are standardly used to evaluate a given society's social and economic development; and in the U.S., high mortality rates have frequently been the catalyst for mobilizing social and government childbearing initiatives. Many decisions about pregnancy, childbirth, and maternity have therefore long been concerns of the state as well of the childbearing woman and her family.
>
> (Treichler, 1990: 120)

Let us return to nineteenth-century Europe in which many women had to find the balance between their reproductive and productive lives. As wives and mothers, they were responsible for the home and the children, but they also contributed financially to the family income by working. There were women for whom lactational amenorrhea took them out of the procreating market whilst not hindering them from work such as sewing, laundry, cleaning. In Germany, the overall number of women in the industrial workforce rose from 400,000 in 1882 to 1.5 million in 1895; by 1907, the number reached 2.1 million. There was a similar trend in other European countries but many governments viewed industrial work for women as harmful to their reproductive capabilities. But it wasn't just in their best interests that policy changed forcing women to spend less time at work and more time at home. Men had to be seen as the breadwinners and women the homemakers. In England, for example, the 1878 Factory and Workshops Acts stated that women were restricted in their working hours. Less time at work was designed to reduce the number of cases of infertility, amenorrhea and miscarriage.

If we turn our attention to post-war economic recovery, we can wonder to what extend a woman's contribution was acknowledged as equal to a man's during a time when women, many of whom again were married and were mothers, worked. The resurgence of the economy depended on an efficient workforce with women performing labour-force tasks. "Nature" took to the backbenches in times of political, economical, cultural and social revolution. Of course working conditions were poor in the mills, factories and mines, and women did suffer from malnutrition, miscarriage, stress amenorrhea and ill health. Irregular menstrual cycles are significantly related to cold exposure and schedule variability, and shift workers do experience menstrual irregularities more than day workers. Exposure to toxicants also cause disruption to menstrual functioning. But these states were deemed easily reversible and when external conditions improved, so too did a woman's health.

It appears that the real enemy holding a woman back from "objective" pursuits and from becoming an independent and accomplished producer was not her biology per se but the manmade cultural interpretation of her constitution being inferior and different to the body, mind and soul of a man. As psychoanalyst Karen Horney (1967) wrote, she is characterised as a debased love object:

> She is said to be at home only in the realm of eros. Spiritual matters are alien to her innermost being, and she is at odds with cultural trends. She therefore is ... a second rate being ... [She is] prevented from real accomplishment by the deplorable, bloody tragedies of menstruation and childbirth. And so every man silently thanks his God, just as the pious Jew does in his prayers, that he was not created a woman.
>
> (Horney, 1967: 114)

The Bulgarian-French psychoanalyst and philosopher Julia Kristeva (1982) explains this in the context of the abject (disgusting) body that threatens a breakdown to a patriarchal system that has a clear distinction between the self and the other. As Breanne Fahs interprets Kristeva in her books of essays *Out for Blood – Essays on Menstruation and Resistance* (2016):

> Prior to when people can establish a clear separation between themselves and others, before people can understand their objects of desire, before they can conceptualize the notion of representation, before they can clearly demarcate themselves from their opposites, before they can divide animals and humans or the primitive from the cultured, they had only the abject: shit, piss, vomit, decay, sweat, blood, pus, animality, murder, sex, leaks and rupture.
>
> (Fahs, 2016: 33–34)

Kristeva's idea is that bodily fluids erupt the "Real" and show us the inevitability of our dying bodies and of death itself. The abject evokes danger to an ordered system. It symbolises power that can weaken and soil. Julia Kristeva observes that in the attention we give to the biological and social aspects of motherhood and the fight for equality and freedom, "we may have become the first civilisation which lacks a discourse on the complexity of motherhood" (Kristeva, 2005).

In our analysis and in our assigning language to the non-verbal and in our attempts to formulate and to understand, we are more removed from the passion and conflict that imbues the experience of motherhood than ever before. Motherhood requires the subject to be both in and out and her passion is the "cleft between the mother's hold over her child and sublimation" (Kristeva, 2005). Following the presentation of her paper "Experiencing the Phallus as Extraneous or Women's Twofold Oedipus Complex" (1998), Kristeva reflected on the concept of *la mère au foyer* (the mother in the home) and on women who, unmoved by the feminist movement that rallies women to reject motherhood so as to acquire sexual freedom, many were rediscovering their femininity through motherhood. With regards to feminism, "although we have a dominant discourse on rights, we have no discourse on the necessity for the human race to guarantee its transmission, its reproduction. Thus we have a discourse on rights, but no discourse on history" (Kristeva cited in Pollock, 1998: 27).

In China, in a culture that prioritises marriage and motherhood, single women over the age of 27 are referred to as "sheng nu" or leftovers. The Chinese government suggests that women can empower and shape their destiny but the reality is they need the birth rate to go up to offset the aging population of a country that appears to be getting older than it is wealthier. By 2040, it is estimated that 24% of the population will be over 65, a slightly higher rate than in the US. Care for elderly relatives in China is taken on by women in the family. They are now expected to combine domestic, productive and procreative duties. In 2015, the

Chinese government announced plans to overturn its one-child-only policy in favour of legalising the rights for families to have two children. In 2016, this became law but the birth rate has not increased as much as was forecast, and there was speculation that the government might soon raise the two-child limit. High living costs, childcare expenses and long working hours are discouraging families from having more than one child. One child has become the cultural norm. Chinese twenty-first-century media is taking a multi-pronged approach. Firstly, they are upholding the traditional stigma of single women. It takes a brave woman to be single in China. The image of the married woman has been undergoing a makeover, re-branded as something desirable. The term "Hot Mum" first appearing in Chinese media in 2003 has become popular, describing an image of the modern feminist that departs from the traditional Chinese portrait of motherhood. Hot Mums are all-rounders who work and take care of the family. Based on an analysis of over 800 articles in the Chinese database *Duxiu*, associate professor at Fudan University, Shanghai Yifei Shen writes in "Hot Mums. Motherhood and Feminism in Post-Socialist China":

> It is argued that this process has not changed power relations between men and women, nor the roles of father and mother. Commercial and market aspects have turned hot mums from an initial expression of women's subjectivity with particular maternal values into subjects of consumerism. The hot mum discourse is apparently contributing to the oppression rather than the empowerment of Chinese women, let alone their increased sense of individuality.
>
> (Shen, 2015, 28)

Reproductive rites can never be fully explored let alone enjoyed when the contribution to society that women make is so heavily monetised. It is estimated that the Chinese government has collected 2 trillion yuan in fines from wealthy families who broke the one-child policy. Overturning the policy bought unexpected economic consequences with companies, used to paying maternity leave for one child, stubbornly reluctant to pay for two. Even though China has labour and women's rights law, some companies advertise men-only jobs. In terms of the laws and policies on menstrual rights, the content is ambiguous, the detail lacking. China is catching up to South Korea, Taiwan, Indonesia, Zambia and Japan on the inclusion of menstrual leave in the workplace. Universally it is not popular with all women as it might be a basis for bias, make it more difficult for women to find work and undermining activism for equality through the medicalising of women's bodies.

Menstrual activism is wide-ranging. In 2015, Kiran Gandhi ran the London Marathon whilst menstruating, not wearing sanitary wear. Tennis player Heather Watson said after losing her game in the 2015 Australian Open that she was off her game because of "girl things". Great Britain's women's hockey team emailed their coach with their period dates so that he could timetable training around them. The companies that make products and services designed to "manage" menstruation commission a lot of research. Most indicate that menstruation does impact performance. So whilst there is a new focus in medical and behavioural science research on "what can be done for women rather than what is wrong with women" (Golub, 1992: xiii), there is still an element of control being exerted on women. Menstruation in the modern era is big business, capitalised on and monetised from every angle, thus stripping it of its power and position. It is in the realms of politics and religion that its symbolism of power, persuasion and possession is at its most heightened.

Dirty protests

Female political prisoners in Northern Island whose bleeds represented a mode of resistance against the state used the symbolism of the menstrual bleed as a powerful weapon in political and religious warfare. Women Provisional IRA prisoners who took part in the "dirty protests" would add their menstrual blood to faecal matter and smear it on the walls and ceilings in their cells, sometimes around the picture frames that contained holy images of the Virgin Mary. They were protesting at the lack of sanitary wear provided by the authorities. "Theresa" is quoted in "Menstrual Blood as a Weapon of Resistance":

> the use of menstrual blood in resisting the state is an act so subversive that it effectively disrupted staunchly entrenched gender norms in Northern Irish society prior to the height of the conflict. This in turn provoked the risk of a distinct form of feminism rooted within the republican movement.
>
> (O'Keefe, 2006: 535)

The prison authorities would try and humiliate female prisoners by refusing to provide sanitary wear. Sophie Laws, in *Issues of Blood* (1990) quotes Teresa Thornhill's description of how one Republican female prisoner was interrogated for the week that she was menstruating. She was made to sit in front of them in the same pair of blood-soaked jeans. In her memoir, *Tell Them Everything*, writer and activist Margaretta D'Arcy describes her time as prisoner in the H-Block in Northern Ireland. D'Arcy writes

> While they thought the authorities were indifferent to their appeals for help when their periods were too heavy or too frequent, a new area of sympathy and understanding had been discovered, from the men in the Blocks. Some of the girls said that they preferred too many periods than none at all: "It is healthier," – anything to indicate that their bodies would not let them down over the no-wash protest.
>
> (D' Arcy, 1981: 80)

The public were not given images or pictorial evidence that showed female prisoners using menstrual blood by way of protest. Regarded as too offensive, the images painted on walls, printed on leaflets and in the press instead were of starving male prisoners, reminiscent of the suffering, pious, pure and clean Christ of Northern Island's Catholic community. As Dearey writes in *Radicalization: The Life Writings of Political Prisoners* (2010), there is a shortage of written accounts by Irish Republican women prisoners perhaps due to

> the deeply entrenched cultural idealizations of women and the importance of cleanliness and purity in the public maintenance of their identities ... the linkage in the public imagination of female sexuality with dirt and the commodification of the female nude (e.g. as bather or odalisque) represents an established cultural mechanism for encountering and negotiating the body and its boundaries.
>
> (Dearey, 2010: 139)

When the public were made aware of protesting female prisoners of Armagh, many reacted with disgust and disbelief. The public found it difficult to negotiate this image of women alongside the more dominant one they were expected to uphold; that of the pure, delicate Irish Republican activist. Female guards inside the prisons did not want to be contaminated by the "filth". The impact on male guards created aggression. In the short story "A Curse" (1985), Republican ex-prisoner Brenda Murphy describes the time when a female prisoner has to tell a male officer that she has her period:

> "I've taken my periods" she said simply. "I need some sanitary napkins and a wash." He looked at her with disgust. "Have you no shame? I've been married twenty years and my wife wouldn't mention things like that." What is the colour of shame? All she could see was red as it trickled down her leg.
>
> (Murphy, cited in Hooley, 1985: 40–41)

Images of menstrual blood running down the legs of Jewish prisoners and inmates in the concentration camps and extermination camps of Nazi Germany forever haunt. The Jewess was redrawn as a carrier and contaminator of filth and disease under Third Reich rule, representing the "other" and a threat to the state. Central to the ideology was the split between pure and impure blood, native and trustworthy, foreign and deceitful. The menstruating body of the Jewess was powerful and dreadful and according to the Nazi doctrine on racial cleansing, Jewish women were like vermin, multiple breeders with the capacity to contaminate and spread disease, biologically, morally. Nazi propaganda created an atmosphere in which their murder was to be regarded as a meritorious act in the service of saving the whole of the human race. Jewish women were to be "exterminated". The strategy of carrying out the "Final Solution" was a subordinate clause: the absolute was in its actual attainment.

Bibliography

Aderman, J. (1985) "Born of Woman: Fantasies of Maternal Power in Macbeth", in M. Garger (ed.), *Cannibals, Witches and Divorce: Estranging the Renaissance*. Baltimore, MD: Johns Hopkins University Press, 90–121.

Aristophanes. (2015) *Women at the Thesmophoria*. trans. S. Halliwell. Oxford: Oxford University Press.

Bannister, J. (1598) *The Historie of Man*. Amsterdam: Da Capo Press: Theatrum Orbis Terrarum.

Belenky, M., Clinchy, B., Goldberger, N. & Tarule, J. (1986 [1997]) *Women's Ways of Knowing: The Development of Self, Voice and Mind*. New York: Basic Books.

Brontë, C. (1847) *Jane Eyre*. New York: Harper Collins. 2010.

Buckley, T. & Gottlieb, A. (eds.) (1988) *Blood Magic – The Anthropology of Menstruation*. Berkeley,CA, Los Angeles, CA & London: University of California Press.

Burrows, G.M. (1828) *Commentaries on the Causes, Forms, Symptoms and Treatment, Moral and Medical, of Insanity*. London: T & G Underwood.

Butler, J. (1990) *Gender Trouble: Feminism and the Subversion of Identity*. New York: Routledge.

Coriat, H. (1912) *Hysteria of Lady Macbeth*. New York: Moffat, Yard & Company.

D'Arcy, M. (1981) *Tell Them Everything*. London: Bloomsbury Publishing.

Davis, A.A. & Nguyen, M. (2014) "A Case Study of Anorexia Nervosa Driven by Religious Sacrifice", *Case Reports in Psychiatry*. doi:10.11552014/512764.

de Beauvoir, S. (1949) *Le Deuxième Sexe, 2 Vols*. Paris: Gallimard. trans. H.M. Parshley (1952) *The Second Sex*, New York: Knopf.

Dearey, M. (2010) *Radicalization: The Life Writings of Political Prisoners*. Abingdon & New York: Routledge.

Delaney, J., Lupton, M.J. & Toth, E. (1976 [1988]) *The Curse: A Cultural History of Menstruation*. Champaign: University of Illinois Press.

Douglas, M. (1966) *Purity and Danger: An Analysis of Concepts of Pollution and Taboo*. London & New York: Routledge & Kegan Paul.

Douglas Murray, T. (1902) *Jean D'Arc: Maid of Orleans Deliverer of France*. New York: McClure, Phillips & Co.

Eghigian, G. (2010) *From Madness to Mental Health: Psychiatric Disorder and Its Treatment in Western Civilisation*. New Brunswick, NJ & London: Rutgers University Press.

Fahs, B. (2016) *Out for Blood – Essays on Menstruation and Resistance*. Albany, NY: SUNY Press.

Fairbairn, W.R.D. (1952) *Psychoanalytic Studies of the Personality*. London: Routledge & Kegan Paul.

Freud, S. (1916) *Some Character-Types Met Within Psychoanalytic Work*. SE, XIV: 310–333. London: Hogarth Press.

Freud, S. (1918) "The Taboo of Virginity", *SE*, XI: 192–208.

Friedmann (Ish-Shalom), M. (ed.) (1890) *Pesikta Rabbati*. Vienna: Verfassers.

Gilmore, D.D. (2001) *Misogyny: The Male Malady*. Philadelphia, PA: University of Pennsylvania Press.

Girard, R. (1979) *Violence and the Sacred*. Baltimore, MD: Johns Hopkins University Press.

Goff, B. (2007) "The Priestess of Athena Grows a Beard: Latent Citizenship in Ancient Greek Women's Ritual Practice", in G. Pollock & V. Turvey-Sauron (eds.), *The Sacred and the Feminine*. London: I.B. Tauris.

Golub, S. (1992) *Periods: From Menarche to Menopause*. London & New Delhi: Sage Publications.

Greer, G. (1971 [1993]) *The Female Eunuch*. London: Flamingo.

Hausfater, G. & Skoblick, B. (1985) "Perimenstrual Behaviour Changes among Female Yellow Baboons: Some Similarities to Premenstrual Syndrome (PMS) in Women", *American Journal of Primatology*, 9(3): 165–172.

Hibbert, C. (1990) *The Virgin Queen: The Personal History of Elizabeth I*. London: Viking.

Hippocrates. (1994) *Epidemics II, IV–VII*. trans. W.D. Smith. Cambridge, MA: Harvard University Press.

Hirsch, B. (2008) *Werewolves and Women with Whiskers: Figures of Estrangement in Early Modern English Drama and Culture*. University of Western Australia, Research Repository Online.

Hogbin, I. (1996) *The Island of Menstruating Men: Religion in Wogeo, New Guinea*. Prospect Heights, IL: Waveland Press Inc.

Hood, K. (1992) "Contextual Determinants of Menstrual Cycle Effects in Observations of Social Interactions", in A. Dan & L. Lewis (eds.), *Menstrual Health in Women's Lives*. Urbana: University of Illinois Press, 83–97.

Hooley, R. (1985) *The Female Line: Northern Irish Women Writers*. Belfast: Northern Ireland Women's Rights Movement.

Horney, K. (1967) *Feminine Psychology*. New York: W.W. Norton and Company.

Jewish Publication Society. (2000) *JPS Hebrew-English Tanakh*. 2nd edition. Philadelphia, PA: Jewish Publication Society.

Kantorowicz, E.H. (1957) *The King's Two Bodies – A Study in Medieval Political Theology*. Princeton, NJ: Princeton University Press.

Kerenyi, K. (1975) *Zeus and Hera: Archetypal Image of Father, Husband and Wife*. trans C. Holme. Princeton, NJ: Princeton University Press.

Kinbrough, R. (1983) "Macbeth: The Prisoner of Gender", *Shakespeare Studies*, 16: 175–190.

Kramer, H. & Sprenger, J. (1484) *Malleus Maleficarum*. trans. M. Summers (1971). New York: Dover Publications.

Kristeva, J. (1982) *Power of Horror: An Essay on Abjection*. Trans. L.S. Roudiez. New York: Columbia University Press.

Kristeva, J. (1998) "Experiencing the Phallus as Extraneous or Women's Twofold Oedipus Complex", *Parallax*, 4(3): 29–43.

Kristeva, J. (2005) "Motherhood Today", [online] www.kirsteva.fr/motherhood.html.

Kuper, H. (1947) *An African Aristocracy: Rank among the Swazi*. London: Oxford University Press for The International African Institute.

La Belle, J. (1980) "'A Strange Infirmity' Lady Macbeth's Amenorrhea", *Shakespeare Quarterly*, 31(3): 381–386.

Lawrence, D. (1982) "Reconsidering the Menstrual Taboo: A Portuguese Case", *Anthropological Quarterly*, 55(2): 84–98.

Lawrence, D. (1988) "Menstrual Politics: Women and Pigs in Rural Portugal", in T. Buckley & A. Gottlieb (eds.), *Blood Magic – The Anthropology of Menstruation*. Berkeley, CA Los Angeles, CA & London: University of California Press, 117–136.

Laws, S. (1990) *Issues of Blood: The Politics of Menstruation*. Hampshire & London: The Macmillan Press Ltd.

Lovering, K. (1995) *Discourses of Menstruation: Girls, Menarche and Psychology*. PhD Thesis London: Goldsmiths University. online.

Lubell, W. (1994) *The Metamorphosis of Baubo: Myths of Women's Sexual Energy.* Nashville, TN & London: Vanderbilt University Press.

Marshack, A. (1972) *The Roots of Civilization.* New York: McGraw-Hill.

Maudsley, H. (1894) "Sex in Mind and in Education", *Popular Science Monthly*, 5: 198–215.

McCracken, P. (2003) "The Amenorrhea of War", *Signs*, 28(2): 625–643.

Moscucci, O. (1990) *The Science of Women: Gynaecology and Gender in England, 1800–1929.* Cambridge, New York & Melbourne: Cambridge University Press.

Murphy, B. (1985) "A Curse", in R. Hooley (ed.) *The Female Line: Northern Irish Women Writers.* Belfast: Northern Ireland Women's Rights Movement, 40–41.

Neumann, E. (1955) *The Great Mother: An Analysis of the Archetype.* Trans. R. Manheim (1963). New York: Pantheon.

Niangoran-Bouah, G. (1964) *La Division Du Temps Et Le Calendrier Rituel Des Peuples Lagunaires De Côte-d'Ivoire.* Paris: Institut d'Ethnologies.

Norris, P. (1990) *Eve: A Biography.* New York: NYU Press.

O'Keefe, T. (2006) "Menstrual Blood as a Weapon of Resistance", *International Feminist Journal of Politics*, 8(4): 535–556.

Ovid. (1986) *Metamorphosis.* trans. A.D. Melville. Oxford: Oxford University Press.

Pankren, S. (1987) *Virginia Woolf and the "Lust of Creation:" A Psychoanalytic Exploration.* New York: State University of New York Press.

Páll, T. (2017) "The Diary of My Period", https://www.boredpanda.com/start-of-the-end/?utm_source=google&utm_medium=organic&utm_campaign=organic.

Parker, R. & Pollock, G. (1987) *Framing Feminism: Art and the Women's Movement 1970–1985.* London & New York: Pandora Press.

Parsons, R.W. (1907) "The American Girl versus Higher Education, Considered from a Medical Point of View", *New York Medical Journal*, 85: 115–119.

Pinckney Stetkevych, S. (1993) *The Mute Immortals Speak; Pre-Islamic Poetry and the Poetics of Ritual.* Ithaca, NY & London: Cornell University Press.

Plowden, E. (1571) *The Commentaries or Reports of Edmund Plowden.* London. 1816.

Pollock, G. & Turvey Sauron, T. (2007) *The Sacred and the Feminine.* London: I.B. Tauris.

Ragnheidarottir, H.J. (2016) *Quest for the Mead of Poetry – Menstrual Symbolism in Icelandic Folk and Fairy Tales.* Asheville, NC: Chiron Publications.

RSVCE (The Revised Standard Version of the Bible: Catholic Edition). (1965, 1966) Washington, DC: The Division of Christian Education of the National Council of the Churches of Christ in the United States of America.

Sadler, J. (1636) *The Sicke Vvomans Private Looking-glasse Wherein Methodically Are Handled All Uterine Affects, or Diseases Arising from the Wombe; Enabling Women to Informe the Physician about the Cause of Their Griefe.* London: Printed by Anne Griffin, for Philemon Stephens, and Christopher Meridith, at the Golden Lion in S. Pauls Church-yard.

Samuels, A. (2015) *Passions, Persons, Psychotherapy, Politics.* London & New York: Routledge.

Sceats, S. (2004) *Food, Consumption and the Body in Contemporary Women's Fiction.* Cambridge: Cambridge University Press.

Shakespeare, W. (2015) *Macbeth.* C. Rutter (ed.), London: Penguin Books.

Shen, Y. (2015) "Hot Mums: Motherhood and Feminism in Post-Socialist China", *Kvinder, Køn & Forskning*, 24(1): 28–41.

Showalter, E. (1987) *The Female Malady.* London: Virago Press Limited.

Shuttleworth, S. (1990) "Female Circulation: Medical Discourse and Popular Advertising in the Mid-Victorian Era", in M. Jacobus, E. Fox Keller & S. Shuttleworth (eds.), *Body/Politics; Women and the Discourses of Science.* London & New York: Routledge, 47–68.

Spivack, C. (2008) "From Hillary Clinton to Lady Macbeth: Or, Historicizing Gender, Law, and Power through Shakespeare's Scottish Play", *William & Mary Journal of Women and the Law,* 15(1): 51–89.

Studd, J. (2006) "Ovariotomy for Menstrual Madness and Premenstrual Syndrome – 19th Century History and Lessons for Current Practice", *Gynecological Endocrinology,* 22(8): 411–415.

Tait, L. (1880) *The Pathology and Treatment of Diseases of the Ovaries.* New York.

Treichler, P. (1990) "Feminism, Medicine and the Meaning of Childbirth", in M. Jacobus., E. Fox Keller & S. Shuttleworth (eds.), *Body/Politics, Women and the Discourses of Science.* New York & London: Routledge, 113–118.

Tsoffar, R. (2004) "The Body as Storyteller: Karaite Women's Experience of Blood and Milk", *Journal of American Folklore,* 117(463): 3–21.

Ussher, J.M. (2006) *Managing the Monstrous Feminine: Regulating the Reproductive Body.* London & New York: Routledge.

Vosselmann, F. (1935) *La Menstruation: Légendes, Coutumes et Superstitions.* Lyon: Faculté de Médicine et de Pharmacie de Lyon.

Warner, M. (1981) *Joan of Arc: The Image of Female Heroism.* Berkeley, CA: University of California Press.

Woolf, V. (1929) *A Room of One's Own.* London & New York: Hogarth Press & Harcourt Brace & Co.

2 Nazi blood ideology, the menstruating woman and war amenorrhea

I

The ideology of German nationalism was constructed on a body of metaphors – the body, genealogies and blood being central themes. As described in Hinton's compilation of papers entitled *Annihilating Difference – The Anthropology of Genocide* (2002): "Nationality is imagined as a 'flow of blood', a unity of substance (Linke, 1999). Such metaphors are thought to 'denote something to which on is naturally tied' (Anderson, 1983: 31)" (Hinton, 2002: 230).

By 1933, it was race that was more important than religion, language, or birth. Race/blood was the precondition for membership into a "social speciation" (Erikson, 1996 cited in Strozier & Flynn, 1996: 55). The Third Reich retraced their steps back to the Germanic people from the Paleolithic period and through this bloodline a reconnection and a reawakening to a genetic superiority upon which they built their Order. Nationhood was represented by the corporeal imagery of blood and bodies and in terms of racial hygiene; blood was the marker of difference. Like dirt, disease and excrement, impure blood had to be expunged. The ideology legitimised elimination. As South African sociologist Leo Kuper writes: "massive slaughter of members of one's own species is repugnant to man, and that ideological legitimisation is a necessary precondition for genocide" (Kuper, 1981: 84).

Hitler, in his earlier decrees, had cited the law in many American states that supported the sterilisation of various physically and mentally ill people. The Third Reich added that anyone who was not eligible to classify themselves as citizens of the Master Race was to be killed. Isabella Leitner writes in *Fragments of Isabella: A Memoir of Auschwitz* (1978):

> The Germans were always in such a hurry. Death was always urgent to them – Jewish death. The earth had to be cleansed of Jews. We didn't know that sharing the planet for another minute was more than this super-race could live with. The air for them was befouled with Jewish breath, and they must have fresh air.

(Leitner, 1978: 30)

The threat of contamination from an impure race, which could spawn impure offspring, was to be done away with:

> It was the Nazi view of all women as cell-bearers that condemned the Jewish ones. Even within the lowest life form – the anti race woman ranked lower still, for spawning it. In Hitler's cliché "Every child that a woman brings into the world is a battle, a battle waged for the existence of her people." Because women in their biology, held history, one gestating Jewish mother posed a greater threat than any fighting man. To be father to a child had no impact on selection. To be a mother in fact or in future – that was the final sentence.
>
> (Felstiner, 1994: 207)

More women than men were the first to be selected for extermination, not just because they were considered less useful workers but also because they were "perpetrators" of the "Jewish race" (Rigelheim, 1998: 348). We know that the selection process was arbitrary, random and illogical, and yet we also know that a woman's sex was precisely the criterion for selection. As historian, writer and author of *To Paint Her Life: Charlotte Salomon in the Nazi Era* (1994) Mary Lowenthal Felstiner writes:

> What helped make the Final Solution a novum – a "new thing" in the history of humankind – was not the open all-male propaganda against a Jewish race but the stealthy intentional murder of a Jewish female sex. Once we see that women did not die of inborn physical fragility – for they lasted longer than men in the Lodz and Warsaw ghettos – then the issue becomes clear. Along the stations toward extinction, from arrest through transport to selection, each gender lived its own journey. It was the weighting of each stage of the Final Solution against women that counted at the end.
>
> (Felstiner, 1994: 138)

Upon arriving at Auschwitz, Miriam Rosenthal watched her mother, her sister and her 1-year-old niece, along with more than 80% of new arrivals who were deemed unfit to work, get a hand signal from Dr Mengele that pointed them to go to the left, for the gas chambers. Rosenthal was sent to the right. A few weeks later, she realised she was pregnant. The Nazis didn't spare Jewish children. The leader of the SS, Heinrich Himmler would often defend the extermination strategy in speeches to his fellow party members. The Posen speeches, given in October 1943 in Posen, German-occupied Poland, are the first known documents in which Himmler, indeed any member of Hitler's Cabinet, speaks openly about a policy of the state to exterminate the Jews:

> I believe, gentleman, that you know me well enough to realize that I am not a bloodthirsty man nor a man who takes pleasure or finds sport in

the harsher things he must do. On the other hand, I have strong nerves and a great sense of duty … and when I recognize the necessity of something, I will do it unflinchingly. As to the Jewish women and children, I did not believe I had a right to let these children grow up to become avengers who would kill our fathers and grandchildren. That, I thought, would be cowardly. Thus the problem was solved without half-measures.

(cited in Friedman, 2012: 398)

Rosenthal hid her pregnancy for as long as possible. When she was around four months pregnant an SS officer picked up his loudspeaker and demanded that all pregnant women line up to receive a double ration of bread. Pregnant and non-pregnant women stepped forward, two hundred of them. All were sent to the gas chambers. Rosenthal did not step forward. Soon after, having been declared fit for work, she was transferred out of Auschwitz and sent to a factory in Augsberg. Her pregnancy was discovered at seven months and she ended up in a sub-camp near Dachau called Kaufering, where prisoners worked in an aeroplane factory on the Messerschmitt plane. With the end of the war approaching, the SS were concerned there would be consequences for their crimes. Rosenthal was put with six other pregnant women in a small hut and by 28 February 1945 seven babies had been born. On 8 May 1945, about a week after Hitler's suicide, the Allies accepted Germany's surrender.

During the Holocaust, Jewish women were sent to seven different concentrations camps across Europe. Ravensbrück camp in north-east Germany was unique in that it had been built just for women prisoners and in some respects is an anomaly in Holocaust discourse on gender selection. This was a camp that had been created for the "deviant". Prostitutes, lesbians and gypsies defined as "asocial", German religious prisoners (primarily Jehovah's Witnesses), the infirm, criminals, those accused of race crimes (sexual relations with an Aryan) and political prisoners, those charged with illegal political activity, communists and socialists and women violating racial hygiene laws were arrested. Until its closure in 1945, over 130,000 women and children were held there. Some of them were Jewish but it was their political affiliations that appeared to be more of a threat to Nazism. Some argue that at Ravensbrück, race and gender were secondary to politics, but the treatment in the camp was undifferentiating. Much of it mirrored what was going on in other camps such as the experiments on men and women to test cures for gas gangrene by creating wounds and infecting them with grit and glass. Some women were trained up to become guards at other camps and others were sent for immediate selection. Olga Benário Prestes, a German Jew and a communist was killed at Ravensbrück at the age of 34. Her father had been a member of the German Social Democratic Party and at 15 she joined the underground Communist Youth Organisation. Whilst operating in Moscow, in 1934, she was given the task of accompanying the Brazilian communist leader Luis Carlos Prestes, then in exile in Moscow, to Brazil. They reached

South America but were captured, following a failed attempt to overthrow the sitting leader Getulio Vargas. Olga was shipped back to Germany as a "gift" to Hitler. She gave birth to a daughter in a Berlin prison from whom she was separated in 1939. She was among the first to arrive at Ravensbrück and in February 1942, she was taken to the Bernburg Euthanasia Centre (*NS-Tötungsanstalt Bernburg*) where she was gassed in April 1942. Her daughter Anita survived the war and she regards her mother more as a political prisoner than as a Jewish victim. According to historian Robert Cohen who has written three books on Olga's life, there are 2,000 Gestapo documents on her, possibly the largest number on any Holocaust victim. Cohen points out that when she was captured in 1936, the documents show how she was referred to as communist and a member of the Comintern. From 1940 onwards, she was referred "almost exclusively as a Jew".

Käthe Leichter was older than Olga Benário, born in Vienna to a wealthy middle-upper-class Jewish family. She was an active socialist who campaigned for social reforms to improve the lives of men and women, especially working-class women. She directed women's affairs for the Viennese Chamber of Workers (*Arbeiterkammer*). She was a prolific writer of articles, reports, statistics and women-related publications. In 1938, she was arrested by the Gestapo, for illegal socialist activities and was sent to Ravensbrück in 1940. In 1942, like Olga, she was sent to the gas chambers of the Bernburg Euthanasia Centre. In her memory, the Austrian government established an annual state prize recognising the work of outstanding Austrian German female historians and in 1998, Gerda Lerner was the recipient of the award. In paying tribute to Leichter, Lerner wrote:

> Käthe Leichter personifies the highest ideals of feminism – lifelong activity on behalf of all women, but especially working-class women; conviction that social reforms are only just if they serve the interests of women as well as men; uncompromising struggle against fascism and National Socialism, which cost her life. In Käthe Leichter's life there was no divide between theory and praxis; she combined her work as a journalist and organizer with her duties as mother and wife, her political leadership role with her research work as a social scientist. Käthe Leichter was heroic in her achievements, for she dared in a time of terror and oppression to organize resistance and to oppose the horrors of Nazi state power with the brave words of humanism on thin leaflets. It was for this she was jailed and finally gassed.
>
> (Lerner, 1998: 50–51)

Different horrors, same hell

Narratives, stories, interviews and testimonies collected from survivors of Ravensbrück and indeed all other camps record daily camp life amongst women and it is clear that there were differences in experience between men and women. One compilation called *Different Horrors, Same Hell* (Goldenberg & Shapiro, 2013) is one such book that views the Holocaust through the lenses of gender analysis and feminist theory. Until the incorporation of female voices into the catalogue of Holocaust literature, the remembering of the Holocaust was incomplete. Much of the male writing approaches the question of what happens when reliable links such as nationality, language, religion, culture, political affiliations and economic status break down, and man is reduced to an animal state. As Brener explains in his MA thesis "An Investigation into the Intergenerational Transmission of Holocaust Effects in South African Survivors" (Brener, 1993):

> both the group and the personal identity of the individual were undermined through the process of dehumanization in the camps, and through the loss of communities, heritage and culture. The estrangement from self and identity impairment leads to severe identity problems (Niederland, 1968; Davidson, 1980a; Kestenberg, 1982). Simultaneously, the elimination of shame boundaries, privacy and deindividuation serves to erode higher ego functioning. The loss of anticipated environmental reliability, the occurrence of senseless events and lack of causality in the camps is threatening to the ego and can lead to the breakdown of internal reality.
>
> (Brener, 1993: 9)

A lot of analysis focuses on idealisation, ways to restore the damaged self, guilt and reparation. After liberation, the defences used in the act of survival in the camps remained in place such as automated ego functions, denial of loss and non-differentiation between past and present. Survivors of the Holocaust such as Bruno Bettelheim found meaning and understanding in characterising the behaviour of inmates by linking them to different stages of infantile behaviour, analysing that the inmates had regressed to such states. For example, he wrote of the concept of oral regression and fixation as a formula linked to the well-fed child. But for some, "A preoccupation with food when one is hungry is not regression. It is the body's attempt to remain alive" (Grossman, 1989: 220 cited in Brener, 1993: 11). Furthermore, the child-like behaviour is not the same as strategies for survival: "the former entails passivity and preference for illusion; the latter demands intelligent calculation and a capacity for quick, objective judgement" (Des Press: 151–152 cited in Brener, 1993: 11).

Bettelheim (1952 [1979]) wrote that surviving requires selfishness, egocentricity and isolation. Interestingly, we know that many women in the camps formed social groups and networks – "camp families". They would tell stories, read poetry, share recipes and so on. For some women who had lost relatives, this communal sharing created replacement families:

The exploration and emphasis should occur not because women's voices are necessarily clearer or better than men's – though in many individual cases they are – but because they are women's voices reflecting on their own particular experiences in ways that no one else can do for them. The need, however, is not just to let women speak for themselves. Of equal, if not greater, importance is the need for them to be heard.

(Rittner & Roth, 1993: 38)

Zoë Waxman's "Unheard Testimony, Untold Stories" (2003) questions why it is that much of the literature, as she reads it, concurs with "preconceived gender roles, patterns of suitable female behaviour, or pre-existing narratives of survival" (Waxman, 2003: 661). Waxman is concerned that historians might have overlooked the accounts of the "full horrors" of experience such as women choosing their own life over their child's or women becoming Jewish kapos (camp prisoners given some privileges in return for supervising other prisoners, labour work and tasks for the SS guards). Similarly, Sara Horowitz argues that narrowly following one interpretative stance "erases the actual experiences of women and, to an extent, domesticates the events of the Holocaust" (Horowitz, 1994: 265).

The horror began long before these women reached the camps and it was the biological functions of the body that threatened to damage the increasingly fragile sense of self. In the trains that took them to the camps the pail overflowed with urine and waste. The stench was overpowering. They had expected to be transferred to ghettos and to be reunited with their belongings and their loved ones. They were disorientated. The women, at first embarrassed about urinating or defecating in front of others, could no longer control their bladders or bowels. Women who were menstruating could not change their sanitary wear. The stench too of dead bodies on the trains created a toxic, hostile environment. But one of the most traumatic events that the women had to endure took place once they got off the trains. They were forced to undress. This was one of the most traumatic of "gender-based wounding" (Horowitz cited in Ofer & Weitzman, 1998: 336). Enforced nudity continued for those that survived another day. Clothes and possessions were taken away, and a number tattooed on their bare arm. It was the compulsory nudity that was the greatest attack on their modesty and privacy, not solely because it was enforced in front of the male guards and in front of one another, but importantly nakedness amongst different generations of women (many from the same family) devalued them. The task was to maintain one's dignity, while trying to survive. As survivor Guiliana Tedeschi writes: "At that time women cared more than nowadays about physical discretion, body care, even about the aesthetic details of their garments, and they could not reveal their nakedness without being traumatised" (Tedeschi, 2005: 13–14 cited in Miglianti, 2015: 44).

Tedeschi's *Questo Povero Corpo* (This Poor Body) recounts the sense of shame (*purdore*) that women in Auschwitz felt as that which represented the dreadful subversion of all that these women had once known. Their modesty, self-protection and sense of shame were attacked and they were raped of their psychological structures and defence mechanisms. Naked, they were then made to have their hair sheared. Hair was a symbol of sensuality, beauty and femininity amongst the Jews. Having their heads shaved transformed these women into a likeness of men. Many of the accounts are written in such a way that they speak the language of an asexual, universal voice. As Bitton-Jackson writes:

> The haircut has a startling effect on every woman's appearance. Individuals become a mass of bodies. Height, stoutness or slimness: There is no distinguishing factor – it is the absence of hair which transformed individual women into like bodies. Age and other personal differences melt away. Facial expressions disappear. Instead, a blank, senseless stare emerges on a thousand faces of one naked, unappealing body. In a matter of minutes even the physical aspect of our numbers seems reduced – there is less of a substance to our dimension. We become a monolithic mass, inconsequential. The shaving had a curious effect. A burden was lifted. The burden of individuality. Of associations. Of identity. Of the recent past. Girls who have continually wept at separation from their parents, sisters and brothers now began to giggle at the strange appearance of their friends ... When responses to names comes forth from completely transformed bodies, recognition is loud, hysterical. Wild, noisy embraces. Shrieking, screaming, disbelief.
>
> (Bitton-Jackson, 1984: 79)

The assault on their exterior was followed by one of an internal nature, one that attacked their body and their psyche. It was the attack on their associations to reproduction. Most prominent in female testimonies are issues surrounding reproduction. Identity for women of this time and notably for Jewish women was very much linked to the body and its function as childmaker. The mind was aligned to the tasks of motherhood and homemaking. The attacks on the body were attacks on self-image and identity. Having stolen everything from them, the Nazis also took away their procreating rights. As Marlene E Heinemann explains in *Gender and Destiny: Women Writers and the Holocaust* (1986),

> Because mothers were especially threatened and because a future for European Jews seemed unlikely to many camp inmates, narratives tend to place a high value on motherhood and fertility. In the context of mass death and compulsory sterility the association of women with reproduction and the preservation of life gives them unique torments and, sometimes, forms of resistance.
>
> (Heinemann, 1986: 34)

Women had to deal with issues of pregnancy, abortions, gynaecological internal examinations enforced upon them by the prison staff in the early period, amenorrhea and infertility. Sterilisations were also done by X-raying women's reproductive organs for sessions of up to 15 minutes. These experiments were conducted on a mass scale. Many women died after these irradiations. Those who survived were examined three months later during which their ovaries were removed and studied. Male victims had one testicle X-rayed and after a month were castrated. Women were usually examined without basic hygiene precautions. Vaginal examinations, often to check for hidden valuables, were regularly done using the same gloves or infected instruments. This would often result in infertility, as did the forced "surgical" sterilisations and other experiments. There are testimonies of chemical substances such as bromide and saltpeter being mixed into camp food to suppress fertility and menstruation. Bitton-Jackson communicates the panic amongst the women upon learning that bromide was likely to have been secreted in their food for sterilisation purposes:

> With amazement we all realized that menstruation ceased in the camps. The first week after our arrival there were many menstruating women … then menstruation ceased abruptly. There is bromide in our food we are told by old-timers. Bromide is supposed to sterilize women. The Germans are experimenting with mass sterilization.
>
> (Bitton-Jackson, 1984: 80)

It is difficult to find evidence amongst Nazi documents attesting to this and not all inmates experienced an interruption of their menstrual cycle. No one as yet has been able to say that they saw the chemicals being administered and put into the food. As Anna Jellyman (2002) interprets in her doctorate "French Women and Nazi Concentration Camps. A Study of the Testimonies of French Female Survivors":

> the concept of mass sterilization via food was in all probability one more product of the active rumour mill which is stressed in so many testimonies. This does not, however, render it any less significant as a feature of the reality of women's concentration camp experience, given that women's belief in the existence of such a systematic structural approach was instrumental in defining their experience and therefore in determining the female testimonial emphasis.
>
> (Jellyman, 2012: 23)

We can see this paralleled in an account from BenEzer's *The Ethiopian Jewish Exodus – Narratives of the Migration Journey to Israel 1977–1985* (2002):

> In the course of the narratives many of my interviewees recalled that pieces of metal and of poison were inserted into pills (and other

medications) given to Jews in the refugee camps in Sudan. This had been done, the interviewees explained, by the Sudanese workers in those camps, causing the death of Jews. While this is not recorded anywhere else, and most probably was not a "reality" of the camps, it is nevertheless a perceived reality, a psychological one.

(BenEzer, 2002: 43)

BenEzer links to the work carried out by Debórah Dwork whose interviews with Holocaust survivors showed that many of them firmly believed that their food had been poisoned. Dwork records that the answers to "Do you think a chemical was added to your food?" were answered differently, unreliably, questionably and inconsistently, although the overall response was in belief that it did happen. Dwork changed her questions to "Why do you think the Germans would have added such a chemical to your food?":

> The women's answers were clear and unequivocal, and nearly identical. Even if the Germans were to lose the war, the women said, and even if each individual speaking survived, the poison she had eaten would prevent her from every conceiving children; thus the Jewish people would die out sooner or later … This construct rationalized their experiences … Thus, if a girl ceased to menstruate she understood this phenomenon within that context, that was the truth.

(Dwork, 1991: xxxvi)

Amenorrhea represented a real threat to a woman's societal role robbing her body of a specific biological function. This then threatened her sense of self and her identity both on a physiological and psychological level. It was a long-term concern. In the short term though, amenorrhea did in some instances protect women from the horrific lewd jokes of the guards who laughed at uncontrolled menses running down women's legs. The guards would often beat these women up for making a mess, comparing them to animals and forcing them to clean up every trace of blood. The flow of menses is reported to have been humiliating. There were no sanitary towels or suitable undergarments nor was there available water to clean off the blood. Rena Kornreich Gelissen was transferred from Auschwitz, where she had used newspaper scraps as sanitary wear, to Birkenau, where no such scraps existed. She recalls:

> My monthly curse wakes me. In the confusion of moving from one camp to another I didn't even think of sneaking newspaper squares with me. I didn't think the latrine in Birkenau would be any different than the toilet in Auschwitz. How naïve I am; newspaper is a luxury that we no longer deserve. Once a month my period still arrives without prior warning. It is something I dread and wait for, never knowing when it will make its appearance. Will I be working? Will I be in the shaving

line on a Sunday, embarrassed in front of the men? Will today be the day I cannot find anything to stop the flow and the SS decide to beat me to death for being unclean? Will today be the day the scrap I find gives me an infection? I hate the smell. I hate not being able to take a bath. The sink in Auschwitz was a relief, but in Birkenau there are no sinks, just faucets … No matter how hard, nor how often I scrub, it always feels as if something is left on my flesh. I worry that the smell of blood will attract the dogs to me. Of all camp horrors, the dogs scare me the most. I pray that if I must die, I do not die screaming.

(Kornreich Gelissen, 2015: 96)

Rena Kornreich Gelissen was one of the few who continued to menstruate in the camps. She believed that some sort of chemical interference was committed against the women but understood the power of undernourishment on the body: "I don't know why the bromide doesn't work on me, but the starvation does" (Kornreich Gelissen, 2015: 130). Her periods did become lighter and shorter and eventually after several months stopped altogether.

Olga Lengyel worked as a medical professional in Auschwitz. Some of the corpses she saw in the morgue had "become abnormally swollen" and she put this down to "menstrual difficulties" rather than malnutrition. She cites a Russian professor involved in post-war research on victims of Auschwitz who found that "nine out of every ten internees revealed a distinct withering of the ovaries." Olga believed this to be a result of the torment and "constant anguish under which we lived" (Lengyel, 1995: 98).

Whilst we can understand the relief at being spared the burden of menstruation, many women who did continue to get their periods counted themselves lucky because it assured them of their continued fertility. The relief though was unhinged by the threat of danger from the SS and camp guards and by the envy of female prisoners whose own periods had stopped. Amenorrhea was the separating factor between the feminine and the defeminised. As an unidentified survivor of Ravensbrück stated: "It hurts, not to have these monthly days, ones doesn't feel a woman anymore, one already belongs to the old ones" (Füllberg-Stolberg et al., 1994: 128).

Their outer appearance was vital to women as well, to assert their femininity and also to give them a better chance at survival. Small wounds, grey hair, lack of personal hygiene could be a risk. They believed that their physical appearance mattered at the selection process. Another anonymous survivor reports:

You know, the most important thing here is that your breasts remain firm. My breasts have saved me more than once … When the Germans look at you, they first glance at your breasts … because as long as your breasts are still good, a person still counts as a work animal.

(Füllberg-Stolberg & Jung, 1994: 126)

Based on a study of 547 Jewish women freed from concentration camps and discovered at an industrial plant in Lenzing, Austria, American sociologist Herbert Bloch noted that personal rehabilitation was boosted by an improvement to the outer physical form. Women expressed the wish "to be women again:"

> People must think we are beggars or animals. I feel so ashamed at being discovered in this way ... It must be difficult to believe that I was once considered a very attractive woman. Now people look at me as if I were dirt under their feet ... People judge you by your appearance and by your manners. Now I'm just a name – nothing. Yesterday when somebody extended a simple courtesy to me that I would have taken for granted formerly, I felt happy all day.
>
> (anon. in Bloch, 1947: 340)

Bloch is regarded as the first of the American officers (and very likely the first professional American sociologist) to enter the camps and he assisted in the organisation of up to a hundred centres and communities for liberated inmates and foreign workers, who numbered in total approximately 500,000. His paper "The Personality of Inmates of Concentration Camps" (1947) showed that many of those liberated from the camps were constantly preoccupied with morbidity, with the breakdown of the family and with their isolation from the world at large. Trauma, shock, apathy, fear, insecurity and an instinctual drive towards the survival were palpable. Rehabilitation relied upon the rediscovery of the fundamental status of what it was to be human:

> Significant in this respect was the pride these women took in the reoccurrence of normal and natural menstruation. At the time of liberation the great majority had ceased having normal menstrual periods. They themselves were under the impression that they had been given drugs in the their food to render them sterile or otherwise incapable of normal physiological functioning. Later medical examination indicated no basis for this belief. With proper diet, rest, and care and with relief from the previous fear and terror, these functions were re-established.
>
> (Bloch, 1947: 340)

Studies in famine and war amenorrhea do verify that malnutrition affects menstruation, propelling the body into an amenorrheic state. But importantly, it is often stress, anxiety and fear that trigger it, far earlier than the effects of malnutrition. Whilst amenorrhea is an anticipated outcome of war on women, it is widely debated as to whether camp internment and associated famine suppresses fertility and whether it effects reproduction long term. A study by Pasternak and Brooks (2007) included the menstrual and reproductive histories of 580 Hungarian female survivors of German concentration camps. Amenorrhea occurred in 94.8% of women during encampment, with

82% experiencing non-menses at the outset. After liberation, 91.1% resumed menstruation within the first year and fecundity was not significantly impacted by imprisonment. Knowing that internment, whilst effecting menstrual function, did not damage reproductive function long term was a huge motivator for women to start the process of recovery and rehabilitation. This was one shard of hope for many who were struggling to reconcile their transformation from an educated and sophisticated people into a crude and rudimentary mass – "living dead".

In contrast, post-war reflection by the Germans was built on the vigour and the energy of reinstating values of normality, amnesty and (re)integration (Frei, 2002). Many Germans came to see themselves as victims of war and Nazism, not the perpetrators: "In this manner, the perpetrators of genocide were associated with the destroyers of Germany, while the Jewish victims were associated with German victims, without, however, creating the same kind of empathy" (Bartov, 1998: 790 cited in Hinton, 2002: 233).

Their message was that all had suffered an assault on human dignity and it was the use of the body as a symbol that came to represent the atrocities of the past. Leftist political protests of the 1960s reclaimed the body through demonstrations of public nakedness. The horror of the Third Reich was exposed, people were being reminded of the legacies of genocide, but so too the protestors were portrayed as victims, burdened by shame, wishing to be free. In West Germany, student protestors' stripping symbolised a taking-off of political armour associated with the Nazi epoch. Nudity was linked to nature and it was natural for them to reject the cultural machination of their nation's murderous past and seek freedom from the unsightly and the blemished. They were seeking freedom from shame. They took pictures of themselves reclining naked and liberated on manicured lawns in Munich. However, the naked white body imagined as truth and purity like Adam and Eve amongst the vegetation was in pictures juxtaposed against clothed others, whose physicality connected them to the corporeal – work, food, reproduction. These clothed immigrants and refugees were a sign of the myth of a re-emerging pollutant. The concept of bodily fluids, urine, faeces, menses and blood, embodied in these clothed figures who shared the same space as the sanitised German naked subjects, were spoilers.

In *Male Fantasies* (1987), Klaus Theweleit examines the writings of men in the Freikorps in Germany. They were private paramilitary groups made up mainly of former military personnel who strongly opposed Communism and were employed by the German government to quash left-wing revolts. With regard to the symbolic power of fluids: "They vacillate between intense interest and cool indifference, aggressiveness and veneration, hatred, anxiety, alienation, and desire" (1987: 24).

It was from the springs of human desire that led a man to be part of the fascist movement. The acts of terror were driven by this unbridled desire. Faced against the threat of Communism, emblematic of immersing blood, the soldier must not let in and he must not let out:

> For the solider-male dam, none of the streams ... can be allowed to flow. He is out to prevent all of them from flowing: "imaginary" and real streams, streams of sperm and desire ... All of these flows are shut off; more important, not a single drop can be allowed to seep through the shell of the body.
>
> (Theweleit, 1987: 266)

Fluids are unpredictable in their nature and potentially dangerous, with the capacity to engulf. But the most dangerous of all is the menstrual blood of a woman. Even though her menses indicates non-pregnancy, therefore she is not a societal contributor but instead just a bleeding vagina, she is nevertheless unpredictable, untrustworthy, conniving and carnivorous. She can create life. She can abort life. She can kill life. And to the Third Reich it was the Jewess, the spellbinding witch, who was a "threat that is absolute" (Felstiner, 1994: 151). Male rational, ordered domination will hunt down and eradicate irrational, mystical femininity. To expunge the nation of a woman's blood, to have a misogynist military that can control menstruation for its dangerous qualities became a vision of fascism.

II

In researching war amenorrhea and the prevalence of secondary amenorrhea in cases of stress, separation, trauma and conflict, I came across papers that cited the works of Hermann Stieve. Stieve was the chairman of the Anatomical Department of the University of Berlin from 1935 to 1952 and he was one of the leading anatomists of his time. He studied prisoners who had been condemned to death to research the ways in which chronic stress impacted on their reproductive organs. Having studied male subjects up until 1933 (Germany did not execute women then), after that time he used the bodies of executed women during the Third Reich to expand his investigations. The "material" he gathered for publication focused on data such as the menstruating and amenorrheic status of these women. He also enquired about the menstrual cycles of those incarcerated in the women's prison Barnimstrasse to study the way in which stress would interrupt their cycles. Stieve's work is starkly conclusive. He found a 100% rate of amenorrhea in young women condemned to death, with total gonadal atrophy at autopsy after five months of incarceration. Many refer to his work exploring the correlates between the "symptom" and the cause, but of course there is the ethical and moral code of conduct that he violently violates in his pursuit of knowledge. Just before my submitting this book for publication, I read in the press that the remains of over 300 of these victims would be buried in Germany in May 2019. The remains consist of one millimetre tissue samples. With this in mind, I cite a paper in *Clinical Anatomy* by German-born anatomist Sabine Hilderbrandt called "The Women on Stieve's List: Victims of National Socialism Whose Bodies Were Used for Anatomical Research" (2013). Hilderbrandt begins:

Bronislawa Czubakowska, Herta Linder and Libertas Schulze-Boysen, all had one last wish on their day of execution: they wanted their bodies to be returned to their mothers. Instead they became subjects of anatomical research and were denied a grave of their own.

(Hilderbrandt, 2013: 3)

Of the 31 anatomical departments in German universities and occupied territories, all of them received bodies from the camps' execution chambers, between 1933 and 1945. They were inanimate objects and their bodies were the foundation of Germany's post-war anatomy research and findings. In researching their age, nationality and reason for execution, Hilderbrandt illustrates a range of personalities, biographies and stories behind the women who were first listed by Stieve, often with mistakes and omissions in their records. Hilderbrandt quotes Snyder: "It is for us scholars to seek these numbers and put them into perspective. It is for us humanists to turn the numbers of people back into people" (Snyder, 2010: 408 cited in Hilderbrandt, 2013: 4).

In writing this chapter I have sought to impart information through witness accounts. Mindful of the elasticity of language, I recalled Ruth Klüger's words from *Still Alive* (2001): "the very act of literature betrays what was experienced in the Holocaust: don't words make 'speakable' what is not?" (Klüger, 2001: 11).

We must never lose sight of the enormity of events – both the grand scale of the horror and torture and the details, particulars, relentless inflictions put upon those sent to the camps. It is only from witnesses that we can grasp any sense of the experience. As Lawrence Langer enquires in *Holocaust Testimonies – The Ruins of Memory* (1991):

> Does a self-conscious literary voice intervene here between the experience and the effect, so that language and imagery obscure even as they seek to clarify? Perhaps: Perhaps not. But as we examine definitions and redefinitions of self emerging from victim narratives, we must keep in mind that each one of them represents a combat, more often that not unconscious, between fragment and form, disaster and intactness, bird-song and pandemonium.
>
> (Langer, 1991: 129)

III

In the 1950s and 1960s, evidence began to emerge about the effects of Holocaust trauma on the children of the survivors. Since then, much has been written on intergenerational aspects of trauma and the narratives inherited by the second and third generations of those who survived the camps. The variable methods by which we come to learn more about how and what has been transmitted are documented:

The mechanism of second generation effects is seen as an extremely complex one in which cumulative trauma of parental communication, the aspect of the parent-child relationship determined by the Holocaust context, and the historical imagery provided by the parent and by other cultural processes are mediated by interaction with normative developmental conflicts, family dynamics independent of the Holocaust, variables of social class, culture, Jewish heritage, and immigrant status.

(Prince, 1985: 27)

Secondary post-traumatic stress disorder is often cited as the syndrome commonly passed on from parent to child. It manifests itself in ways concerned with the question of "who am I?". Offspring struggle with impaired self-esteem, issues of identity, over-identification with the "victim/survivor" status, the idea that they are the "replacement" for murdered relatives and often many are high achievers hoping their accomplishments can somehow make up for what has been lost. In other cases, the trauma is all encompassing, with the threat of annihilation and catastrophic expectancy dominating their thoughts. This in some ways enables children to feel connected to their parents, vicariously reliving the dread.

Each account is different. Helen Motro recalls conversations from a group for children of Holocaust survivors that meet each year on Holocaust Memorial Day:

We gather to talk about our ability and our inability to love, to be lovable, to deserve love. We hardly mention the war at all. We don't have to; it's always there in the background, axiomatic. After all the war is our template. One of us might say, "when I was 6 and wouldn't eat enough, my mother shouted at me: '"Mengele I survived – but having you will kill me!"' And we others listening will nod and know what our friend means. Not all of our fathers beat their sons when their boys came into the house wearing black boots. Not all of our mothers froze us out as teenagers because they themselves survived by abandoning their own mothers at 15 in the camps. No, most of us had parents who loved too much, who smothered us with their care, their solicitude, their ever-present, all-enveloping anxiety.

(Motro, 1996 cited in Kellermann, 2001)

Natan Kellermann, in his paper "Transmission of Holocaust Trauma" (2001), juxtaposes Motro's account with a very different one – the daughter of two survivors of Auschwitz who was born in a DP-camp in 1948. She was clinically depressed for her entire life. The support from the family she went on to have and the anti-depressants she took were of little help. Her parents had lost five children in the camps and she was their only surviving child. She suffered severe deprivation for most of her childhood. Survival was a constant struggle. Suicidal ideation and dreams of the horrors her siblings had endured in the camps before they were killed dominated her internal world.

The internal world of patients who enter into psychoanalytic treatment is often burdened by the child's need to live in the parent's past. Furthermore, the repressed grief of the parents and the reservoir of emotions that have not sufficiently been worked through are held in their children who act as repositories. Many of these children become "memorial candles in Holocaust cape" (Wardi, 1992). When the parent projects feelings into the child, the child then must do something with those feelings that he/she has introjected. This process can often result in the emotional content being transformed and metabolised into problems, symptoms, illnesses and so on. The trauma is relived by a traumatised psyche and many individuals redraw the scars on their body.

In his paper "Psychophysiological Sequaelae of Holocaust Trauma in a Jewish Child" (1980), psychoanalyst Moshe Halevi Spero writes about his patient "Sara". She is a 26-year-old married Orthodox Jew, presenting with noncyclic uterine bleeding. Her physician, who is "suspicious of psychogenic origins of the symptoms", refers her to Spero whose subsequent paper begins by exploring the complexities in differentiating Sara's presenting symptom as either psychosomatic, hysterical, or both. Understanding the environment in which Sara grew up is key:

> As Sara began to focus more clearly on childhood issues, she began to challenge earlier denials of her family's destructive emotional atmosphere and her repression of traumatic childhood fantasies and nightmares. These were partly stimulated by her parents' frequent and detailed descriptions of concentration camp experiences and by their use of these descriptions to enforce discipline.
>
> (Spero, 1980: 59)

The emotional atmosphere during Sara's childhood was largely one of depression and solitude. Her mother was emotionally withdrawn and self-punishing. Her father was "passively seductive yet prohibitive". In the ninth week of her psychoanalytic treatment:

> Sara was now able to less defensively confront her intense hatred of her father for rejecting her femininity at puberty. Sara related that her mother would emphasize that menstrual blood was "the blood of death" synonymous with infertility, disease, human destruction, and Hitler's vengeance against the Jews. "In those horrible months," Sara's mother once told her daughter of her "I never saw the Guest" (Jewish tradition employs "the Guest" as a euphemism for the regularly recurring menstrual cycle). Sara's mother often told her that "Beauty like yours cannot exist for long … there are always Hitlers who would love to spill Jewish blood. Already strong oedipal fears and bodily preoccupations onto hatred of her father, men in general, and finally her own husband. Paternal and maternal introjects that plagued Sara and compromised a more appropriate identity formation

gained additional tenacity through unworked grief for her mother, who died three years earlier; Sara's guilt manifested itself in self-destructive fantasies and in a functional uterine anomalie which also caused a temporary inability to have children.

(Spero, 1980: 59–60)

In therapy, Sara recollected her mother miscarrying a 3-month-old foetus in the bathroom. Her mother screamed, "This is my blood, your blood, Jewish blood, spilled by Hitler." Sara, age 11, gagged and "almost fainted" and ran to her father for help but her call was rejected. He instead called the police. Spero writes:

> The disgust with which she perceived matters sexual was strongly related to the extreme death anxiety created by her mother and fostered by Sara's own need for punishment in the face of violently angry feelings towards her parents. In this setting, the trauma of the mother's miscarriage came almost as a confirmation of both women's pathological fantasies and expectations. During the next two weeks of therapy, Sara dreamed and spoke of wanting the symptom to reappear, but it did not.
>
> (Spero, 1980: 60)

In addition to Sara's hysterical characteristics and her specific symptom of uterine bleeding, she presented with other conversion symptoms such as gagging, swooning and the inability to talk. Somaticising overlaid expressing feelings. Sara's bleeding was linked to a fear of castration or bleeding to death, power, control and an identification with her mother's pathology. So too the reality of her own childbearing stirred up repressed feelings of guilt and a fear of retribution by her mother who miscarried. Sara adhered to the strict menstrual laws of Orthodox Judaism not as a religious Jew but as a neurotic one. She thus had "incorporated a powerful defensive structure allowing her to continuously re-experience the psychological and historical conflicts of her childhood, while appearing to function as a scrupulous and appropriately observant Jewish woman" (Spero, 1980: 64).

Spero explains that conversion reaction, a somatic dysfunction with no physical cause, is the classic hysterical symptom. Hysterical conversion symptoms tend to have symbolic associations and meanings for the patient. This bearing of symbolism and the task of subject against anxiety is sometimes that which distinguishes hysteria from psychosomatic illness, which is arrived at when other defence mechanisms have failed to protect the ego against the anxiety. The failure causes the psychosomatic disorder. It is difficult to separate the two out, as the way in which we view manifestations of psychophysiology is through seeing the totality of the mind/body process which involves multiple organisational, developmental, social, endocrinological, biological factors, and so on. And of the anxiety itself, from a Lacanian perspective it is not necessarily about what has been lost through separation, but instead about looking in the mirror and discovering that what you see/what you are is more than what you had bargained for.

Bibliography

Albeck, H.J. (1993) "Intergenerational Consequences of Trauma: Reframing Traps in Treatment Theory: A Second Generation Perspective", in M.O. Williams & J. F. Sommer (eds.), *Handbook of Post-Traumatic Therapy*. Westport, CT: Greenwood Press, 106–125.

Bartov, O. (1998) "Defining Enemies, Making Victims: Germans, Jews, and the Holocaust", *American Historical Review*, 103(3): 771–816.

BenEzer, G. (2002) *The Ethiopian Jewish Exodus – Narratives of the Migration Journey to Israel 1977–1985*. London & New York: Routledge Publishing.

Bettelheim, B. (1952 [1979]) *Surviving and Other Essays*. London: Thames & Hudson.

Bitton-Jackson, L.E. (1984) *Elli: Coming of Age in the Holocaust*. London: HarperCollins Publishers.

Bloch, H.A. (1947) "The Personality of Inmates of Concentration Camps", *American Journal of Sociology*, 52(4): 335–341.

Brener, L. (1993) *An Investigation into the Intergenerational Transmission of Holocaust Effects in South African Survivors*. MA Thesis Dept. of Psychology: University of Cape Town.

Dwork, D. (1991) *Children with a Star: Jewish Youth in Nazi Europe*. New Haven, CT & London: Yale University Press.

Erikson, K. (1996) "On Pseudospeciation and Social Speciation", in C.B. Strozier & M. Flynn (eds.), *Genocide, War and Human Survival*. Lanham, MD: Rowman & Littlefield Publishers, 51–58.

Felstiner, M. (1994) *To Paint Her Life: Charlotte Salomon in the Nazi Era*. Berkeley, CA & London: University of California Press.

Frei, N. trans. J. Golb (2002) *Adenauer's Germany and the Nazi Past – The Politics of Amnesty and Integration*. New York: Columbia University Press.

Friedman, J.C. (2012) *The Routledge History of the Holocaust*. London & New York: Routledge Publishers.

Füllberg-Stolberg, C., Jung, M. & Riebe, R. (1994) *Frauen in Konzentrationslagern: Bergen-Belsen, Ravensbrück*. Bremen: Temmen.

Goldenberg, M. & Shapiro, A.H. (eds.), (2013) *Different Horrors Same Hell: Gender and the Holocaust*. Seattle, WA: University of Washington Press.

Grossman, F.G. (1989) "The Art of the Children of Terezin – A Psychological Study", *Holocaust and Genocide Studies*, 4(2): 213–229.

Heinemann, M.E. (1986) *Gender and Destiny: Women Writers and the Holocaust*. New York & London: Greenwood Press.

Hilderbrandt, S. (2013) "The Women on Stieve's List: Victims of National Socialism Whose Bodies Were Used for Anatomical Research", *Clinical Anatomy*, 26(1): 3–21.

Hinton, A.L. (2002) *Annihilating Difference – The Anthropology of Genocide*. Berkeley, CA & London: University of California Press.

Horowitz, S. (1994) "Memory and Testimony of Women Survivors of Nazi Germany", in J. Baskin (ed.), *Women of the Word: Jewish Women and Jewish Writing*. Detroit, MI: Wayne State University Press, 258–282.

Jellyman, A. (2002) *French Women and Nazi Concentration Camps. A Study of the Testimonies of French Female Survivors*. [online] https://ir.canterbury.ac.nz/handle/10092/4593.

Kellermann, N.P.F. (2001) "Transmission of Holocaust Trauma – An Integrative View", *Psychiatry: Interpersonal and Biological Processes*, 64(3): 256–267.

Klüger, R. (2001) *Still Alive – A Holocaust Girlhood Remembered*. New York: The Feminist Press.

Kornreich Gelissen, R. (2015) *Rena's Promise: A Story of Sisters in Auschwitz*. Boston, MA: Beacon Press.

Kuper, L. (1981) *Genocide: Its Political Use in the Twentieth Century*. New Haven, CT: Yale University Press.

Langer, L.L. (1991) *Holocaust Testimonies – The Ruins of Memory*. New Haven, CT: Yale University Press.

Leitner, I. (1978) *Fragments of Isabella: A Memoir of Auschwitz*. New York: Crowell.

Lengyel, O. (1995) *Five Chimneys: A Woman Survivor's True Story of Auschwitz*. Chicago, IL: Academy Chicago Publishers.

Lerner, G. (1998) *Why History Matters: Life and Thought*. Oxford: Oxford University Press.

Linke, U. (1999a) *Blood and Nation: The European Aesthetics of Race*. Philadelphia, PA: University of Pennsylvania Press.

Linke, U. (1999b) *German Bodies: Race and Representation after Hitler*. New York: Routledge Publishers.

Miglianti, G. (2015) "Tracks of Shame: 'Pudore' in Writings of Female Holocaust Survivors in Italy", *Tropos*, 3(1).

Motro, H.S. (1996) "Children of Holocaust Survivors Remembering in Their Own Way", *International Herald Tribune*, 19 April.

Ofer, D. & Weitzman, L.J. (eds.), (1998) *Women in the Holocaust*. New Haven, CT & London: Yale University Press.

Pasternak, A. & Brooks, P.G. (2007) "The Long-Term Effects of the Holocaust on the Reproductive Function of Female Survivors", *Journal of Minimally Invasive Gynecology*, (14): 211–217.

Prince, R.M. (1985) "Second Generation Effects of Historical Trauma", *Psychoanalytic Review*, 72(1): 9–29.

Rigelheim, J. (1998) "The Spilt between Gender and the Holocaust", in D. Ofer & L. J. Weitzman (eds.), *Women in the Holocaust*. New Haven, CT & London: Yale University Press, 340–350.

Rittner, C. & Roth, J.K. (eds.), (1993) *Different Voices: Women and the Holocaust*. New York: Paragon House.

Snyder, T. (2010) *Bloodlands: Europe between Hitler and Stalin*. New York: Basic Books.

Spero, M.H. (1980) "Psychophysiological Sequaelae of Holocaust Trauma in a Jewish Child", *American Journal of Psychoanalysis*, 40(1): 53–66.

Strozier, C.B. & Flynn, M. (1996) *Trauma and Self*. Lanham, MD: Rowman & Littlefield Publishers.

Tedeschi, G. (2005) *"Qesto Povero Corpo" (This Poor Body)*. Alessandria: Edizioni dell'Orso.

Theweleit, K. (1987) *Male Fantasies Vol. 1: Women, Floods, Bodies, History*. Minneapolis, MN: University of Minnesota Press.

Wardi, D. (1992) *Memorial Candles: Children of the Holocaust*. London: Routledge Publishing.

Waxman, Z. (2003) "'Unheard Testimony, Untold Stories': The Representation of Women's Holocaust Experiences", *Women's History Review*, 12(4): 661–677.

3   A far cry from a no thing

Commentaries on secondary amenorrhea

This chapter will present and review the literature that explores secondary amen-orrhea as both a concrete and symbolic representation of a woman's physical and mental health. In fact, the stopping of the menstrual blood flow can be *the* giveaway clue of an underlying organic disorder and it can also indicate that the psychic apparatus designed to safeguard and contain is flooded. Trauma, loss, deprivation, helplessness, hopelessness, fear and shock are all possible "truths" behind the supposed blank canvas of the body that has stopped bleeding. So too, omnipotence and impotence, symbiosis and individuation, desire and a repulsion of that desire are possible routes to be explored. Secondary amenorrhea is multi-faceted, as should our approach to understanding it.

On the surface, it would appear that the work of psychoanalysis deals with a selection of shared themes. Patients bring to the consulting room feelings associated with depression, anxiety, loss, frustration, fixation, and so on. When they speak of illness, pain, symptoms and bodily function, so too the content, broadly speaking, might sound familiar from one patient to the next. But importantly, the analyst will focus on the experience of each individual because each individual is unique. From an existential point of view, each person's reality can only be understood if it is viewed from each individual's unique perspective. And in psychoanalysis, the analyst is often required to put him/herself in the patient's shoes in an attempt to feel what it is like to be them. Analysis can then go deeper to ascertain what lies beneath the surface, in the thinking (direct thinking) and in the imagining (fantasy thinking) of the experience. As Carl Jung writes in *Symbols of Transformation*:

> We have ... two kinds of thinking: directed thinking, and dream or fan-tasy thinking. The former operates with speech elements for the purpose of communication, and is difficult and exhausting; the latter is effortless, working as it were spontaneously, with the contents ready to hand, and guided by unconscious motives. The one produces innovations and adap-tation, copies reality and tries to act upon it; the other turns away from reality, sets free subjective tendencies, and as regards adaptation, is unproductive.
>
> (Jung, 1911/1912 [2014]: para. 20)

The skilful analyst will be capable of reading between the lines, interpreting what is amidst the interplay between phantasy and reality and between the realities of self and other. Nothing is taken for granted and nothing is presumed. There is a whole other narrative – that of the unconscious, – and a whole new discourse, that are there to be explored. In *Time Present and Time Past* (2005), British psychoanalyst Pearl King skilfully explains a key component of an analysis, which is called the transference phenomena. Within, the patient

> repeats and re-lives in the present of the psychoanalytic relationship unconscious conflicts, traumas and pathological phantasies from his past and re-experiences them – together with affects, expectations, and wishes appropriate to those past situations and relationships – in relation to his analyst, who is then felt to be the person responsible for whatever distress he is re-experiencing. In this way, the symptoms of the patient's illness are given a new transference meaning.
>
> (King, 2005: 138)

If we apply this in the context of working with a patient who is amenorrheic, the analytic couple can reconsider and re-examine the aetiology of amenorrhea and can locate the points at which it appears in the patient's narrative. Importantly though, when it comes to amenorrhea, as with many other biological conditions, we must not overlook the essential structure of the very thing that presents itself. We can't just rush to explore what we perceive amenorrhea to be or to represent or what we hypothesise as being the psychological components behind its formation. We must study the experience (Husserl, 1915 [1989]), its essential structure from a phenomenological point of view (Giorgi, 2009). What's more, we need to describe it if we are going to go on to interpret it and evoke further meaning (Heidegger, 1927 [1962]; Merleau-Ponty, 1948 [1962]; Gadamer, 1975).

Let us think about this in the context of women who have polycystic ovary syndrome (PCOS), which is often accompanied by secondary amenorrhea or oligomenorrhea (irregular, unpredictable periods) because the body is producing high levels of androgens, i.e., male sex hormones. It is estimated to affect one in five women of reproductive age and as a heterogeneous condition it has diverse and significant clinical implications for women: reproductive, metabolic and psychological. Because some women who display the hallmark symptoms of PCOS don't actually have cysts on their ovaries or fluid in the sacs, some doctors want to reclassify the condition as reproductive metabolic syndrome. It is crucial that the aetiology of this condition is fully understood so that the medical team can provide the best treatment in each patient's case. From a psychological, psychoanalytic point of view, we must look at it through the phenomenological viewfinder if we are to fully apprehend the actual "lived experience" including the experience of "embodiment and emotion" (Kruks cited in Jagger & Young, 1998: 66). What is PCOS? What is it like living with PCOS? In what way does it play on a woman's mind? What feelings are stirred up by the symptoms? In other words, the biological and the physiological along with the psychological must be pieced together:

> Most research has focused on the biological and physiological aspects of the syndrome. The challenges to feminine identity and body image due to obesity, acne and excess hair, as well as infertility and long-term health related concerns compromise quality of life and adversely impact on mood and psychological well-being. Limited studies to date have reported that women who have PCOS are more prone to depression, anxiety, low self-esteem, negative body image and psychosexual dysfunction. The other critical aspect of psychosocial impact in PCOS is the negative impact of mood disturbance, poor self-esteem and reduced psychological wellbeing on motivation and on ability to implement and sustain successful lifestyle changes that are critical in this condition. These issues all need to be explored and addressed as part of PCOS assessment and management.
>
> (Teede et al., 2010)

PCOS is the most prevalent endocrine disorder amongst fertile women and a 2014 Italian study, "Personality and Psychiatric Disorders in Women Affected by Polycystic Ovary Syndrome" (Scaruffi et al., 2014), showed that many of the 60 subjects had personality and psychiatric disorders compared with a control group of 40 "normal" subjects. Women with PCOS displayed "elevated dysphoric feelings, chronic emotional stress and several difficulties in social skills and daily life". Treatment might involve lifestyle changes (weight loss, structured exercise, modified diet), or taking the oral contraceptive pill, cyclic progestins, or specialist drugs such as Metformin. For women wanting to have children, infertility therapies are usually discussed. The reality of all of this weighs heavily on the patient's mind. Throw into the mix the unconscious and we cannot but appreciate all that the body must do as an active, not passive conduit of psychic traffic,. It is a synthesis of the psychogenic and the hormonal, the biological and the cultural. French existential phenomenologist Maurice Merleau-Ponty brilliantly writes about the way in which all these vitals "gear into each other". In "The Body as Object and Mechanistic Physiology", in his enquiry into what accounts for the phenomena of phantom limbs, he writes: "no psychological explanation can overlook the fact that the severance of the nerves abolished the phantom limb. What has to be understood, then, is how the psychic determining factors and the physiological conditions gear into each other" (Merleau-Ponty, 1945 cited in Mooney & Moran, 2004: 428).

Siri Hustvedt uses Merleau-Ponty's thinking to further her own understanding of hysteria. She writes in her paper "I Wept For Years and When I Stopped I was Blind" (2014):

Merleau-Ponty argues against the physicalist notion of the body as a passive extended machine with a dis-embodied Cartesian ego, a model that stubbornly persists in representationalist cognitive science with its computational metaphors, albeit often implicitly. If, as Merleau-Ponty argued so passionately we are active "body-subjects" in a world with others, equipped with pre-reflective intentionality and enveloped capacities that form over time, rather than isolated subjects inhabiting corporeal machines, then the "no-man's land" between the psychological plane and the physiological plane begins to close. If thought, ideas, and speech are embodied, psychobiological, intersubjective realities, not floating abstract representations but embedded in a bodily sensorimotor dynamic, then "conversion disorders" may cease to look quite so supernatural. Rather than charting correspondences between two distinct realms, psyche and soma, we can look for meanings in a live body that is socio-psycho-biological, with each hyphenated segment mingled into the other, rather than neatly stratified.

(Hustvedt, 2014: 309)

We know that the psychosomatic interrelationship is stronger in some regions more than in the Euro-American cultures and amenorrhea resides here. For example amongst the Yoruba in Nigeria, for whom reproduction is a task that *must* be experienced, anxiety is rife. In his study "Physical Health and Psychiatric Disorder in Nigeria" (1966), Robert Collis refers to Lambo's work "Neuropsychiatric Observations in Nigeria" (1956) to emphasise the significance of reproduction: "Failure to accomplish this function seems to be the key to the understanding of some of the neurotic conflicts that would otherwise be puzzling to a European observer" (Lambo, 1956 cited in Collis, 1966: 14). Collis writes about impotence and infertility as barriers to reproduction and to the desired social status that accompanies the production of children. These barriers lead to psychiatric disorders:

A continual state of fertility for women and an extraordinary sexual prowess for men must always be present if they are to have peace of mind. The most minor deficiency of these functions can lead to morbid degrees of anxiety and depression, often with the worsening of the defect.

(Collis, 1966: 42)

The Yoruba responded better to physical treatment as a curative method, than to psychological intervention. A settled mind comes about when all the parts of the body function harmoniously with one another. Physical illnesses are precipitants of psychiatric disorders. For example, many post-menopausal Yoruba women, in their hope to become pregnant, develop pseudocyesis (phantom pregnancy) and "Even amenorrhea of three years duration may fail to convince them that they are not pregnant" (Collis, 1966: 15).

Pseudocyesis, as we shall discuss further on in this chapter, is an example of the way in which the body enables the mind to avoid facing up to a new reality. Body memory is a powerful tool in this process. In "Body Memory and the Unconscious" (2012) Thomas Fuchs writes:

> In body memory, the situations and actions experienced in the past are, as it were, all fused together without any of them standing out individually. Through the repetition and superimposition of experiences, a habit structure has been formed; well practised motion sequences, repeatedly perceived gestalten forms of actions and interactions have become an implicit bodily knowledge and skill. Body memory does not take one back to the past, but conveys an implicit effectiveness of the past in the present. This approach converges with the results of recent memory research on the central significant of implicit memory which is just as much at the basis of our customary behaviour as of our unconscious avoidance of actions.
>
> (Fuchs, 2012: 91)

The unconscious is absence in the presence, the unperceived in the perceived, and as Wittgenstein reflects, "If someone says 'I have a body' he can be asked, 'Who is speaking here with this mouth?'" (Wittgenstein, 1969: 244).

Trauma and emotionally induced amenorrhea

In Buchan's 1797 *Treatise on the Prevention and Cure of Diseases* on what is now commonly referred to as stress or emotional amenorrhea, formally classified as psychogenic, functional or hypothalamic amenorrhea, Buchan writes, "Barrenness is often the consequence of grief, sudden fear, anxiety or any of the passions which tend to obstruct the menstrual flux" (Buchan, 1797: 368).

In many cases psychic factors influence endocrine functioning: This disrupts the reproductive system and periods stop, often abruptly. Psychogenic amenorrhea is also linked to nervous disorders "frequently interwoven in the aetiology of neuroses or some psychotic states" (Björo, 1966: 78).

There are several striking examples of trauma-induced amenorrhea. In "'Symbolic' Amenorrhea – Emotional Factors in Secondary Amenorrhea" (1979), Coldsmith writes about a woman who was menstruating regularly but became amenorrheic after she was severely beaten and abused by her husband on their wedding night. For the whole of the six-year marriage and for the two years following the divorce, she did not have a menstrual bleed. When she got engaged to a man whom she then went on to marry her periods came back (Coldsmith, 1979 cited in Thompson, 1988: 60). In "The Etiology of Some Menstrual Disorders: A Gynaecological and Psychiatric Issue" (2007), Sheinfeld et al. give an example of an orthodox Jewish woman forced to have intercourse with her husband when menstruating. Jewish law states that husband and wife should not have contact with one another whilst the woman is "unclean". Sheinfeld interprets the woman's amenorrhea as a "defence" against her feelings associated with being made to suffer in sin. In her thirteenth year of amenorrhea, she feels relieved rather than annoyed. Is it not also that her condition somatises and anaesthetises the rage that exists cornered by the impotent stance she must adopt, framed by Jewish law that states a bride is the property of her husband?

In *Psychosomatic Aspects of Gynaecological Disorders, Seven Psychoanalytic Case Studies* (1969), Ludwig, Murawski and Sturgis focus their writing on integrating psychoanalysis with medicine. One of the cases they present is of a 32-year-old woman who had her first period at 14; her periods stopped around the age of 18, soon after her father was involved in a car accident. The driver of the other car was killed and the patient's father's face was "smashed". He lost sight in one eye and his sense of smell, and the depression that took hold of him had a long-lasting impact emotionally and financially. Ludwig writes, "During the course of this patient's psycho-analysis, one theme recurred: death wishes to herself and more particularly to others ... Women seemed to be outstanding targets for her aggression" (Ludwig et al., 1969: 27). This patient often envisaged herself as a heroine. Like Joan of Arc, her amenorrhea was a sign of her strength. Recurring fantasies were of having a penis and urinating standing up. At the time of the accident, with the onset of her amenorrhea "she died as a girl" (Ludwig et al., 1969: 32).

In Helke Sander's "Remembering/Forgetting", which is an essay taken from *Liberators Take Liberties: War, Rapes Children* (Sander & Johr, 1992), the reader is shown examples of women and the soldier "liberators" who raped them during and after the war in Germany, notably in Berlin in 1945. One witness reports:

> The women's hysteria set in once the rumour started about the black troops who would be the first to march in if the Russians were not faster. I also witnessed the ways in which mothers who tormented us with warnings about washing made themselves unattractive and dirty to repel the conquerors.
>
> (Sander, 1995: 16)

Venereal disease, contracted through rape, was widespread, with many women being subjected to forced examinations and medication. Of these women, many became amenorrheic, often for some years. Most remained silent, developing "a distance from socially proclaimed truths and a sense of absurdity associated with withdrawal, mistrust and the reflexes of those who play dead" (Sander, 1995: 25).

Perhaps the amenorrhea developed as an organic symptom following invasive and unhygienic examinations. Perhaps too it was the result of the shock and trauma that caused a schism in the previously well-regulated hypothalamic-pituitary-adrenal (HPA) axis or might we think of it in symbolic terms as the emergence of a most powerful and evocative symbol of playing dead? The body is dead, shut off to life and to all men who wish their sperm to impregnate her. Is not her amenorrhea an act that diffuses the acute pain and creates a watertight defensive system that is defiant, even scornful, aspiringly transcending of nature? At the same time, we have Sander's point that many women "forgave" their rapists and perhaps in these instances, the amenorrhea was a state that subscribed to being outside the natural order of things yet at the same time inside a societal system governed by law but where that law did not clearly, definitively oppose transgression. She is compromised by a perverse version of Freud's notion of "turning towards the father" (Freud, 1931, *SE*, XXI: 221–46). Whilst many women who had been raped had to decide whether to abort an unborn child or to give birth to it, amenorrhea could signify at the very least a barrier to entry, the prevention of future unwanted pregnancies and a defence against reliving the primary trauma.

It is often difficult to cut through the culture of silence that inhibits many women from talking about their experiences; menstruation itself is "commonly invested with a variety of sociocultural, ethnic, and other highly personal beliefs" (Youngs & Reame, 1985 cited in Rosenthal & Smith, 1985: 25).

By taking a multi-disciplined approach, where the patient feels her case is much more to the clinician than just cause, effect and treatment, she might feel enabled to resolve that which inflicts on both body and mind. The next part of this chapter will be a compilation of research and clinical work to illustrate and examine cases of secondary amenorrhea. They come from studies in psychiatry, psychoanalysis and psychosomatic medicine. The theories and the clinical examples in many ways interlink and formulate a dynamic of interplay. We shall begin with hysteria, as it is one of the most richly documented conditions in which amenorrhea features.

Historical treatises on amenorrhea and hysteria linked to trauma

Whilst looking through the books on hysteria at Senate House library in London, in and amongst the more familiar ones was a treasure of a find that had not as yet been signed out; *Hysteria Complicated by Ecstasy – The Case of Nanette Leroux* (2010). Its author Jan Goldstein, whilst rummaging around a Paris archive, came across a manuscript from the 1820s, which she suspected was terra incognita. Goldstein discovered over 200 pages of notes recording and narrating the case of Nanette Leroux. Nanette's hysterical catalepsy was, according to her French physician, the renowned Antoine Despine, caused by fright. The first entry in the medical diary reads

> The patient attributed the onset of her malady not without reason to the repeated frights caused by an evil person, a rural policeman (*garde champêtre*) who on several occasions had attempted to offend her modesty. The first time he pursued her, she was having her period, and the flow stopped immediately. She was at the time, seventeen years old.
>
> (Goldstein, 2010: 138)

The blocked and suppressed fluids caused the catalepsy and hysteria, which led to a loss of speech and *"transport des sens"* (sensory transportation). Despine had called his case study "History of the Catalepsy of Nanette Leroux", but his co-author, Alexandre Bertrand, renamed it "Hysteria Complicated by Ecstasy". The title was somewhat misleading as neither author made any interpretations of a sexual nature for fear of being incriminated. They sought to dispense of Nanette's symptoms with a series of shock therapies, cold showers and magnetism. It was as if the body was an intricate system of currents, some of which had short-circuited, that could be fixed and re-circuited. This was common in those days (Shorter, 1992) but not all practitioners were convinced. French midwife Marie-Anne Victoire Gillain Boivin thought it imprudent to believe a cold shower could kick-start menses when in fact it might even re-ignite the hysteria.

Years following her treatment, Nanette married and became pregnant, ful-filling the role of what society deemed sensible and healthy for a woman. However her old symptoms returned, refuting the belief that the best remedy for menstrual malady was marriage and motherhood. Jan Goldstein interprets Nanette's attachment to ill health as a wish to be cared for by her doctors in a place described by Erik Erikson (1968) as a "moratorium". She had already once displayed such yearning during her treatment when she had created a symbiotic co-dependency with her carer Maillard. He attended to her every need and engaged with Nanette in a way that Despine, frustratingly, would/could not: "By the force of his folksy eloquence, he succeeded in getting through to the patient and reassuring her. But he becomes her 'misplaced accomplice'" (Goldstein, 2010: 180).

Despine and Bertrand will have known other practitioners such as Louyer-Villermay who were exploring the eroticised aspects of hysteria with the patient communicating "insufficient sexual satisfaction and an overactive imagination" (Goldstein, 2010: 54). Unmet eroticism with nervous spasms were at the root of the etiology of hysteria. Nanette's cataleptic symptoms were apt in dramatising this. Despine and his team had refused to explore her hysteria as anything more than an articulation of friction between psyche and soma. Their goal was for their patient to resume menses. That was the indi-cator of a good health.

Michael Foucault famously named medicine of the nineteenth century, a time of "hysterization" of the female body (Foucault, 1978: 104), but contrary to his assertion that this was going on only amongst the bourgeoisie, there are many records that prove the poor, just as much as the rich, were concerned with their bodies and sexual function. In "Hysteria At the Edinburgh Infirmary – The Con-struction and Treatment of A Disease, 1770–1800" (1988), Professor Risse uncovers the ambiguous constructions of disease formulae and reveals that work-ing-class women sought treatment for hysteria. Nearly 80% of women at admission were amenorrheic. Having taken into account nutritional and environmental fac-tors, most of these women were still proscribed a daily dose of electrical shocks to the lower abdomen, a method known as "drawing sparks". But physicians noted that whilst the hysteria might subside, "most menstrual irregularities, especially the amenorrheas, remained unchanged" (Risse, 1988: 13).

Désiré Bourneville observed this in 1873, when working on the theory of a uterine etiology of hysteria. He wrote of one patient:

> Her periods are sometimes accompanied by attacks, but not in any absolute way. Often the attacks occur in the interval between periods. Delays in menstruation do not appear to have any action. Finally a very long amenorrhea (19 months) did not prevent the attacks from returning for ten months.
>
> (Bourneville, 1877: 164 cited in Bogousslavsky, 2014: 72)

Bourneville is often thought of as a pioneer in neuropsychology and is credited for his capacity to listen to and empathise with his patients, developing a social analysis of the condition of hysteria rather than just making it accountable to clinical diagnostics. Bourneville introduced the older physician Jean-Martin Charcot to the Saltpêtrière Hospital in Paris. It is Charcot's work with hysterical patients, one that gradually evolved over a 20-year period, that has caused us to see hysterics as specimens, theatrically posing their hysterical wares in front of their physicians and their audiences. Despite all of the theatrics, there were some major advancements taking place. French scholar Asti Hustvedt crucially points out in *Medical Muses: Hysteria in Nineteenth-Century Paris* (2011) that Charcot was linking neurology with somatics and the psyche. Many of his patients refused food, many were diagnosed with depression, multiple personality disorders and some self-harmed. They were assimilated into his thinking about patient work and they complied with his treatment of conditions, many of which are common today. Hysteria is no longer classified as a disease or diagnosed as a medical entity in its own right, but it remains in our consciousness and aspects of it have been broken off and reclassified into disorders each with their own separate names. In "The Body and The Mind, The Doctor and The Patient: Negotiating Hysteria", Porter asks

> So what of hysteria? Are historians to think of hysteria as a true disease, whose rise and fall can, in principle, be plotted down the centuries, so long as we exercise vigilance against anachronistic translation or archaic concepts? Or is it a veritable joker in the taxonomic pack, a promiscuous diagnostic fly-by-night, never faithfully wedded to an authentic malady – or worse, a whole spurious entity, a fancy free disease name, like Prester John, independent of any corresponding disease-thing, a cover up for medical ignorance? Or worse still, may hysteria truly have been the doctor's Waterloo: a real disorder, but, as Alan Krohn hints, one so "elusive" as to have slipped our nosological nets?
>
> (Porter, 1993: 226)

Charcot's contemporaries, Janet and Freud, advanced the theory of hysteria as "*maladie mentale*" but this theory was long in the making. In "Hysteria – The History of a Disease" (1965), Ilza Veith commends the seventeenth-century physician and chemist Edward Jorden for writing about hysteria as a psychological malady. For Jorden (1603), hysteria, often arising from uterine and menstrual blockages, was the result of "peturbations of the minde". He offered up sexual abstinence (a traditional Galenic theme) as one frustration and prescribed a treatment that was designed to enable the patient to release their emotional tensions. Around 150 years later, William Cullen (1769) classified hysteria under a new category of illness termed "neuroses". Cullen and fellow medics such as James Gregory explored psychological factors such as fear, anger and disappointment as triggers that might cause a fit. To be clear, however, Cullen coined the term but was not the father of neurosis. His work was predominantly on hypochondriasis to which he referred to hysteria in describing its uniqueness not from a distinct nervousness but from "its combined effects on the vital and intellectual functions" (Dyde, 2015: 230). Menstrual disturbances flagged up physical and psychic discord. In 1781, Dublin obstetrician Edward Forrester linked amenorrhea with "a vehement desire of venery, attended with melancholy or mania" (Forrester, 1781 cited in Shorter, 1992: 17).

In the 1800s, amenorrhea was steadfastly cited as "a cause of insanity". In 1873, Thomas Clouston, a lecturer on mental diseases at the University of Edinburgh, identified 35 different types of insanity, a quarter of which were specific to women, including "amenorrheal insanity", "puerperal insanity", "insanity of pregnancy", "lactational insanity" and "hysterical insanity". Many medics incorporated early psychoanalytic theories of sexual desire and sexual function into their treatment of the "female maladies" (Showalter, 1985 [1997]). As they understood it, during important stages in a woman's life cycle, notably puberty, a failure of the impulse or libido to direct mental energy resulted in mental illness such as hysterical or puerperal insanity. This theory was later on put to use at the Maudsley Hospital between 1923 and 1938. Patients were given glandular extracts taken from animal sources as one form of treatment. The practice of administering hormonal secretions to the body was commonplace in the early twentieth century. Alongside this, a psychological enquiry took place to discover what might have caused the illness, what was lacking and what they were in need from their environment. One case study was of a 21-year-old woman, admitted in April 1923, under the care of Doctor Isabel Emslie Hutton. The patient was diagnosed with "compulsion neurosis" caused by the "condition of [her] sex organs". Hutton stated that a stay at Maudsley would allow this patient the space she needed away from her mother:

> Her mother fussing at puberty about her amenorrhea and warnings about men appeared to have made her regress towards childishness and she says she "wanted to remain a child", cared for by and dependent upon her

mother. Her fear of going out of her mind is associated with her amenorrhea and with masturbation, which she feared had injured her. The compulsion to touch things, and her own body, are also connected with this (CFM 003.1125).

(Evans & Jones, 2012)

After eight months of treatment with glandular and hormonal extracts, the patient was reported as being in better physical health, menstruating regularly although "the obsessive doubt and slowness persist more than ever."

It seems that throughout history, many medical doctors have wanted to reaffirm womanhood in their patients, patching up the physical and stabilising the emotional. Stabilising the menstrual cycle is classified as a stabiliser of the mind, reducing hysterical insanity or other such female maladies. Psychoanalysis has always been concerned with delving much deeper into the root causes of an illness and Freud, Breuer, Janet and their colleagues had been exploring hysteria seeking to reveal the layers of psychological pain and conflict that had gone into creating the hysterical masterpieces they witnessed in Charcot's scenes. Pierre Janet focused on trauma.

The talking cure

Janet worked on the principle that a person could not move on and develop their personality if they had not successfully integrated traumatic memories from the past. In one of his treatment methods, he substituted the content of the original picture of the trauma with replacement images. In other words, he changed his patients' traumatic memories. One of his first patients at the Salpêtrière in Paris was Marie who had been deeply shocked by her first menstrual bleed (Janet, 1889 cited in Leys, 2000: 106). The act of menarche as a traumatic event and menarcheal insanity were common concepts at the time of Janet publishing his first insights in *Revue Philosophique* (Janet, 1887). To stop her menarcheal bleeding, Marie had jumped into a tub of cold water (believed to congest bodily and menstrual fluids) and she did not bleed again for another five years. Although in consciousness, Marie had forgotten this event, each time she did get a period in some way she was reminded of an original trauma. Under hypnosis, Marie regressed to the age before menarche and Janet told her that her having periods was normal. However, her anxiety persisted and later on in the treatment they uncovered another trauma. Aged 16, Marie had seen an old woman fall down the stairs and die. Whenever Marie heard the word "blood" her somatic sensations relating to this event returned. Janet suggested the old woman had not died but had only tripped and as a result of this directive hypnotic substitution technique, Marie's anxiety attacks stopped. Many praised Janet's 1889 paper and his treatment of Marie but criticism was and continues to be never far away:

The questions whether such approaches lead to further dissociation of traumatic memories, as Janet thought, or to their implicit assimilation remains unanswered. Contemporary authors (Kluft, personal communication) have warned that in patients with a history of incest where the child was denied validation of the trauma because of threats by the perpetrator, the substitution technique could easily be misunderstood by the patient as an extension of the process of negation of trauma.

(Van der Hart et al., 1989: 9)

There was also the need to reflect on the fact that many of Janet's patients would eventually start remembering the original trauma and become disturbed again. He would give additional sessions of hypnosis, but his faithfulness to the process waned and in 1919 he wrote "Hypnosis is quite dead until the day of its resurrection" (Janet, 1919 [1976]: 203).[1]

What was increasingly evident was the quality and intensity of the rapport between patient and clinician impacting the treatment. Janet recognised the dependency of the patient to his/her therapist, referring to it as an "act of adoption" (Janet, 1919: 1154). The rapport was tantamount to the cure and when we read Janet we cannot miss the links to Freud's understanding of transference love. Janet writes of the therapeutic relationship: "In all these cases, what is involved is a kind of love, but it must be emphasized that it is a very special kind which is involved" (Janet, 1925: 465f).

For Freud, central to the conflict expressed in a patient's symptom was her yearning for the love from the man, an authority figure. The doctor/analyst role was the perfect blank screen on which to transfer this longing and love. Freud asked that his patients consider the part they played in the creation and unfolding of events. He showed them a lot of interest and gave them a lot of time in the hope that an attachment would build. He observed in his patients "a combination of exclusive attachment and credulous obedience is in general among the characteristics of love" (Freud, 1890 [1905], *SE*, VII: 296).

His method was arguably subtly seductive in nature and he believed that the patient yearned for the seducer who represented a figure from the past, unmatched and unequalled by any other. Yielding would move the treatment on. In the account of his treatment of Ilona Weiss, whom he treated in the autumn of 1892 and July 1893 for severe pains in her legs and fatigue:

> When one starts upon a cathartic treatment of this kind, the first question one asks oneself is whether the patient herself is aware of the origin and the precipitating cause of her illness … The interest shown in her by the physician, the understanding of her which he allows her to feel and the hope of recovery he holds out to her – all these will decide the patient to yield up her secret.
>
> (Breuer & Freud (1893–1895), *SE*, II: 138)

Emma Eckstein, arguably Freud's first analysand, was another of Freud's patients who complained of difficulty in walking. She also presented with irregular heavy or painful periods and hysterical tendencies. In Chapter 6 of this book, we shall look in detail at Freud's treatment plan, which resulted in a catastrophe causing her to haemorrhage from the nose and nearly bleed to death. Freud's treatment approach in curing Eckstein's hysteria and her menstrual irregularities created a setting in which she could transfer her search for the lost object and seek out the love of the doctor. His time, his attention and his intellect represented his love. Freud was certain that her persistent abnormal menstrual bleeding was caused by unrequited sexual longing.

In terms of the "talking cure", while Janet convinced his patients to take false memories as truth, Freud, in contrast, insisted his patients face the truth, as he understood it. However, his patients' communications were often mis-heard, mis-read or overlaid with male-orientated interpretations. Even if the hysterical feminine body of the nineteenth century was viewed as a "privileged object of knowledge" (Foucault, 1978: 104–105) she was never-theless subordinate to and reliant on man. In *Rewriting The Soul: Multiple Personality and the Science of Memory* (1998), Ian Hacking suggests that Freud himself was deluded, so resolutely was he attached to his theories. Many patients ended up believing things that were false, things that were frankly bizarre. And what Freud himself knew to be lies, many of his patients would not accept as truth. As Hacking puts it: "Janet fooled his patients; Freud fooled himself" (Hacking, 1998: 196).

Whilst Janet favoured a theory of dissociation, Freud believed that conver-sion arose out of the repressed conflicts and phantasies expressed through the somatic and behavioural symptoms. The motivation behind the symptoms was the libido. Such symptoms, like dreams, are an expression of wishes. Freud distinguished between two main types of somatisation: actual neurosis (neurasthenia and anxiety neurosis), and conversion hysteria. As described by psychoanalyst Joyce McDougall, in "The Psychosoma and the Psychoanalytic Process":

> In a sense one was the antithesis to the other. Whereas in hysterical con-version we witness the "mysterious leap" from mind to body, in the con-cept of the actual neurosis there is a leap in the opposite direction from the somatic to the psychic sphere. In either case an invisible barrier is crossed. The problems raised by this transition have, to this day, lost little of their mystery.
>
> (McDougall, 1974: 440)

Marilia Aisenstein, closely observing the work on psychosomatic phenomena at the Paris school of psychosomatics, explains that Freud's view of hysterical conversion was of psychological conflict that was too unbearable to bring to the surface of conscious thought and was repressed in the unconscious and "converted" into physical symptoms such as recurring movements, tics, etc. The dissociation and the conversion were unified by the hysteria. What they shared was what Breuer termed "double conscience". Freud does not focus on the conflict between the desire of the body on the one hand set against the wishes of the psyche on the other, but rather a single somatic site locates the conflict of contradictory forces: "Hysterical conversion makes the body into a language, the symptoms telling an unconscious story, and all mental activity finds its source in the erotic libido" (Aisenstein, 2006: 668). We shall now look at those narratives in which deprivation, loss and abuse feature in the analysis of the symptom of amenorrhea.

Contemporary studies of amenorrhea associated to loss and deprivation

A study in 2015 that looked at the associations between adverse experiences during childhood and fertility difficulties in adulthood claimed to be the first of its kind. Published in *The Journal of Psychosomatic Obstetrics and Gynecology*, "Adverse Childhood Event Experiences, Fertility Difficulties and Menstrual Cycle Characteristics" concluded that "The effect of childhood stress on fertility may be mediated through altered functioning of the HPA axis, acting to suppress fertility in response to less than optimal reproductive circumstances" (Jacobs et al., 2015: 46).

The stress triggers were aligned to traumatic family events such as parents separating, death, or abuse. The interactions of children with those around them were said to be critical psychosocial stressors. Such life events elevated cortisol levels and also impacted on menstruation, causing disruption to the cycles and to fertility in general (Mangold et al., 2010). Furthermore, for each additional adverse event experienced, the risk of fertility difficulties increased as well: "The child abuse subscale, sexual abuse and physical abuse more specifically, and experiencing parental substance use or neglect during childhood, showed stronger associations with fertility issues than the full ACE (adverse childhood experiences) scale" (Jacobs et al., 2015: 50).

Women in the high and low adversity groups were more likely to report fertility difficulties and a history of amenorrhea than those who reported no childhood adversity. Cumulative exposure to four or more childhood adversities was strongly associated with fertility difficulties and amenorrhea. Ten years or so earlier, a study charting 20 girls with functional hypothalamic amenorrhea (Bomba et al., 2007) found that "early traumatic experiences" were evident in many of the interviews. The team at the Department of Gynaecological Endocrinology of the University of Brescia were looking to find out if early life experiences had anything to do with present non-menses. The Children's Depression Inventory and the Eating Disorder Inventory were the two tests given to the girls who were also interviewed by a specialist in child and adolescent neuropsychiatry, as were the parents. Eighteen couples (90%) of parents reported incidences of psychopathology such as anxiety or depression in at least one close relative of their daughter. Eleven reported familial conflict, five of which were domestic violence. High too on the list (55%) was the reference to a house change during the first year of their daughter's life. The study concluded that psychic conflicts were transformed into somatic symptoms and the change in the endocrine levels was proportional to the degrees of the psychosomatic disturbances. Notably, 80% of girls when interviewed reported to have an "excessively demanding, controlling and intrusive mother" and 50% reported conflict in the family. The data also showed that all the teenagers were concerned about body image with a desire to be thin and there was a general theme of disordered eating of a "restrictive type".

One theory is that, for some, amenorrhea is the successful exertion of control. It offsets the feelings of disempowerment instigated by the control of others to which they must be subjected. The amenorrhea also refutes any conflict associated with separation and loss that is otherwise represented by the cyclical nature, the comings and goings of menstruation. Unlike menses and its associate fantasies to other fluids such as urine and sweat that rekindle orality and anality (extensively commented on in the literature on eating disorders), amenorrhea again overrides any feelings of passivity and helplessness. We know that this surmounting is undertaken with such precision in eating disorders. As Joyce Kraus Aronson writes in her introduction to *Insights in the Dynamic Psychotherapy of Anorexia and Bulimia* (1993):

> Some anorexics and bulimics who have complied with dominating and controlling parents all of their lives silently, unconsciously exercise their own need to control at a neuroendocrine level through amenorrhea. Menstrual bleeding can represent loss and separation from the patient's childhood attachment to the maternal object. Amenorrhea can serve to deny menstruation and allow the patient to hold to a childlike self image.
>
> (Kraus Aronson, 1993: xxv)

In "Hyperprolactinemic Amenorrhea – Insights From a Case Cured During Psychoanalysis" (2005), the reader is offered an insight into hyperprolactinemia and weight gain that is commonly present after a significant life event and predominantly effects women bought up in conditions of paternal deprivation. A loss usually triggers the symptoms. The authors of the study present a case of a 27-year-old woman with "idiopathic hyperprolactinemia, amenorrhea, binge eating and rapid weight gain following the death of her father" (Cardoso & Sobrinho, 2005: 44). The woman, referred to as "Helen" undergoes psychoanalysis. Here she describes how her grandparents had looked after her and her younger sister until the age of 12 at which point the two girls were sent back to live with their parents. The grandmother was described as a strong woman "reassuring but not affectionate, obsessed with stuffing her grand-daughters with food". Helen described her mother as "insecure, beautiful, distant", frequently intruding on Helen's life, even trying to make an appointment with the psychoanalyst. The father was impatient and sometimes violent. He warned his daughter away from boys and Helen believed that she was a surrogate for his stillborn son who had died before she was born. Her father died suddenly (Helen having only "discovered" him in her adolescent years) and her boyfriend who had promised to care for her during this time of mourning broke off their relationship. Amenorrhea and binge eating started immediately. The importance of the absence of a "true" Oedipal phase was noted. During the analysis, Helen's ambiguous and unsatisfactory relationships were explored and when she felt sad or upset she would get up from the couch needing to see the analyst with her own eyes whilst expressing her doubts about the analyst's competence. As the work progressed, she one day confronted her boyfriend with whom she was having a "sticky, asexual relation" and he confirmed that he no longer wanted to be with her. Whilst she was sad about this she was "willing to face the situation". The following day the first of a series of menstrual bleeds came. This signified the restoration of a normal neuroendocrine state based on the patient's new capacity to mourn an unsatisfactory relationship. In the concluding commentary, the authors emphasised how important it was for this patient to have first met with the endocrinologist who then referred her on for psychoanalysis:

> The endocrinologist reassured the patient about the innocence of her bodily symptoms and offered a solid, but peripheral, support. By doing so, this doctor became a strong reference to the patient while, in the same process, she was freed to establish a massive transferential relationship with the psychoanalyst. This situation, however unplanned, turned out to be the patient's first opportunity for a healthy triangulation.
>
> (Cardoso & Sobrinho, 2005: 50)

In 2011, Sobrinho and colleagues presented a research paper that they described as robust in its evidence that linked an absent or violent father with coping strategies formulated by the child that favoured specific neuroendocrine responses used later on in life. In "Paternal Deprivation Prior to Adolescence and Vulnerability to Pituitary Adenomas", Sobrinho writes up the data on an observational control multi-centre study of 830 patients, male and female, with pituitary adenomas, of which 395 patients tested for prolactinoma and 1130 with acromegaly. It was found that compared to control populations these patients with higher-scoring pituitary adenomas had a history of paternal deprivation. In addition,

> We found that absence of fathers is primarily associated with prolactinomas while violence is primarily associated with acromegaly, a finding which is of itself new and unexpected. Absence of father early in life is not necessarily deleterious. Foster families, stepfathers or other persons may fulfil a satisfactory parental role in some cases. Violence may have a more damaging potential.
>
> (Sobrinho et al., 2011: 55)[2]

Sobrinho cites McGowan et al. (2009) who reported abnormal regulation of hippocampal glucocordicoid receptor expression in suicides of those who had been abused as children compared to non-abused suicide controls – the point being that neuroendocrine responses later on in life might be conditioned by early life experiences. Fascinatingly, the secretion of prolactin, perhaps stimulated by adverse environmental and psychological factors rooted in childhood, is itself a hormone that optimises the survival of the young. Amenorrhea is a condition of the nursing mother: "Whether adaptive, as in the case of surrogate maternity, or pathological, as in the case of pseudo-pregnancy, prolactin responds to a perceived need to take care of a child" (Sobrinho, 1998: 133)

Pregnancy, pseudocyesis and secondary amenorrhea

Missed periods are symptomatic of pregnancy and breastfeeding. The amenorrhea in these instances is of a physiological nature (i.e., in the normal course of life). Most women who report missed periods are offered a pregnancy test by their GP because pregnancy is the most common cause. Some of these women are shocked when the test result comes back negative because they are convinced that they are pregnant. Viewed through a psychoanalytic lens, their unconscious content reveals fantasies of pregnancy. In "Emotional Settings of Functional Amenorrhea" (1964), Engels, Pattee and Wittkower present the theory that amenorrhea is linked with the fantasies of young women who wish to mobilise organisational patterns from a pre-genital age, so that they might return to the time before things went awry. One amenorrhea patient in their study reported a conscious fear of pregnancy, which they interpreted as an unconscious wish colliding with an unconscious fear of being impregnated by her father. In *The Ego Ideal, Being in Love And Genitality* (1985), Janine Chasseguet-Smirgel refers to the work of gynaecologist Hélène Michael-Wolfrom who reported several amenorrheic patients thinking they were pregnant. They were in fact menopausal and this denial of reality, Chasseguet-Smirgel explains that "mutilation and the wish for a child that replaces it can be directly linked to the oedipal situation" (Chasseguet-Smirgel, 1985: 51).

She goes on to write about a patient, a woman doctor and mother, who came back to see Chasseguet-Smirgel eight years after the end of her first analysis. This patient's periods had stopped for a few months previous to her returning to analysis and she had been experiencing "hypochondriacal anxieties and fears due to the beginning of the menopause" (1985: 51). They worked together over four sessions and discovered mainly through analysing dreams that the menopause was a symbol of her desire to have a child by her father. It was also a symbol of a punishment inflicted upon her by her mother for having such guilty wishes:

She had comes to ask me – in the maternal transference – not to punish her by depriving her of her procreative powers. Needless to say this wish and these fears had been elaborated at length during her analysis. Her periods recommenced during the week of this brief treatment, and I have every reason to suppose that she accepted their subsequent disappearance better, since she had no further recourse for my help.

(Chasseguet-Smirgel, 1985: 51)

In some cases of women who believe themselves to be pregnant, alongside the amenorrhea, their bodies experience other pregnancy symptoms. The body is in a false, phantom pregnancy and this is a condition termed "pseudocyesis" (from the Greek words *pseudes* (false) and *kyesis* (pregnancy). The Diagnostic and Statistical Manuel of Mental Disorders (DSM-5) categorises it within "Other Specified Somatic Symptom and Related Disorder" and defines it as

a false belief of being pregnant that is associated with objective signs and reported symptoms of pregnancy, which may include abdominal enlargement, reduced menstrual flow, amenorrhea, subjective sensations of foetal movement, nausea, breast engorgement and secretions, and labor pains at the expected date of delivery.

(American Psychiatric Association, 2013)

What we have here is an example of a marriage between the psychological and the somatic that goes on to bear a false pregnancy. It is a state that is difficult to refute, its symptoms proving so deceptive. In fact, as Aldrich writes in "A Case of Recurrent Pseudocyesis", "Symptoms are often related with such complete conviction by the patient that the physician or obstetrician is led to omit examinations or tests he might otherwise perform" (Aldrich, 1972: 11).

Pseudocyesis is not an imagined pregnancy (officially termed "delusions of pregnancy", more a belief of a thought). In pseudocyesis, an intense desire to be pregnant triggers the pituitary gland to secrete elevated hormones that mimic those of a pregnant body. In 50–70% of cases, amenorrhea is tied to the hyperprolactinemia and so a medical "disease" or hormonal disorder goes a long way to explain the condition. But in terms of psychopathology, it's the trigger, the desire, the stress, the "regressed impulse" (Marty & de M'Uzan, 1963), that finds an outlet when no other option (physically or behaviourally) is available to them.

Incidence of pseudocyesis is higher in rural and underdeveloped countries where access to medical care is limited. Cases in India are linked to the pressure women are under to produce a male heir to secure the generational line and social status and to provide economic security in old age. The psycho-socio-cultural context of pseudocyesis is important to note, so too the depth of the desire and the need to bear a male heir. In cultures such as the Igbo of south-east Nigeria, where pregnancy and childbirth confirm womanhood and a married woman's place in her husband's family, "societal pressure may precipitate pseudocyesis as a psychological defence to intense stress if the woman proves to be infertile" (Tarín et al., 2013: 39).

The rates of incidence are higher in most African black cultures compared to others, given the significance that is placed on fertility as well as lower levels of education and sterility problems. It is estimated to present in 1 of 160 maternity admissions in many African countries and 1 in 22,000 cases in the United States. Interestingly, the lower number of incidences reported amongst women from developed countries who can access diagnostic procedures at an early stage was also put down to the fact that they are open to a wider set of cultural references and "their emotional conflict will seek a more 'refined' mode of expression than that of spurious pregnancy" (Pawlowski & Pawlowski, 1958: 440). It is as if pseudocyesis has fallen out of fashion, with numbers far less than what they were during the late eighteen century when 1 in 200 pregnancies were diagnosed as being cases of pseudocyesis. As Aldrich explains:

> Earlier psychodynamic formulations considered pseudocyesis to be a manifestation of hysterical conversion. Later formulations viewed the condition as an organ neurosis. A more recent view implicates depression as a major determinant. Childhood deprivation, the need to avoid the abandonment or loss of love object, and the fear of losing the capacity to bear a child (most cases occur in childless women of an average age of thirty three) have been implicated as potential contributors to causation.
>
> (Aldrich, 1972: 11)

Pseudocyesis has been called a "paradigm of psychosomatic research". In terms of the physical mimicking the psychological, what is being expressed or denied still remains much of a mystery. Perhaps the psychoanalytic hypothesis that suggests it reveals the unconscious wish or dread for a child is outdated? Research is more commonly linking pseudocyesis with clinical depression, because tests on these women show lower levels of dopamine with consequently higher levels of luteinizing hormone and prolactin. This neuro-endocrinological picture is markedly different to other forms of secondary amenorrhea.

Amenorrhea and psychiatric disturbance

Through the advancement of medical research, we now know that neuro-endocrine pathways impair the HPA axis, which then leads to secondary amenorrhea. Depression and schizophrenia display similar hypothalamic-pituitary-axis abnormalities.[3] Anorexia, depression, stress amenorrhea and exercise-induced amenorrhea share similar alternations to the HPA axis patterning. Stress from separation and psychic conflict over body image are linked. In Osofsky and Fisher's "Psychological Correlates of the Development of Amenorrhea in a Stress Situation" (1967), the authors wrote up their longitudinal study of "normal" menstruating women beginning their freshman year at nursing school, focussing on the question of whether the move from home to college would in itself bring on amenorrhea. They looked at those who did not have a history of menstrual disturbance. The results of their study showed that it was the psychological parameters specifically linked to the woman's body image or body concept that impacted their menstrual flow. The more "distorted" their view of themselves was, the greater chance of there being a distortion in their menstrual cycle. So too women with low body awareness and conflicts about their feminine identity and role in society were more likely to develop menstrual disturbances in stressful situations.

Bipolar disorder and depression show similar disruptions of function in the HPA (Rasgon et al., 2000). Up until the point when endocrinological processes were found to be responsible for menstrual cycling, psychotic disorders were put down to a dysfunction of the gonads. Whilst it has been widely accepted that psychiatric morbidity and amenorrhea share a commonality, what is less certain is whether an amenorrheic landscape feeds the development of psychiatric disturbances or if, on the flip side, the psychiatric morbidity is fertile fodder for the growth of amenorrhea and other menstrual disorders. The uncertainty surrounding this was cloaked over by medics of the late nineteenth century who subjected many women presenting with amenorrhea to surgical removal of their ovaries, so as to save them from insanity. Various menstrual cycle disturbances, anomalies of the genital organs, and masculinisation were seen in conjunction with psychotic disorders so genital abnormalities and menstrual cycle disturbances were considered possible causes of psychosis. The terms uterine and amenorrheal insanity illustrate the hypothesis that "insanity in some few cases actually results de novo from this [amenorrhea] as an exciting or predisposing cause" (Clouston, 1883).

In recent studies of women with bipolar disorder, around one-third are reported to have had menstrual disturbances during adolescence before they are diagnosed and treated for bipolar (Joffe et al., 2006). Once again, amenorrhea could be seen as the vital sign and gynaecological investigations might be an opportune moment to detect a psychiatric complaint that deserves attending to early. Brockington (2011) lists the illustrative monographs of the clinical features of menstrual psychosis, generally those of manic-depressive (bipolar) disorder. His argument is that investigations of menstrual psychosis can better inform us of bipolar disorder.

Engel's paper "Emotional Settings of Functional Amenorrhea" (1964), notes that amenorrheics referred for observation on psychiatric grounds showed histories and incidents of neurosis, psychosis, oral and psychosexual conflict and schizophrenic thinking. Often for "Les aménorrhées de cause psychique" (Decourt & Michard, 1953) the prognosis of recovery was poor:

> There is a fundamental difference in the personality structure and in the psychodynamics between these patients and patients with amenorrhea resulting from an acute emotional distress … while some patients are severely disturbed

emotionally, most do not display overtly neurotic traits [however] a neurotic "terrain" must pre-exist when such unremarkable events as a change of environment or an examination failure can precipitate amenorrhea.

(Engels et al., 1964: 683)

Medication used for neurologic and psychiatric disorders such as epilepsy, migraines and bipolar disorder often disrupt the HPA axis which can then go on to disrupt the menstrual cycle and cause amenorrhea. These drugs are highly effective but for adolescents the worry is that prolonged amenorrhea with hyperprolactinemia can risk healthy bone development. Not everyone thinks this is a side effect worth risking. Many women who take part in studies on antipsychotic-induced amenorrhea view the cessation of menses as not "normal" associated with sterility. The risk of the delusion of pregnancy is increased. For schizophrenics, gender identity is affected by amenorrhea and many patients believe themselves to have changed sex – delusional pseudo-transexualism – and other sexual delusions. The amenorrhea and the hirutism, common side effects of antipsychotic drugs concretise their experiences of sexual delusions (Seeman, 2011). It is fundamental that the meaning of amenorrhea for these patients be explored in a psychotherapeutic setting.

Hide and seek it

In 1912, James Walsh's 832-page book, with its lengthy title *Psychotherapy Including The History of The Use of Mental Influence, Directly or Indirectly, In Healing And The Principles For The Application of Energies Derived From the Mind To the Treatment of Disease*, amenorrhea is described as the clearest example of menstrual difficulty derived from the influence of the mind over the body. Walsh documents the case of a woman frightened by a "maniac" waving a revolver around: "She dared not make a move nor a sign." Her menstruation stopped completely and when it came back irregularly it bled through the ear, from the pierce in the lobule, made for earrings. In another case, a woman whilst on her period was frightened by "an insane person flourishing a knife" and for many years her irregular periods bled through her nose, "and usually only the molimina in the genital tract" (Walsh, 1912: 436). Earlier, in 1840, Dr James Blundell had written about "Amenorrhea in Adults" in *Observations on some of the More Important Diseases of Women*. He cited the cold, an accident, or a fright as the main triggers, a commonly held view in those days:

At first, perhaps, no inconvenience is experienced beyond the alarm, but afterwards the general health seems to give way, and the habit becomes sallow and emaciated, and there is darkness around the eyes, and the cheek bones rise into notice … at the same time the stomach and bowels get into an unhealthy condition, and perhaps there are irregular determinations of blood to different parts of the system: the chest, bowels, and stomach … but where the determination takes place to other parts where the vessels seem to be less secure, effusion is by no means infrequent, therefore bleeding from the nose, bowels and lungs, are by no means uncommon.

(Blundell, 1840: 183)

Dr Blundell (one of the first physicians to perform blood transfusions on humans) suggests one method for treating amenorrhea would be to make another part of the body bleed, such as the arm. "Excitement of the uterus" is also recommended, so too a remedy of ammonia and if all else fails "warm hip baths, or general immersion of the body and horse exercise" (Blundell, 1840: 184–185).

Termed "vicarious menstruation", the phenomena of menstruation as an organism bleeding from orifices other than the uterus has its roots in Hippocratic texts stating that a nosebleed was a good thing as it released menses that were hitherto suppressed. Haemorrhages of these kinds relieved the pressure and were "the body's attempt to regain equilibrium" (Skultans, 1985: 712). Gynaecological works discussed the mutual relationship between the genital and nasal mucous membrane with other exit routes such as the mouth, anus, gums, ears, lungs, brain and eyes being able to "restore the disturbed equilibrium of blood distribution" (Kisch, 1910: 165).

In terms of studying the transactional relationship of bodily functions, the findings in historic sources are interesting for contemporary studies. Menstrual disturbances, notably amenorrhea, are now linked to constipation and irregular bowel movements. Psychoanalytic enquiry will seek to ascertain the role the psyche plays on the bleeding/non-bleeding body. In "Varieties of Somatization – Psychological Components in Psychosomatic Bleeding" which is a chapter in *Psychodynamic Symptoms: Psychodynamic Treatment of the Underlying Personality Disorder* (1989), Ira L Mintz outlines the case of a 22-year-old nurse with severe ulcerative colitis, suffering from cramps, mucus, diarrhoea and bleeding. Blood was usually found in her stools in small amounts:

One day she reported that she was five weeks overdue with her period. Before this she had been regular. I encouraged her to associate to the overdue period. This resulted in a serious of childhood memories about bleeding, bodily injury, and loss of control … She remembered wondering where her menstrual blood came from and whether it would stop. Initially she wondered whether she was bleeding or whether the blood came from a bowel movement. It all seemed to come from the same hole. I suggested that unconsciously, she might still have the same fantasy – that it all came from the same hole. In her strong attempt to stop the rectal bleeding, thinking in the back of her mind that it all came from the same hole, she stopped her menstrual bleeding. She thought about the possibility of that fantasy for a few moments and allowed that it might be so. Shortly thereafter, the session ended and she left.

(Mintz cited in Wilson & Mintz, 1989: 172)

Fifteen minutes later, whilst on the bus, the patient's period came. Mintz concludes that the amenorrhea was not primarily related to drives, anxieties, or indeed "transference phenomena", but was an attempt to stop the rectal bleeding with the patient wanting to "work constructively in treatment". Previous to this treatment the patient had been seeing a physician who proctoscoped her every week and during this time she was experiencing up to 35 stools per day.

Conflict and its resulting outcomes are a given but we can turn to Fenichal's *The Psychoanalytic Theory of Neurosis* (1946) to clear up some confusion associated with the role of the unconscious finding expression through various organ systems. Fenichal warns that, sometimes, hormonal functions are influenced by unconscious instinctual conflicts "and thus produce secondary somatic symptoms not intended as such" (Fenichal, 1946: 240). With regards to menstrual or premenstrual mental disorders in women he writes:

> somatic factor always plays a part, namely, the physical alternations at the source of the instinctual drives. But on the other hand the unconscious significance of the idea of menstruation and the mental reaction to this significance may likewise alter the hormonal events. In cases of disturbances, the premenstrual body feeling represents tension, retention (sometimes pregnancy), dirt, pregenitality, hatred; the menstrual low may bring relaxation, and is felt as evacuation (sometimes birth), cleanliness, genitality, love; but it may also represent loss of anal and urethral control, Oedipal guilt, castration, the frustration of wishes for a child, and humiliation.
>
> (Fenichal, 1946: 240)

Castration, conflict and the cloak of amenorrhea

In classical psychoanalysis, menstruation was thought to represent a woman's castration. It was symbolic of "no child and no penis" (Deutsch, 1925: 39). Psychoanalyst Helene Deutsch maintained that the female castration complex impacted on a girl's reaction to menstruation but this reaction was in part down to the information she had consciously absorbed from those around her. In "A Short Study of the Development of the Libido" (1924), Karl Abraham wrote of one patient: "during menstruation which used to excite her castration complex in a typical way ... she scarcely ever stopped crying" (Abraham, 1924 [1927] cited in Grigg et al., 2015: 78). This patient's tears in part mourned the loss of her masculinity. In a footnote, Abraham added that the tears of patient "X" were "her unconscious wish to urinate like a man" (Abraham, 1924 [1927]: 501).

One of Abraham's first patients was Karen Horney who later became a psychoanalyst and an active member of the Berlin Psychoanalytic Society. Horney was irked by Abraham's assumption that women felt inferior because of their genitalia. She criticised him for viewing things through a male narcissistic gaze. She developed her own theory in which the menstrual bleed represented the castration of woman that masks her phantasies to bear her father's child (1926). Melanie Klein, suggested that the girl envied her mother's possession of the penis and her hatred of her was disguised as anxiety. Only this time though, as a menstruating woman, she really could bear her father's child. Adolescent turmoil was indeed a replica of earlier Oedipal strivings and puberty might realise those incestuous wishes. In a paper for the *Psychoanalytic Review* "Penis Envy and the Female Oedipus Complex: A Plea to Reawaken an Ineffectual Debate", authors Zepf and Seel (2016) propose that the Oedipal conflict is the result of the parents' complexes projected into their children. In containing this projective identification, the rivalry with penis envy is both the girl's wish for father and for her own maternal power, and a wish to have the penis so as to satisfy mother.

In terms of linking menarche (the first menstrual bleed) to unconscious fantasy and castration fears, Deutsch writes that it symbolises the dangers of female sexuality and reproductive capabilities and is in itself unclean and dangerous:[4]

> All observations suggest that, whether or not the girl is given intellectual knowledge even when she has the best possible information about the biological aspects of the process, and despite its wish fulfilling character, the first menstruation is usually experienced as a trauma.
>
> (Deutsch, 1945: 157)

Often the first rip in a young woman's sense of self comes with the first tear from the first menstrual bleed. In its most rudimentary form, menarche can represent the thief that steals away her freedom, her position, her place in the family. Menarche is a real threat. As Elaine Showalter writes of a time when people shuffled around in the shadow of knowledge: "Many of these young innocent women, notably in Victorian times, were left in what they could only construe as vaginal haemorrhaging" (Showalter, 1987: 56).

Menarche was thought to be a trigger for "adolescent insanity" by thinking men such as Kant as well as many medics. It has been proven to be a hotbed for mental breakdown and depression, with delinquency in part bought on by an internal conflict between the girl's need for independence and her dependency on others to help her fulfil this goal. Menstruation might pose a threat to the adolescent's task of becoming independent and unique whilst remaining connected to the group and the group's ideology.

In many cases of amenorrhea the constitution of the non-menstruating body might be a way to realise the wish for an uninterrupted, cohesive state. So too it might symbolise a regression to a desired pre-pubertal state. All the meanwhile, under this cloak what is often hidden is a more complex state of being. Returning to Engel, Pattee and Wittkower's paper, "Emotional Settings of Functional Amenorrhea" (1964), we are presented with a patient whose menses stopped when she had to start caring for her dying father. For this patient, adult sexuality was associated with sin and damnation because of a real or imagined incestuous experience as a child. Menstruation associated to womanhood was a source of conflict. Her menses had been irregular for a long time but she stopped bleeding altogether when her father became gravely ill. Engels writes:

> Menses returned within forty eight hours of the interview, in which for the first time she disclosed her secret probably because the doctor's condoning attitude served temporarily to lessen her guilt. Reasoning that there had been no real resolution of the conflict, we rightly predicted a return of amenorrhea.
>
> (Engels et al., 1964: 687)

Another example Engels gives is of a 31-year-old postgraduate nursing student who presented with amenorrhea of four years and with anorexia. She was the youngest of four children born into a "very close and loyal family". She was her father's favourite and she looked like her mother "whom he deeply loves". He was intolerant of any mention of the children having sexual relationships. At age 12, she was very anxious at the thought of separation from her mother. She liked the idea of being normal in menstruating, but also viewed this as "weakening" which she would have to offset with controlled eating. The idea of relaxing this control, and the control she had over feelings for others, panicked her with the notion that it would lead to complete sexual abandon. The thought of medication to bring on a period caused great anxiety and anger. Engels's thoughts were that this patient was made anxious by an awareness of her instinctual impulses

> and gravely limited her life in order to avoid such feelings. Her family relationships bespoke of unresolved Oedipal complex, and her defences, particularly reaction formation, were characteristic of her pregenital adjustment. Amenorrhea and compulsive dieting began as she sacrificed more and more of the conflict-producing aspects of normal life in her ascetic role as a hardworking student nurse.
>
> (Engels, 1964: 692)

Anorexia, eating disorders and amenorrhea are often linked and we shall study this in detail in Chapter 4. Here though we can briefly consider the mechanism of starvation employed to avoid psychobiological maturity and keep the person in an uninterrupted state.

Anorexia

Psychoanalysis in the 1940s and '50s linked psychological motives behind the disorder with themes based on orality. Anorexia, like a form of conversion hysteria, repudiated oral sadistic fantasies. But some argued that many of these young girls did not display a conflict or show an interest in such issues. Alan Goodsitt (1997) proposed that the condition was more concerned with a deficient ego and a lack of cohesion to the overall structure of the psyche. The eating disorders are better understood as "attempts to drown out the anguished feelings by frantic self-stimulatory activities … The symptoms are misguided attempts to organise affects and internal states meaningfully" (Goodsitt, 1997: 59).

If this is a condition that is about self-regulation and autonomy (Bruch, 1973), then surely it is amenorrhea that best acts this out, divorced from the uncertainty and unpredictability of menstrual bleeding? As an embodied state devoid of erraticism, amenorrhea becomes a reliable marker of a permanent state of totality. In this way, it can be thought of as symbolising the early childhood characteristics of obedience and conformity that many of these patients displayed, deficient in their sense of separateness. The anorexia and the amenorrhea offset all such deficiencies, enabling the unconscious to exert control.

In her paper "What It Means to Bleed: An Exploration of Young Women's Experiences of Menarche and Menstruation" (2013), Kate Donmall argues that menstruation is not an organising experience as may would have us believe and many women in fact want no part in it. She gives us the example of Laura who "longs to make it stop" and longs for a "totally empty womb". Donmall helpfully writes about Laura's wish to be castrated:

> Linking this to classical theories of female masochism, a psychic refusal to accept menstruation, or to long for it to cease, may be a refusal to accept the kind of femininity that, in the theories of Deutsch and Horney (and one might argue extant in today's society) is linked to passivity and pain. The discomfort and pain, and the guilt induced by repressed and potentially incestuous desires, cause the woman to draw back from the feminine erotic function or to hide her sexuality and the menstruation that may symbolize it. We might consider how the "mess" of menstruation might awaken unconsciously the sadistic conception of coitus (Bonaparte, 1935; Klein, 1932) and thus a fear of sexuality, or reawaken feelings of confusion and shame in relation to the mess of infantile incontinence. Alternatively, if menstruation may indeed be unconsciously interpreted as a punishment for masturbation (Deutsch, 1925) this offers another explanation for the intimate connections between menstruation, mess and shame as seen across the sample.
>
> (Donmall, 2013: 213)

For many specialists, eating disorders and issues of femininity cannot be separated. Amenorrhea can be thought of as a symptomatic rejection of a particular type of femininity stained with menstruation. As Malson and Ussher explain, it is "alien, out of control, emotional, sexual, vulnerable and dangerous. It is argued that amenorrhea in anorexia may signify a rejection of this particular negative construction of "femininity" rather than of adulthood or femininity per se" (Malson & Ussher, 1996: 505). Malson and Ussher's research showed that amenorrhea as a symptom of anorexia cannot be viewed as simply biological but instead represents a psychological communication. For one of their studies, they interviewed 23 women with anorexia aged 17 and over, many in their early twenties. Most were white British and of "middle-class" background. The participants were asked to discuss their ideas and experiences of anorexia, the body and gender identity. The interviews were analysed using a discourse-analytic methodology, the results of which found that many of the participants viewed amenorrhea positively, as "not being a woman anymore" (Malson & Ussher, 1996: 512).

Defiance against the feminine

The menstruating body can represent "the locus of all that threatens our attempts at control. It overtakes, it overwhelms, it erupts and it disrupts" (Bordo, 1992: 94). In the *Bulletin of the Menninger Clinic*, Gill wrote up "Functional Disturbances of Menstruation" (1943). He had observed that amenorrheic patients consciously or unconsciously regarded their menses as a degrading visible sign of a feminine inferiority. Psychoanalytic enquiry from the 1930s regarded amenorrhea as a simple statement of an unconscious repudiation of women. Linked with sterility, frigidity, dysmenorrhea and vomiting, Menninger (1939) wrote in "Somatic Correlations With the Unconscious Repudiation of Femininity in Women"

> All of them, I think, may be visualized as representations in different spheres of a profoundly influential drive, the subjective aspect of which is a wish to repudiate, or destroy one's own femininity, one's femaleness, expressing at the same time self-directed aggression and self punishment.
>
> (Menninger, 1939: 526)

Menninger also wondered why it was that many women volunteered for the invasive treatments offered by male doctors. Using the theme of penis envy, Menninger outlined the strivings of a little girl who must give up her wishes to emulate the men in her household whilst at the same time managing the envy she might feel for them. Thus, with hostility towards men "some women wish to destroy or to have destroyed the femaleness within them" (Menninger, 1939: 524).

Christopher Bollas, like Menninger, explores psychoneurotic illness as a motive for avoiding the realms of the maturational process. The alignment to the male is something he questions in the self's erotic life in *Hysteria* (2000): The hysteric's "demi-erotic transference" to her doctor suggests that the illness is rooted in the mother's rejection of her daughter's sexuality. To overcome this, a man's love is sought after:

> When he or she is pleased to have an ailment confirmed as real, possibly even to have some small surgery, the hysteric feels that he or she will be the recipient of the doctor's intelligent love. Casting aside the paradox of a love that would remove a part of the body – in the unconscious always the genital – the hysteric finds in the surgeon's attentions a hand that seems to much more alive to the body's needs than that of the mother.
>
> (Bollas, 2000: 59)

If we suppose that amenorrhea is a rebellion against societal dictates of what a woman should be, then it can also be seen as an assertion of what a woman wants. Amenorrhea provides a legitimate space separate from the one assigned to her by a societal system that curbs her rights and limits her possibilities. Indeed, the space that is on offer to women can be experienced as castrating to them as much as it is virile to men. And with menstruation being the quintessential symbol, who needs it?

Victoria, a patient of Italian psychoanalyst and psychiatrist Riccardo Lombardi, had come for analysis. She, with her husband, was hoping to one day have a child. As the analysis progressed, a deeper meaning behind the difficulty to conceive was starting to unravel. In one session, Victoria said to Lombardi:

> My husband says that my uterus bleeds because I mortify my femininity by not having a baby. I told him "It's really clever, this thought of yours, what a pity that it doesn't correspond in the least with reality! If you really want to know, I don't have the least intention of having a baby. Despite what you think, it's possible to be a woman even if you don't have babies.
>
> (Lombardi, 2011: 11)

I emailed Dr Lombardi to ask for his thoughts on why too often discussions of menstruation are left out of the consulting room. He replied:

> I see the cessation of menses of what I call the Body Mind Dissociation. When the body and most primitive bodily emotions are integrated into the mind's horizons, the menses come back … In my view it is not only, as you say, that it seems that psychoanalysis unconsciously props up the menstrual taboo by leaving all discussions of menses and non menses out of the consulting room, BUT that psychoanalysis leaves the real body out of the consulting room, stimulating self-referential working through based on metaphoric and symbolic linking. This is specifically counterproductive especially now, since most analytic patients need to integrate the body into their personality and to work through the most concrete and elementary level of functioning.
>
> (Lombardi, pers. comm. 17 March 2017)

Perhaps a shift in thinking from the analyst might enable one in the patient, if she feels they are in some way attuned to one another. I am thinking about cases of extreme eating disorders where the patient believes the analyst cannot possibly know what it feels like to be in their shoes. Analysts are often experienced as talking the talk but can they really walk the walk, or are they just flip-flopping in between sessions, patients and consulting rooms?

When a patient is prepared to express herself through a bodily state, and in some circumstances when only death will do, where in the patient's frame of mind is the analyst? Are you with me, or without me? How much can you truly bear?

Notes

1 In a 2003 clinical study, twelve women presenting with functional hypothalamic amenorrhea (FHA) were given a single session of hypnotherapy and observed for twelve weeks afterwards; within that time frame nine out of the twelve patients menstruated. All reported an increased feeling of well-being and self-confidence (Tschugguel & Berga, 2003: 982). The authors of the study report that hypnosis is a therapy that improves the subject's psychological equilibrium and "reverses the physiological effects of stress within an acceptable period of time". Hypnosis in these instances sets about to reduce stress, reset the homeostasis and the body's equilibrium enabling the body to self-correct. Similarly with cognitive behavioural therapy that attributes functional hypothalamic amenorrhea to metabolic and psychogenic stresses, success rates in correcting neuroendocrine aberrations and reversing anovulation are good. Addressing "problematic behaviours and attitudes" a study in 2006 set about to substantiate the role of CBT in the treatment of FHA and to highlight CBT as an alternative to commonly prescribed corrective sex hormone therapy: "Health truly depends upon developing healthy attitudes and healthy behaviors. Misattributions, negative images of self and other, unrealistic expectations, and emotional disharmony can cause neuroendocrine havoc" (Berga & Loucks, 2006: 124).

   In the study of a group of women who were offered 16 sessions with a therapist, physician, or nutritionist over a 20-week period, 88% of those who underwent CBT had evidence of ovulation compared to 25% of those who were observed with no intervention (Berga et al., 2003).

2 Pituitary adenomas are benign tumours that arise from cells in the pituitary gland (considered to be the master hormone gland that regulates the body's hormones). Over-production of hormones by the pituitary tumour cells results in "functional" adenoma. These include prolactinoma, the over-production of prolactin, and acromegaly, an excess of growth hormone. Prolactinoma causes loss of menses in women. Symptoms in men include lower testosterone levels leading to diminishing sexual interest (UCLA Health Pituitary Tumor Program).

3 Estradiol levels are lower in depressed women than in euthymic women likely to be caused from the HPA function. In a three-year study of women aged 36–45, those with a history of depression had a higher rate of peri-menopause compared with non-depressed women. This suggests that depression might impact on a woman's ovarian function, causing it to cease in her 30s or 40s (Harlow et al., 2003).

4 In *Helene Deutsch: Psychoanalysis of the Sexual Functions of Women* (1991) editor Paul Roazan comments on the psychology of puberty: "With the giving up of the clitoris as an organ of excitation and with the appearance of menstruation one might say that a real castration has taken place, in the sense of the loss of a pleasurable organ that has functioned as s surrogate penis" (Roazan, 1991: 38).

Bibliography

Abraham, K. (1924) "A Short Study of the Development of the Libido, Viewed in the Light of Mental Disorders", in K. Abraham (ed.), (1927) *Selected Papers of Karl Abraham*. trans. D. Byran & A. Strachey London: Hogarth Press, 418–502.

Aisenstein, M. (2006) "The Indissociable Unity of Psyche and Soma: A View from the Paris Psychosomatic School", *International Journal of Psychoanalysis*, 87(3): 667–680.

Aldrich, C.K. (1972) "A Case of Recurrent Pseudocyesis", *Biology and Medicine*, 16: 11–21.

American Psychiatric Association. (2013). *Diagnostic and Statistical Manual of Mental Disorders*. 5th edition. Washington, DC: American Psychiatric Association Publishing.

Appignanesi, L. & Forrester, J. (2005) *Freud's Women*. London: Orion Books, Ltd.

Berga, S.L. & Loucks, T.L. (2006) "Use of Cognitive Behavior Therapy for Functional Hypothalamic Amenorrhea", *Annals of the New York Academy of Sciences*, 1092: 114–129.

Berga, S.L., Marcus, M.D., Loucks, T.L., Hlastala, S., Ringham, R. & Krohn, M.A. (2003) "Recovery of Ovarian Activity in Women with Functional Hypothalamic Amenorrhea Who Were Treated with Cognitive Behavior Therapy", *Fertility & Sterility*, 80(4): 976–981.

Björo, K. (1966) "Amenorrhea: A Study with Particular Attention to the Problems of Ovarian Failure", *Acta Obstetrica Et Gynecologica Scandinavica*, 45(S1): 68–124.

Blundell, J. (1840) in T. Castle (ed.), *Observations on Some of the More Important Diseases of Women*. Philadelphia, PA: A. Waldie.

Bogousslavsky, J. (2014) "Hysteria: The Rise of an Enigma", *Frontiers of Neurology and Neuroscience*. 35. Montreux: Karger Books.

Bollas, C. (2000) *Hysteria*. London: Routledge Publishing.

Bomba, M., Gambera, A., Bonini, L., Pernoni, M., Neri, F., Scagliola, P. & Nacinovich, R. (2007) "Endocrine Profiles and Neuropsychological Correlates of Functional Hypothalamic Amenorrhea in Adolescents", *Fertility and Sterility*, 87(4): 876–885.

Bonaparte, M. (1935) "Passivity, Masochism and Femininity", *International Journal of Psychoanalysis*, 16: 325–333.

Bordo, S. (1992) *Unbearable Weight – Feminism, Western Culture, and the Body*. Los Angeles, CA: University of California Press.

Breuer, J. & Freud, S. (1893–1895). "II Case Histories (5) Fraulein Elisabeth von R. (Freud)", in *Studies on Hysteria, SE* II. London: Vintage Hogarth Press.

Brockington, I.F. (2011) "Menstrual Psychosis: A Bipolar Disorder with A Link to the Hypothalamus", *Current Psychiatry Reports*, 13: 193–197.

Bruch, H. (1973) *Eating Disorders: Obesity, Anorexia Nervosa and the Person Within*. New York: Basic Books.

Buchan, W. (1797) *Domestic Medicine or a Treatise on the Prevention and Cure of Diseases by Regimen and Simple Medicines*. 20th edition. New York: James Lyon & Co.

Cardoso, G. & Sobrinho, L.G. (2005) "Hyperprolactinemic Amenorrhea – Insights from a Case Cured during Psychoanalysis", *Revista Portuguesa De Psicossomática*, 7 (1–2): 43–51.

Chadwick, M. (1932) *The Psychological Effects of Menstruation*. New York: Nervous and Mental Disease Publishing Company.

Chasseguet-Smirgel, J. (1985) *The Ego Ideal: A Psychoanalytic Essay on the Malady of the Ideal*. trans. P. Barrows. London: Free Association Books.

Clouston, T.S. (1873) "The Morisoman Lectures on Insanity for 1873 by the Late David Skae", *Journal of Mental Science*, xix: 340–355.

Clouston, S. (1883) *Clinical Lectures on Mental Disease*. 1st edition. London: J and A Churchill.

Coldsmith, D. (1979) "'Symbolic' Amenorrhea – Emotional Factors in Secondary Amenorrhea", *Medical Aspects of Human Sexuality*, 9: 95–112.

Collis, R.J.M. (1966) "Physical Health and Psychiatric Disorder in Nigeria", *Transactions of the American Philosophical Society*, 56(4): 1–45.

Cullen, W. (1769) *Synopsis nosologiae methodicae*. Edinburgh.

Decourt, J. & Michard, J.P. (1953). "Les aménorrhées de cause psychique", *Revue du Practician*, 3: 27.

Deutsch, H. (1925) "The Psychology of Women in Relation to the Functions of Reproduction", in R. Fliess (ed.), (1973) *An Anthology of Essential Papers with Critical Introductions.* New York: International Universities Press, 192–206.

Deutsch, H. (1945) *Psychology of Women, Volume 2: Motherhood.* New York: Grune & Stratton.

Donmall, K. (2013) "What It Means to Bleed: An Exploration of Young Women's Experiences of Menarche and Menstruation", *British Journal of Psychotherapy,* 29(2): 202–216.

Dyde, S. (2015) "Cullen, a Cautionary Tale", *Medical History,* 59(2): 220–240.

Engels, W.D., Pattee, C.J. & Wittkower, E.D. (1964) "Emotional Settings of Functional Amenorrhea", *Psychosomatic Medicine,* 26(6): 682–698.

Erikson, E.H. (1968) *Identity, Youth and Crisis.* New York: W.W. Norton & Company Inc.

Evans, B. & Jones, E. (2012) "Organ Extracts and the Development of Psychiatry: Hormonal Treatments at the Maudsley Hospital 1923–1938", *Journal of the History of the Behavioral Sciences,* 48(3): 251–276.

Fenichal, O. (1946) *The Psychoanalytic Theory of Neurosis.* London & New York: Routledge Publishing.

Foucault, M. trans R. Hurley (1978) *The History of Sexuality, Volume 1: An Introduction.* New York: Pantheon.

Freud, S. (1890 [1905]) "Psychical (or Mental) Treatment", in *A Case of Hysteria, Three Essays on Sexuality and Other Works,* SE VII. London: Hogarth Press, 281–302.

Freud, S. (1896) *The Aetiology of Hysteria. SE,* III: 189–221. London: Hogarth Press.

Freud, S. (1931) *Female Sexuality. SE,* XXI: 221–246. London: Hogarth Press.

Freud, S. & Breuer, J. (1895) *Studies on Hysteria.* New York: Basic Books.

Fuchs, T. (2012) "Body Memory and the Unconscious", in D. Lohmar & J. Brudzínska (eds.), *Founding Psychoanalysis Phenomenological Theory of Subjectivity and the Psychoanalytic Experience.* Dordrecht: Kluwer, 69–82.

Gadamer, H.G. (1975) *Truth and Method.* London & New York: Continuum International Publishing Group.

Gill, M.M. (1943) "Functional Disturbances of Menstruation", *Bulletin of the Menninger Clinic,* 7: 6–14.

Giorgi, A. (2009) *The Descriptive Phenomenological Method in Psychology: A Modified Husserlian Approach.* Pittsburgh, PA: Duquesne University Press.

Goldstein, J. (2010) *Hysteria Complicated by Ecstasy – The Case of Nanette Leroux.* Princeton, NJ & Oxford: Princeton University Press.

Goodsitt, A. (1997) "Eating Disorders: A Self-Psychological Perspective", in D. M. Garner & P.E. Garfinkel (eds.), *Handbook of Treatment for Eating Disorders.* 2nd edition. New York: Guilford Press, 205–228.

Grigg, R., Hecq, D. & Smith, C. (eds.), (2015) *Female Sexuality: Psychoanalytic Controversies.* London: Karnac Books.

Hacking, I. (1998) *Rewriting the Soul: Multiple Personality and the Science of Memory.* Princeton, NJ & Oxford: Princeton University Press.

Harlow, B.L., Wise, L.A., Otto, M.W., Soares, C.N. & Cohen, L.S. (2003) "Depression and Its Influence on Reproductive Endocrine and Menstrual Cycle Markers Associated with Perimenopause: The Harvard Study of Moods and Cycles", *Archives of General Psychiatry,* 60: 29–36.

Heidegger, M. (1927 [1962]) *Being and Time.* trans. J. Macquarrie & E. Robinson. New York: Harper & Row.

Horney, K. (1926) "Review of Zur Psychologie Der Weiblichen Sexualfunktionen", *International Journal of Psychoanalysis*, 7: 92–100.

Husserl, E. (1915 [1989]) *Ideas Pertaining to a Pure Phenomenology and to a Phenomenological Philosophy*. trans. R. Rojcewicz & A. Schuwer. Dordrecht & Boston, MA: Kluwer Academic Publishers.

Hustvedt, A. (2011) *Medical Muses: Hysteria in Nineteenth-Century Paris*. London & New York: Bloomsbury Publishing Plc.

Hustvedt, S. (2014) "I Wept for Years and When I Stopped I Was Blind", *Neurophysiologie Clinique*, 44: 305–313.

Jacobs, M.B., Boynton-Jarrett, R.D. & Harville, E.W. (2015) "Adverse Childhood Event Experiences, Fertility Difficulties and Menstrual Cycle Characteristics", *Journal of Psychosomatic Obstetrics and Gynecology*, 36(2): 46–57.

Jagger, A.M. & Young, I.M. (eds.), (1998) *A Companion to Feminist Philosophy*. Oxford: Blackwell Publishing.

Janet, P. (1887) "L'anaesthésie Systemmatisée et la Dissociation des Phénomènes Psychologiques", *Revue Philosophique*, 23: 449–472.

Janet, P. (1889a) *L'automatisme Psychologique*. Paris: Felix Alcan. reprinted Société Piere Janet, Paris, 1973.

Janet, P. (1889b) "L'automatism Psychologique: Essai de Psychologie Expérimentale sure les Forms Inférieures de L'activité Humaine", Reprinted 1989, Paris: 410–412, in R. Leys (ed.), (2000) *Trauma: A Genealogy*. Chicago, IL & London: University of Chicago Press, 106.

Janet, P. (1919) trans. E. & C. Paul (1976) *Psychological Healing: A Historical and Clinical Study*. 2 vols. London: George Allen & Unwin.

Janet, P. (1925). "L'influence somnambulique et la besoin de direction", in idem (ed.), *Névroses et idées fixes*, Vol. 1. 4th edition. Paris: Alcan, 423–480. (Original work published in 1898).

Joffe, H., Kim, D.R., Foris, J.M., Baldassano, C.F., Gyulai, L., Hwang, C.H., McLaughlin, W.L., Sachs, G.S., Thase, M.E., Harlow, B.L. & Cohen, L.S. (2006) "Menstrual Dysfunction Prior to Onset of Psychiatric Illness Is Reported More Commonly by Women with Bipolar Disorder than by Women with Unipolar Depression and Healthy Controls", *Journal of Clinical Psychiatry*, 67: 29304.

Jung, C. (1911/1912 [2014]) *Symbols of Transformation – An Analysis of the Prelude to a Case of Schizophrenia*. trans. R.F.C. Hull (ed.), (1969). Princeton, NJ: Princeton University Press.

King, P. (2005) *Time Present and Time Past*. London & New York: Routledge Publishing.

Kisch, E.H. (1910) *The Sexual Life of Women in Its Physiological, Pathological and Hygienic Aspects*. New York: Rebman Company.

Klein, M. (1932) *The Psychoanalysis of Children*. trans. A. Strachey (1963). London: Hogarth Press.

Klein, M. (1952a) "Some Theoretical Conclusions regarding the Emotional Life of the Infant", in M. Klein (ed.), (1975) *Envy and Gratitude and Other Works, 1946–1963*. London: Hogarth Press, 61–93.

Klein, M. (1952b) "The Mutual Influences in the Development of Ego and Id", *Psychoanalytic Study of the Child*, 7: 51–53.

Kraus Aronson, J. (1993) *Insights in the Dynamic Psychotherapy of Anorexia and Bulimia: An Introduction to the Literature*. Northvale & London: Jason Aronson Inc.

Kruks, S. (1998) "Existentialism and Phenomenology", in A.M. Jagger & I.M. Young (eds.), *A Companion to Feminist Philosophy*. Oxford: Blackwell Publishing, 66–74.

Lambo, T.A. (1956) "Neuropsychiatric Observations in Western Nigeria", *British Medical Journal*, 2: 1388–1394.

Langer, M.M. (1989) *Merleau-Ponty's Phenomenology of Perception: A Guide and Commentary*. London: Palgrave Macmillan.

Leys, R. (2000) *Trauma: A Genealogy*. Chicago, IL & London: University of Chicago Press.

Lombardi, R. (2011) "The Body, Feelings, and the Unheard Music of the Senses", *Contemporary Psychoanalysis*, 47: 3–24.

Ludwig, A.O., Murawski, B.J. & Sturgis, S.H. (1969) *Psychosomatic Aspects of Gynaecological Disorders – Seven Psychoanalytic Case Studies*. Cambridge, MA: Harvard University Press.

Malson, H. (1998) *The Thin Woman: Feminism, Post-Structuralism and the Social Psychology of Anorexia Nervosa*. London & New York: Routledge Publishing.

Malson, H. & Ussher, J.M. (1996) "Bloody Women: A Discourse Analysis of Amenorrhea as A Symptom of Anorexia Nervosa", *Feminism and Psychology*, 6(4): 505–521.

Mangold, D., Wand, G., Javors, M. & Mintz, J. (2010) "Acculturation, Childhood Trauma and the Cortisol Awakening Response in American Adults", *Journal of Hormones and Behaviour*, 58(4): 637–646.

Marty, P. & de M'Uzan, M. (1963) "La Pensée Opératoire (Operational Thinking)", *Revue Française De Psychoanalyse*, 27(Special Issue): 345–456.

McDougall, J. (1974) "The Psychosoma and the Psychoanalytic Process", *The International Review of Psycho-Analysis*, 1: 437–459.

McGowan, P.O., Sasaki, A., D'Alessio, A.C., Dymov, S., Labonté, B., Szyf, M., Turecki, G. & Meaney, M.J. (2009) "Epigenetic Regulation of the Glucocorticoid Receptor in Human Brain Associates with Childhood Abuse", *Nature Neuroscience*, 12: 342–348.

Menninger, K.A. (1939) "Somatic Correlations with the Unconscious Repudiation of Femininity in Women", *Journal of Nervous and Mental Disease*, 89: 514–527.

Merleau-Ponty, M. (1948 [1962]) *Phenomenology of Perception*. trans. C. Smith. London & New York: Routledge & Kegan Paul.

Mooney, T. & Moran, D. (eds.), (2004) *The Phenomenology Reader*. London & New York: Routledge Publishing.

Osofsky, H.J. & Fisher, H. (1967) "Psychological Correlates of the Development of Amenorrhea in a Stress Situation", *Psychosomatic Medicine*, 29(1): 15–23.

Pawlowski, E.J. & Pawlowski, M.M. (1958) "Unconscious and Abortive Aspects of Pseudocyesis", *Wisconsin Medical Journal*, 57: 427–540.

Porter, R. (1993) "The Body and the Mind, the Doctor and the Patient: Negotiating Hysteria", in S.L. Gilman, H. King, R. Porter, G.S. Rousseau & E. Showalter (eds.), *Hysteria Beyond Freud*. Berkeley, CA: University of California Press, 225–285.

Rasgon, N.L., Altshuler, L.L., Gudeman, D., Burt, V.K., Tanavoli, S., Hendrick, V. & Korenman, S. (2000) "Medication Status and Polycystic Ovary Syndrome in Women with Bipolar Disorder: A Preliminary Report", *Journal of Clinical Psychiatry*, 61(3): 173–178.

Risse, G.B. (1988) "Hysteria at the Edinburgh Infirmary: The Construction and Treatment of a Disease, 1700–1800", *Medical History*, 32(1): 1–22.

Roazan, P. (ed.), (1991) *Helene Deutsch: Psychoanalysis of the Sexual Functions of Women*. trans. E. Mosbacher. London & New York: Karnac Books.

Rosenthal, M.B. & Smith, D.H. (eds.), (1985) *Psychosomatic Obstetrics and Gynecology*. Basel: Karger Books.

Sander, H. (1995) "Remembering/Forgetting", trans. S. Liebman, *October 72*: 15–25, originally in.

Sander, H. & Johr, B. (1992) *BeFreier Und Befreite: Krieg, Vergewaltigungen, Kinder (Liberators Take Liberties: War, Rapes Children)*. Munich: Verlag Antje Kunstrmann.

Scaruffi, E., Gambineri, A., Cattaneo, S., Turra, J., Vettor, R. & Mioni, R. (2014) "Personality and Psychiatric Disorders in Women Affected by Polycystic Ovary Syndrome", *Frontiers in Endocrinology*, 5: 185.

Seeman, M.V. (2011) "Antipsychotic-induced Amenorrhea", *Journal of Mental Health*, 20(5): 484–491.

Sheinfeld, H., Gal, M., Bunzel, M.E. & Vishne, T. (2007) "The Etiology of Some Menstrual Disorders: A Gynaecological and Psychiatric Issue", *Health Care Women Int.*, 28(9): 817–827.

Shorter, E. (1992) *From Paralysis to Fatigue: A History of Psychosomatic Illness in the Modern Era*. New York: The Free Press.

Showalter, E. (1985 [1997]) *The Female Malady*. London: Virago Press Limited.

Skultans, V. (1985) "Research Note. Vicarious Menstruation", *Social Science and Medicine*, 21(6): 713–714.

Sobrinho, L.G. (1998) "Emotional Aspects of Hyperprolactinemia", *Psychotherapy and Psychosomatics*, 67(3): 113–139.

Sobrinho, L.G., Duarte, J.S., Paiva, I., Gomes, L., Vicente, V. & Aguiar, P. (2011) "Paternal Deprivation Prior to Adolescence and Vulnerability to Pituitary Adenomas", *Pituitary*, 15(2): 251–257.

Tarín, J.J., Hermenegildo, C., García-Pérez, M.A. & Cano, A. (2013) "Endocrinology and Physiology of Pseudocyesis", *Reproductive Biology and Endocrinology*, 14: 11–39.

Teede, H., Deeks, A. & Moran, L. (2010) "Polycystic Ovary Syndrome: A Complex Condition with Psychological, Reproductive and Metabolic Manifestations that Impacts on Health across the Lifespan", *BMC Medicine*, 8(41): 1–10.

Thompson, J.G. (1988) *The Psychobiology of Emotions*. New York: Springer Science + Business Media.

Tschugguel, W. & Berga, S.L. (2003) "Treatment of Functional Hypothalamic Amenorrhea with Hypnotherapy", *Fertility & Sterility*, 80(4): 982–985.

Van der Hart, O., Brown, P. & Van der Kolk, B. (1989) "Pierre Janet's Treatment of Posttraumatic Stress", *Journal of Traumatic Stress*, 2: 356–380.

Veith, I. (1965) *Hysteria – The History of a Disease*. Chicago, IL: University of Chicago Press.

Walsh, J.J. (1912) *Psychotherapy Including the History of the Use of Mental Influence, Directly or Indirectly, in Healing and the Principles for the Application of Energies Derived from the Mind to the Treatment of Diseases*. New York & London: D. Appleton & Co.

Wilson, C.P. & Mintz, I.L. (1989) *Psychodynamic Symptoms: Psychodynamic Treatment of the Underlying Personality Disorder*. Northvale, NJ: Jason Aronson.

Wittgenstein, L. (1969) in G.E.M. Anscombe & G.H. von Wright (eds.), *On Certainty*. New York: Harper & Row.

Youngs, D.D. & Reame, N. (1985) "Psychoendocrinology and the Menstrual Cycle", in M.B. Rosenthal & D.H. Smith (eds.) *Psychosomatic Obstetrics and Gynaecology*. Basel: Karger Books, 25–34.

Zepf, S. & Seel, D. (2016) "Penis Envy and the Female Oedipus Complex: A Plea to Reawaken an Ineffectual Debate", *Psychoanalytic Review*, 103(3): 397–421.

4 The body boundary, the ego boundary, non-menses and patterns of relating in anorexia and eating disorders

Introduction

Anorexia is often thought of as the body bearer of psychic contradictory states in conflict; a two-fold system of submission and resistance. It is a "confused and confusing opposition of signals" (Becker, 2008: 145). It is a system of control, differentiation and autonomy. The more successful the anorectic is, the more she disappears. The more she disappears, the more she is seen. I am reminded of the work of poet Louise Glück. As a patient, psychoanalysis had provided Glück with a frame that could replace the anorexia she had developed from the age of 16. She later turned to poetry, perhaps finding psychoanalytic "truths" too abstract or indeterminate. Poetry, like anorexia, focuses on form. In one poem, "Widows", she writes about a card game that her mother and aunt are playing. It's a game their mother taught them:

> My grandmother thought ahead; she prepared her daughters.
> They have cards; they have each other.
> They don't need any more companionship

The aunt wins the game and the final lines of the poem read

> Her cards evaporate: that's what you want, that's the object: in the end,
> The one who has nothing wins.
>
> (Glück, 1990)

To what extent is the form of secondary amenorrhea a game changer in the developing patterns of disordered eating? This chapter will consider this question.

Menstrual markers

What is the position and place of secondary amenorrhea (SA) in the identities and subjectivities of women presenting with anorexia (AN) and with other eating disorders (EDs), SA being a key component in these complex systems?

In looking at both historic and current analysis on the subject, I hope too to enable an easy transition into a way of thinking that supports the view that some patterns of relating, as exemplified in this case with food, can serve as a framework in which an autistic mind can find some sort of container. Whilst looking at most recent research that links eating regimes with autism, might we also consider that the non-menstruating body is itself another way in which an autistic state of mind can find representation? The neat, clean, unblemished, untarnished, consistent non-attributes of the non-menstruating body can house a psyche that fastidiously demands a body that mirrors a psychical method of thinking that operates with clear and exacting parameters. It's a match made in heaven. But this pathway to heaven, as we see with anorexia, can be deadly.

It is now widely accepted that eating disorders are deadly diseases. Research into the National Death Index clearly shows that the cause of death extracted from death certificates and the monitoring of crude mortality rates are such that they underscore the severity of all types of eating disorders. A review of nearly fifty years of research in the paper "Mortality Rates in Patients with Anorexia Nervosa and Other Eating Disorders" (Arcelus et al., 2011) confirms that AN has the highest mortality rate of any psychiatric illness, including major depression. Importantly, conversations are constantly taking place as to what are the most effective ways to treat anorexia, bulimia and other eating disorders. Researchers are rightly challenged to validate their quantitative data with qualitative (narratives/stories/interviews) placing the issue in the wider context of mental as well as physical health. Often conflicting and contradicting evidence emerges, but most experts agree that a patient treatment plan that includes psychotherapy or a talking therapy is best practice. One of the linchpins in the success of the psychotherapeutic model is that an alliance be formed between therapist and patient, "not an alliance designed to control symptoms, but an alliance designed to understand the emotional meanings of the patient's verbal and somatic expressions" (Levin, cited in Siegal, 1992: 48).

In "Somatic Symptoms, Psychoanalytic Treatment, Emotional Growth" (1992), Ronald Levin comprehensively illustrates the alliance by presenting a case study of a 22-year-old woman suffering from seizures and an eating disorder. He introduces the chapter with a firm position that a technical treatment approach can actually be harmful:

> Technological medical care leads caretakers to conceptualize physical and behavioural symptoms as disease, while overlooking the level of emotional development of the patient; the unconscious meaning of the patient's words, actions, and somatic processes are also ignored … patients treated technologically often do not develop emotionally. Conflicts remain unresolved and actively contribute to symptoms.
>
> (Levin cited in Siegal, 1992: 44)

Perhaps the patient also needs to experience the therapist as someone unafraid; this is important when the stakes are high and the patient is demonstrating a defiant stance against moving away from the place that she knows might eventually kill her. Perhaps it's about sitting alongside her on that ledge, however many storeys (stories) up for as long as it takes. I think it's right and proper for the medics and not the therapists to be concerned with the details of a patient's weight and other physical indices. The therapist is there to deal with matters of the psyche. Paradoxically, they are not there to cathect the bodily state into an emotional one but rather (as Christopher Bollas explained to me) to use the act of interpretation to reach the patient and for them both to find a common language. I understand this not just as "what are you telling me" but "what are you trying to do to me?" This is the question that acknowledges the severity of the illness and allows room for the exploration of that which supports and that which opposes the illness. We are with that old and crucial adage – ambivalence.

Rachel

Twelve-year-old "Rachel" was an outpatient at an eating disorder clinic, presenting with very erratic eating patterns. After a couple of menstrual cycles from the age of around 11, her periods stopped. Neither anorexic nor bulimic with no clear plan or execution in terms of dieting, her eating mirrored her thinking. Her emotions were all over the place, as was her eating with swings from days of eating nothing to days of replenishing and refuelling, but never bingeing. "Rachel" never made herself sick. When she looked in the mirror, she could see parts of her body, notably her legs and ankles, getting bigger. Of that she was absolutely sure. She was a tall girl, not the tallest in her primary school, but taller than most. The transition from a small primary school to a much larger secondary school was the catalyst for her discombobulation and the new social politics and game playing amongst her peers left her disorientated and feeling exposed. The process of transition profoundly frightened her and that's when she started "messing about with food". The details of her treatment plan are with the clinic but I was able to speak to "Rachel" when she was 15 and I asked her what she thought had gone on. She was non-committal about her experience at the clinic and said that it made her fear endings because the trainee psychologist with whom she was working had left to move on to another placement. They had worked towards an ending and at the last session "Rachel" had given her a card which she had made herself. When I asked her about her periods and how she felt about them returning she replied, "What do you mean feelings? I don't like how they come back because it meant I was eating enough for it to happen … Is that what you mean?" When I asked what her periods symbolised she replied, "End of cycle, no? I'm not scared of getting it, I just don't like how it relates to my weight … The cleaning out of your body yes but the weight no" (pers. comm., 2017).

I met "Rachel" again in 2019, aged 17. She appeared happy in herself, working well at a sixth form college (having managed the transition out of her secondary school not only far better this time round but with much aplomb). She says she still hates the thought of a bloated stomach and she goes to the gym at least three times a week plus extra exercises at home to ensure a flat tummy. She eats and on the whole her mother reported that she eats well, enjoying her food but careful to stay within the remit of how much is good enough and how much would tip her into bad eating. She has regular periods which although "painful and annoying" she welcomes as cleansing and a positive symbol of womanhood, sisterhood and adulthood.

"Rachel" is a young woman making progress, adapting so as to live a full life, more able to contain a wider spectrum of feelings. Her ambivalence no longer eats away at her. That the tension between love and hate, that can be so powerful so as to destroy, is being managed by this young woman is a good thing. In my mind, the practice of psychoanalysis accommodates this ambivalence. It think it is useful to refer to Bleger's work (1967 [2013]) that describes the difference between ambivalence and ambiguity. Ambivalence acknowledges that there are contradicting and conflicting associations whereas ambiguity (a pre-ambivalent state) does not allow for discrimination between several possible meanings existing at the same time. To consider the way in which a patient thinks about her menses is a useful tool in our assessing her capacity to be in a state of ambivalence rather than ambiguity. It might be a useful part of the eating disorder puzzle for therapists to become more acquainted with.

Let us consider the puzzle at large. One: is anorexia a wish to be thin or the repulsion against being fat? – Refer to Bruch (1973). Two: to what extent is anorexia, like hysteria, a language used by the patient because she knows no other? – Refer to Shoenberg (1975). Three: how are we to decode anorexia as linked to obsessive compulsive disorder, when obsessional ways of behaving transform any possible communication into something abstract and beyond the spoken word? – Rothenberg (1990). Four: what are the multifactorial aspects to the aetiology of eating disorders? – Hsu (1984).

What I want to suggest is that the cessation of menses is a clue too often overlooked or dismissed. It is a relevant and meaningful symbol that partners the eating disorder. However, it is too often engaged with in a concrete way along with the monitoring of the patient's weight and body mass index. When a young girl stops menstruating and when she regains her menses, these are dates that are noted down as markers at two polar points along a patient's journey, bookending like an entrance and exit. As specialist psychotherapist Cynthia Rousso clarified in our communications, menstruation is often used as a benchmark indicator to assess a patient's health. At the time of our speaking (November 2016), Cynthia Rousso was working in the Child and Adolescent Mental Health Service at the Royal Free Hospital in London, UK. It has one of the largest eating disorder services in the country with up to 11 referrals each week. Often, even when eating disorder patients achieve their minimum required weight, it is only when their menses returns that the clinic is more confident about discharging them. One anecdotal clinical motif Rousso gave me was of women preparing to go to college or university. They gain their minimum weight and want to be discharged but they are asked to put on more weight so as to trigger a menstrual bleed. Many agree to increase the weight incrementally. Menstruation is "a marker of good health". This compromise and working together between patients and clinicians is a statement of better health reflecting a more developed intrapsychic system more in tune with reality. It goes without saying that decisions are made on a case-by-case basis as it cannot simply be that a return of menses, relating to body mass index and biological variables, necessarily means the patient has recovered from the eating disorder. What I took away from my speaking with Rousso and from my observations of the service was that the conversations provided by menses and non-menses on one level acted as a line of discourse, a container and clearly demarked boundary with which the multidisciplinary staff and the patients could engage with during treatment. But to what degree were opportunities to unpack the meaning of menses taken? And whilst discharged and free from the clinic, to what degree were some patients really well enough, psychically stable for the long-term challenges ahead of them? A return of menstruation does not necessarily mean a return to better health. More specifically for Rousso, "while a return of menstruation is a return to better physical health, this does not necessarily apply to emotional health" (Cynthia Rousso, pers. comm., 22 May 2017).

The referral process

It is widely accepted that early treatment of eating disorders leads to better prognosis (Hay, 2013). However, a systematic review carried out in 2011 showed that only 23% of those with eating disorders sought help and most of them did so because they wanted support to lose weight (Hart, 2011). In "Stigmatizing Attitudes and Beliefs About Anorexia and Bulimia Among Italian Undergraduates", Caslini et al. (2016) argue that these diseases are still heavily burdened by stigma, which creates social distance between "us and them":

> Dimensions of stigma in relation to AN and BN are different as compared with other mental health disorders. Although stigma about mental illness generally includes avoidance of social interaction, perceived dangerousness, unpredictability and poor diagnosis … For EDs it mainly involves guilt and blame, personal responsibility and minimizing attitudes regarding the seriousness of the illness.
>
> (Caslini et al., 2016: 216)

Out of a study of 10,123 adolescents aged 13 to 18 in the US, the majority (73–78%) with eating disorders reported some contact with service providers such as their GP, school services, or mental health speciality care unit. However only between 3 to 28% had specifically talked with a professional about their eating or weight problems. This study by Swanson et al. (2011) published in the *Archives of General Psychiatry* was picked up by many eating disorder prevention and treatment organisations because it clarified the situation in terms of the difficulties sufferers face to be seen

> whether this is due to denial, shame or stigma, or a lack of recognition of eating symptoms by professionals treating other targeted problems, it shows that adolescents do use services. This suggests possible avenues for prevention and early intervention if recognition could be improved.
>
> (National Eating Disorder Association)

In the UK, around 15% of middle-aged women have experienced disordered eating at some point in their life (https://www.nhs.uk/news/mental-health/ eating-disorders-in-middle-aged-women-common/) with three in one hundred middle-aged women affected in 2017. Whilst we are increasingly more aware of the prevalence amongst 40- and 50-year-old women, we also learn that few in this age bracket access the healthcare provision, as shown in the study "Lifetime and 12 Month Prevalence of Eating Disorders amongst Women in Midlife: a Population-Based Study of Diagnoses and Risk Factors" (Micali et al., 2017). The results of this study showed that

> Although some risk factors differed across ED subtypes, childhood sexual abuse and poor parenting were associated to binge/purge type disorders, whilst personality factors were more broadly associated with several diagnostic categories … The evidence that lifetime and active EDs are common amongst women in mid-life, compounded by the lack of healthcare access and treatment, highlights the likelihood of high disease burden and unmet needs.
>
> (Micali et al., 2017)

The key factor is making sure that experts are alert to this. The advice is reminiscent to that given in the 1970s, for example in Fries's "Studies in Secondary Amenorrhea, Anorectic Behaviour and Body Image Perception": Fries wrote:

> We know that every woman with anorexia nervosa has had a starting point. Thus it is important that physicians and especially gynaecologists pay great attention to a history of dieting behaviour and weight loss in women who consult them for secondary amenorrhea.
>
> (Fries, 1977)

Fries explains that a characteristic feature of AN is the endocrine disorder which is signalled by the loss of menstruation. Analysing the data of several leading research papers Fries shows how secondary amenorrhea is an early symptom (70% of 628 cases) that either coincides with other symptoms such as weight loss and changes in eating patterns or precedes them:

> However most authors have difficulties differentiating retrospectively between the onset of the feeding disorder (i.e. the anorectic behaviour) and the onset of weight loss, which causes uncertainty regarding the amount of weight really lost before the onset of amenorrhea. It has been concluded that menstruation ceases early in anorexia nervosa but usually after some real weight loss, which would be in agreement with the hypothesis of a "critical body weight" necessary for the maintenance of regular menstruations.
>
> (Fries, 1977: 163–164)

Many studies show that amenorrhea does occur before an appreciable amount of weight has been lost. With this as a backdrop to the referral process, historically amenorrhea has distinguished patients that need to be referred to a specialist eating disorder unit from their thin (but healthy) counterparts. By the time most patients get to the clinic, they are of a very low weight. They display a disordered way of relating to food and have individual persistent and strict ideas of the body beautiful. Most have stopped menstruating. This is interesting because the newly revised fifth edition of the *Diagnostic and Statistical Manual of Mental Disorders*, (American Psychiatric Association, 2013) (*DSM-5*) removed amenorrhea as a diagnostic criterion for anorexia, challenging its diagnostic usefulness. Reasons for this included that men have anorexia as do postmenopausal women, some women take contraceptives and some girls are anorexic premenarche: Amenorrhea does not distinguish between groups on a number of important measures of clinical severity" (Roberto et al., 2008: 559).

The chart review of 240 inpatients carried out by Roberto et al. found that 25% of underweight ED patients did not have amenorrhea and in applying the DSM-5 criteria, 36% of female AN patients did not have amenorrhea. The "prognostic value of menstrual status" does impact and complicate the original set of attitudes towards treatment. For example:

> the presence/absence of menstruation does not influence the procedures and the therapeutic strategies used to address the eating disorder psychopathology and behaviors, as well as the treatment of psychiatric comorbidities. Secondly, the inclusion of amenorrhea as one of the criteria for the diagnosis of AN could delay the diagnosis and the beginning of appropriate treatment.
>
> (Dalle Gave et al., 2008: 1293)

In the UK, waiting times for a space in an eating disorder unit in some areas of the country are up by 120% since 2015 and girls are having to be treated hundred of miles away from their families. Many clinics are flooded with cases that are "not specified". We should be alert to the fact that these cases are also imbued with psychic angst and to catch these patients before they slip further away from good health is imperative. A dangerous time is around menarche, when periods and subsequent weight gain appear to be risk factors for the onset of eating disorders. Added to this is low self-esteem amongst adolescents and increased body-image awareness that leaves young teenagers susceptible. If we think again about "Rachel", the transition from primary to secondary school, the bombardment of images on social media, a weakened sense of self and lowering self-esteem makes her and others like her vulnerable. The body boundary starts to weaken and erode. An eating disorder offers a place of refuge. When researching for my PhD, I spoke with 13-year-old non-identical twin girls. Twin A had not started her periods and was upset that she was one of the last in her class to do so. Wanting to be like her peers and curious to know what it felt like to menstruate, she asked her mother to take her to a specialist. They were told by the specialist paediatrician not to worry. If she hadn't started menstruating by 16 they would start investigations. She did in fact get her period at 15. Twin B had started menstruating at 13, but her sporadic, non-uniformed bleeds with the accompanying weight gain and bloating made her want to lose weight. Desiring a body for herself that was thin and not fat, she stopped eating, stopped going to school and soon developed dysmorphia. She felt and saw the fat piling on. Her accompanying aggressive verbal attacks and her demonstrating of a young girl at war with herself resulted in the twins feeling miles apart from one another, for the first time in their lives. This sense of separation was overwhelming. Twin B had been Queen Bee at primary school, but in secondary school she was simply one of many. Mirror mirror on the wall, she was by far not at all the fairest of them all. What a cruel world she imagined she lived in. She struggled with individuation and whilst she sought solitude from the masses, Twin A wanted to join a group and be part of a shared experience, just not the one her sister was offering. Their experience will define their future but it need not shape it. The twist to this tale is that at the first meeting with the GP, Twin B was incorrectly measured, her height set against her weight miscalculated. The GP put the figure much lower than it actually was causing alarm bells to ring. Once the girl was in the CAMHS system could we argue that this propelled her into an illness that might never have taken shape? What if this was a teenager displaying typical teenage foibles? Was it the GP's anxiety projected onto the girl, the girl having to metabolise it for them all? Was the outcome of this slip two years of misery and heartache for the family or was it on the horizon, caught early, unconsciously so, by the GP?

Amenorrhea – a badge of truism?

Despite what the manuals advise, for many patients secondary amenorrhea is the marker of "true" anorexia. We see this in Karin Eli's paper "An Embodied Belonging: Amenorrhea and Anorexic Subjectivities" (2014). Eli interviewed 23 women aged between 17 and 38, all of whom had anorexia nervosa, bulimia nervosa, or sub-threshold anorexia or bulimia. Her study showed "Notably, although the participants invoked amenorrhea as a defining sign of illness, they did not cast menstruation as a sign of health, rather, they spoke of their menstrual periods as contradicting their anorexic-identified selves" (Eli, 2014: 53).

Eli, a medical anthropologist, explains that neither menstruation, nor its lack, were key points to the study and the participants were not directed to discuss it. Nevertheless, 18 of the 35 women volunteered their discussion of it at least once. They used it as a way to help narrate their illness. It was linked to disorder and was a vital component in the articulation of their anorexic identity. Amenorrhea was almost synonymous with anorexia. Furthermore, a return to menses did not signify recovery. It frightened many. For "Oryan", as Eli understood it, her newly menstruating body was "acting in opposition to her will, imprisoning her disordered wish within an unrelenting, deceptively recovered frame" (Eli, 2014: 70).

Psychoanalytic explorations into eating disorders

"We" no longer know what a child is. So we do not know the incredible challenge for our self during that era to comprehend the biological demand of adolescence. I totally understand an adolescent boy who feels he does not know how to be a man much less that he wants to be one. I think the pressure on the girl is far greater. Why should she accept the push into menses???? Given all that means in the eyes of the others? Why not say "nope, I am staying here and I am prepared to die for it." I think unless we get this basic fact – for both "genders" – we miss the core point.

(Bollas, pers. comm., 12 September 2016)

How is the unconscious using food to feed its own hunger? The list of ideas is exhaustive amongst classical psychoanalytic thinkers: Eating may be equated with gratification, impregnation, intercourse, performance, growing, castrating, destroying, engulfing, killing, cannibalism. Food may symbolise the breast, the genitals, faeces, poison, a parent, or a sibling" (Minuchin et al., 1978: 15).

Bulimia can be interpreted as an impulsive action that is habitualised. It can be an unconscious wish for repetitive masturbatory activity and a resolution to some sort of conflict. In "Bulimia: Psychoanalytic Perspectives", Schwartz focuses on "the pathology of early object relations and later intra-psychic conflicts over incestuous impregnation fantasies … and associations with masturbatory conflicts and early adolescent phallic activity" (Schwartz, 1986: 439).

Also suggested is the theory that for those children who have witnessed "primal scene stimuli", they react to this by doing to themselves what was done to the parents; in other words sticking a finger down the throat to induce vomiting.

The beauty of psychoanalysis is that nothing is untouchable. Our conscious thoughts might be no match for the unconscious but we endeavour, we return, revisit, repeat and so on, so that we might repair. Often though the rally cry is that eating disordered patients are concrete thinkers. Many experts advise that psychoanalytic treatment should start only when the patient has put on weight, or it should be avoided altogether. They imagine that the silences in the consulting room would be unbearable and annihilating and for concrete thinkers unable or unwilling to symbolise, the emergence from a chrysalis could be damaging. But this is only one strand of thinking, perhaps itself too concrete. I have never underestimated reparative potential of the analytic rapport. A patient can feel truly empowered.

Issues of power and control are often sited within the idealised, fictitious, mental picture of the anorectic. To imagine a process of transformation requires us to think about the paradox in which her symptoms and her condition both give and deny her control. Her power is both real and imagined:

> For a human being to experience his or her self as powerful requires that s/he experience being in the world as meaningful. We can note two significant consequences of this conception of human agency. Firstly, it entails that an increased feeling of power may denote a decrease in actual power and vice-versa. In other words, my way of rendering my experience as meaningful may generate an increased feeling of power, yet this may undermine my actual capacity for autonomy agency.
>
> (Owen, 1995, cited in Hauke, 2000: 179)

In *Jung and the Postmodern: The Interpretation of Realities* (2000), Hauke refers to Elizabeth Grosz's book *Volatile Bodies: Toward a Corporeal Feminism* (1994) to emphasise the care needed in analysis when we extrapolate the "I" out from that which is "still tangled up with the 'reactive forces in the governance of the body' rather than going on to become a 'speaking' 'I'" (Hauke, 2000: 184).

The perilous journey to the realisation of a "speaking I" must take into account the reasons why the body in the first instance served as the choice communicator. I would add that to enable the patient to transcribe and translate that which her body speaks into actual words requires precision and skill on the analyst's part so that they are not experienced as yet another intruder. The analyst needs to be experienced as a benign interlocutor. As Rizzuto explains:

> The patient's most persistent defence is an ever-present attempt to control the analyst. The motive for the defence seems to be to prevent the analyst from making emotional contact with the patient. In fact, if such contact is not introduced very gradually it evokes massive anxiety.
>
> (Rizzuto, 1988: 371)

When considering this alongside "restrictor or bulimic fat phobia", Wilson warns that "these patients do not suffer from a lack of appetite but the opposite, a struggle to avoid being overwhelmed by their impulses, including voraciousness" (Wilson, 1988: 443). It goes without saying that the analyst needs to demonstrate the skill and dexterity to withstand the might of the patient's pull. Impulse (like perversion) can be catchy. As Thomä expertly writes:

> Instead of becoming aware of any positive or negative transference, they try to lure the physician into assuming certain roles. The more successful they are in inducing him to pamper or punish them, the more chaotic the situation becomes. For in "counteraction," the analyst now represents those very emotional impulses which the patients have to fend off within themselves.
>
> (Thomä, 1967: 309)

Perhaps what the patient wants to know from the outset is who goes first? Where I lead, will you follow? What will the analyst put words to that others have not? How do we help in the transferring of the patient's taking in of our interpretation from nil by mouth, to liquids, to solids, to then independent feeding as demonstrated in their willingness to challenge the analyst and show willing towards doing it for themselves? Will the analyst be able to surmount his own narcissism and offer the patient meat and two veg, even though the projective identification instils in him his own ravishing desire to provide a flamboyant sickly rich analysis that could choke them both? Remember, she knows how to vomit it up and expel it. He might not! It is tempting to get busy interpreting eating disorders and to tidy up the mess, unconsciously displaying a mastering of the technique that can rival hers but the patient, sick at the sight of this, will bolt.

Amenorrhea as a denial of female sexuality

In "The Psychoanalytic Treatment of Anorexia Nervosa and Bulimia" (1988), Wilson illustrates how anorexia is "an emotional disturbance that emerges as a retreat from the developing adult sexuality via a regression to the prepubertal relation to the parents" (Wilson, 1988: 443).

There is a deep distress towards maturation and developing female sexuality. As Freud noted in "From the History of an Infantile Neurosis" (1918), neurotic tendencies in adolescent and pubertal girls expressed an "aversion to sexuality by means of anorexia" (Freud, 1918, *SE*, XVII, 7: 122).

The young girl with anorexia is trying hard not to grow up. She must override her body that is moving in a direction against her will. Experiencing this at a primitive level, this battle is far more dangerous than death itself. Many clinicians say that the problems originate long before the classical Oedipal set-up, and are rooted in a disturbance in the symbiotic dyad between mother and child. Perhaps the eating disorder reunites mother and daughter, with mother as the transitional phenomena in the hope that the girl's memories of her as a good enough mother do not disappoint.

Secondary amenorrhea signifies a successful protest against growing up and fits with the anorectic's model. It provides a narcissistic defence against affects and gives her a trick to play with in the creation of an illusion of self-sufficiency. German psychoanalyst Helmut Thomä advocated the use of secondary amenorrhea as a reliable early indicator that anorexia nervosa was more than just a matter of weight loss. His work in this field led him to believe that many anorectics were still living unconsciously as though tied to their nursing mother. (This might in part explain why so many inpatients make a strong attachment to tube feeding; take away the tubes and they stop eating.) In one case study, Thomä presents "Henrietta A", a 19-year-old who has had 289 sessions of psychoanalysis over two years:

> Torn between her inability to be a boy and her dislike of being a girl she bolstered up her confidence with a new ideal of sexuality … By denying "dangerous" aspects of the outside world and by repressing her drives, the patient eventually attained a state of the ego that was free from anxiety … .
>
> (Thomä, 1967: 20)

Regression to the magical childlike body that avoids psychobiological maturity brings relief from turmoil and from anxiety. Unresolved pre-oedipal fixations to the mother arrest the child's development and sexual and masturbatory conflicts from the genitals are displayed to the mother with food and eating being forbidden sexual objects and actions (Sperling, 1978: 139–178). Others suggest the issue lies in early dependency needs that were not sufficiently gratified (Fairbairn, 1952; Guntrip, 1969 [2011]). The amenorrheic body can serve as a container and a symbolic representation of a successful repudiation of psychosexual conflict. It displays a successfully crafted, rigid, non-erratic, non-erotic body boundary. The body boundary and the ego boundary are in unison with one another. They are important components in AN, which close off and protect the adolescent girl from being penetrated from the outside (unconsciously by mother, mother's food, mother's feminine identity). Many obsessive and compulsive traits are linked with a rigid ego boundary, so too anxiety disorders. Patients who present with these, often present with disordered eating too. Thomas A Loftus's paper "Psychogenic Factors in Anovulatory Women III. Behavioral and Psychoanalytic Aspects of Anovulatory Amenorrhea" (1962) presents data on five anovulatory amenorrheic patients who have entered or completed psychotherapy. Aged between 15 and 25, they displaced obsessional behaviour. Two had anorexia (one in remission). The analysis of psychodynamics revealed a pattern of the following

1. Repressed rage at mother as manifested by infantile sadistic fantasies and impulses;

2. Guilty fear, due to the assumed inevitable loss of parental "love and pro-
    tection" (i.e. gratification of stronger-than-usual dependency needs)
    through one's own misdeeds. This guilty fear, in turn, causes further
    repression and intensification of the aggressive energy absorbed by the
    non-reporting fantasies of enraged behaviour. The developing child
    finally escapes imperfectly from this vicious cycle by the adoption of
    exactly opposite traits of gentleness (reaction-formation) or by isolation
    (obsessional thoughts and actions without the proper emotion). When
    therapy has been successful, this pattern has been corrected.

(Loftus, 1962: 26)

Four of the five responded to psychoanalytically orientated psychotherapy with
spontaneous menstruation. Similarly, in the work by Engels (cited in Chapter 3)
and his colleagues, menses resumed during the patients' work with psychiatric
investigations. They too presented with obsessional personalities, histories of anorexia and amenorrhea. Engels uses the term "emotional anorexia obsessional". Con-
flictual anxiety is avoided by renouncing femininity and "normal" life.

Beyond the need for control is a deficient sense of self. If we consider
a sense of self-cohesion based on the principle of successfully differentiating
between inside and outside (Lichtenberg, 1978), we can suppose then that
secondary amenorrhea in anorexia presents the ego's flawed pursuit of self-
cohesion. Just as narcissistic personality disorders are driven by fear of the
threat or loss of a sense of self, with an ego boundary between inside and
outside too confining or too capacious, then perhaps similarly anorexia with
its associative need to split rather than distinguish between has a rigidity and
non-permeability to its ego boundary that serves a purpose. I would add that
the exacting absence of menstruation is highly symbolic of that which lacks
movement and flow. It is a declaration of absolute control and is a signal that
the outsider cannot enter. The anorectic's relationship, real or imagined, with
external objects is central. As Thomä explains

Both in fact and in subjective experience, the biological act of taking in,
of incorporation, is a prototype of object finding, of making contact and
of assimilating an outside thing onto oneself. In the subjective experience
of hunger, the ego depends on nature in a twofold way: the need which
is satisfied comes form the inside, whilst the satisfaction of the drive is
provided by an object, which in early life is supplied by another person,
usually the mother. This dependency of the inside on something outside
brings about an unbearable conflict in anorectic patients and explains
why they do not acknowledge any needs or bodily desires.

(Thomä, 1967: 441)

Hilda Bruch mirrors this in her findings and states that the patient has "the
basic delusion of not having an identity of their own, of not even owning

their body and its sensations, with the specific inability of recognizing hunger as a sign of nutritional need" (Bruch, 1973: 50).

Anorexia is a statement of an impairment of the developmental phase of separation-individuation. By repudiating menstruation and thus procreation, amenorrhea leaves the girl tied to mother's cord, in the pre-oedipal phase. This can be burdensome on the mother, especially if they have their own unresolved issues. In "Attacks on Linking: Stressors and Identity Challenges for Mothers of Daughters with Long Lasting Anorexia Nervosa", the subjective experience of ten mothers of daughters with chronic eating disorders were explored. It was found that the quality of the network of relationships they had with others was an important aspect, as was the mothers' relationship with themselves. It was difficult for them to feel that they were "good mothers" or to maintain a "positive maternal self-perception") (Tuval-Maschiach et al., 2014: 613). Many felt incompetent, ill equipped and powerless to help their daughters as they could no longer identify or connect with them or their illness. Perhaps the daughter unconsciously is challenging the mother to scrap the well-warn template of ideals and instead envisage a new reality of womanhood. Michelle Doughty writes about this in relation to menstruation in *The Bath*, which won her Best Undergraduate Writing Prize in 2014:

> I am in seventh-grade biology class when I feel a release of pressure just below my stomach. I hate my period immediately. Not just the inconvenience or even the brutal pain – I hate the entire concept that I am a woman now and a part of me is ready to have a child. I am a cross country runner; I already exercise too much, and with just a hit of dieting I become amenorrheic. The less I eat, the less I bleed, and I love it. I refuse to be the latest in a long line of Russian dolls, another child inside a child inside a child. Each mother creates a daughter, and each daughter fits perfectly inside the mother to whom she belongs. For months in middle school, I still cramp once a month, but the sensation blends into hunger pains. Again and again I dream of sticky red blood pooling over my hips, so thick it sinks me into the mattress and glues me to the bed. I wake up hungry, but that doesn't mean that I have to eat. I am anorexic for many years.
>
> (Doughty, 2014)

In *Vital Signs: Nature, Culture, Psychoanalysis* (2000), Charles Shepherdson writes about the handing-down process as an

> intimate transmission of the signifier, inherited at the level of the flesh … An inheritance between generations of women, which functions at the level of the body, without answering to physiology; a history, then, which at the same time is not susceptible to the usual, broad cultural analysis … .
>
> (Shepherdson, 2000: 18)

This is an important point if we consider the lack of female authorship in medical and gynaecological accounts. As it is clear from testimonies like Doughty's, many women do not want the meaning of their lives to be liquefied into one colossal, universal womb.

By way of contrast, discussions in psychoanalysis can enable women's bodies to "emerge as critical matters of concern" (Butler, 1993: 4). And we find what they are concerned with are issues that have a strong psychic component, often inherited and haunting. Interviews with AN patients show many of them perceive dysfunction in the family, stressful life events and patterned behaviour of dieting as the main causes of their condition. Many have been caught up in parental marital disharmony, with the illness serving as a means to minimise the conflict or locate it elsewhere, away from the marriage. It is also common that the anorectic is in an "enmeshed relationship ... especially when the parental relationship (is) poor" (Crisp, 1980: 186). A sick child can bring about stability and provide focus for family members to regroup to help tackle the illness. In many cases, the trigger exists before the patient's own birth, with an earlier traumatic obstetric loss. Mothers identify their child with a dead sibling or parent "to whom death wishes and ambivalence had been entertained" (Falstein et al., 1956: 766).

Whilst Falstein was referring to males, for many bereaved families, the child freezes in time like a perfect picture, capturing a time that once was male or female. Many anorectic girls are "good" girls. Professor of psychiatry and eminent researcher Arthur Crisp found in a study of 102 female anorectic patients (1980) that 81 were described as good, compliant children "with no discipline problems" (Crisp, 1980: 183)

To what extent does the compliant girl become the compliant patient? To what extent does she feel able to speak, free associate, talk feeling and unedited whilst those around her, in charge of her care, wave forms around for signing, book appointments, get out the blood pressure monitor and weighing apparatus, manage calls from anxious parents, etc.? To what extent does the clinic act in the role of the hysterical mother whose reason for being takes centre stage? It is hard to rebel in an eating disorder unit when you are told that there are hundreds of others queuing for your place. In a setting where compliancy is key, can some young girls actually feel brave enough to rebel and demonstrate a defiant, non-cooperative stance of a "normal" disgruntled teenager? Then again, if she does, maybe she is being compliant in acting out what is expected of her, what we want to see in her so that we might try and reach her. Is this not potentially the stuff of madness? That's why many analysts advocate for a separate therapeutic space outside of the clinic for meeting their patients.

Bodies and image

In "Body Appreciation and Attitudes to Menstruation", Chrisler et al. (2015) found that of a sample of 72 women across the US, broadly, the results showed that "women with the most positive attitudes towards the body also have more positive (and less negative) attitudes towards menstruation" (Chrisler et al., 2015: 79).

Noted though was the fact that the study could not determine if negative attitudes towards menstruation lead to negative views about the body. An earlier study "Body Image In Secondary Amenorrhea" (1997) compared 21 women with SA of at least six months with a control group. Interestingly, the data

> did not confirm the body overestimation previously found among amenorrheics … The lack of significant differences in ideal body values and in dissatisfaction indices between the two groups could confirm that all women are influenced by cultural models, following the "thin body cult" promoted by mass media.
>
> (Orlandi et al., 1997: 50)

A key question has always been whether anorexia, as with other eating disorders, is a reaction or a syndrome? And in a choice of "language" with the dictum to be thin, to what extent are these women influenced by the language and the desires of those around them? Paradoxically, the anorectic is serving a purpose beyond that which is her own, especially so long as society views thinness as perfect. Social critic and psychoanalyst Susie Orbach, in the 1980s, put forward the explanation that in opting our of one system, the anorectic is in fact "conforming to society's demand for women to be thin" (Orbach, 1982 [2016]: 155).

And for author Naomi Wolf, our interest in the bodies of women exists "in order to take over the work of social coercion that myths about motherhood, domesticity, chastity and passivity no longer can manage" (Wolf, 1991: 11).We partake in a new political script in which "the cultural fixation on female thinness is not an obsession about female beauty but an obsession about female obedience" (Wolf, 1991: 187).

I find that this links well with French philosopher Jacques Derrida's observations on society's interest in those who are excluded and those who make up the margins (something we shall see in the next chapter as occupying the writings of Bernard Shaw). Derrida wrote: "Every culture and society requires an internal critique or deconstruction as an essential part of its development … Every culture is haunted by its other" (Derrida cited in Kearney, 1984: 116).

The identity of man is currently haunted by the rapid growth of obese populations. Politicians, medics and think tanks have declared a war on obesity, saying it should be at the top of their "to do" list, alongside terrorism, as a threat to society. A global report published by *The Lancet* (2016: 1377–1396) analysed the trends in mean body-mass index of over 19 million adult participants in 200 countries from 1975–2014. The numbers clearly revealed a change in tide:

Over the past four decades, we have transitioned from a world in which underweight prevalence was more than double that of obesity, to one in which more people are obese than underweight, both globally and in all regions except parts of sub-Saharan Africa and Asia.

(*The Lancet*, 2016: 1389)

This "epidemic of severe obesity" is often linked to poor diet and low levels of physical activity. That it is a mental disease about which we are ill educated is a reason less readily accepted. Uncontested is the burden and the threat that obesity brings on a nation and its resources. It is estimated to cost the UK's National Health Service over £6 billion every year. Whilst obesity, and its associated secondary illnesses, rule the medical headlines, the anorexic is nevertheless a key "other" upon which that which is projected onto her is perceived as unattainable. We can see this with the super-skinny fashion models and the way they are both vilified and worshipped. Their bodies are believed to supersede the bodies of normal women who bloat, bleed, tear, leak, etc. They model clothes and peddle images that many women aspire to buy into. At the same time, they are accused of being dangerous role models because of their thinness. What intrigued me in 2015 was the sudden removal of *Playboy* playmates from the infamous "men's magazine". Women once so abhorrent to many feminists were being binned off. *Playboy* took the decision to stop printing pictures of completely nude women in its magazines. The editors had realised that men were not necessarily buying copies for the pictures because they could access whatever they wanted for free online. As the media bombarded women with the idea that a thinner, leaner, manicured woman was one of great feminine beauty, *Playboy* magazine had been mirroring this by showing much thinner women in its centrefolds. However, men were put off. In "Cultural Expectations of Thinness in Women" (1980), the concept of societies aspiring towards a "thinner standard" (Garner et al., 1980: 483) was evident and both the *Playboy* magazine models and the Miss America Pageant contestants had become significantly thinner over a 20-year period. *Playboy* centrefolds "changed shape", the models having a smaller bust size, and larger waist and smaller hip measurements. Meanwhile in terms of the actual sizes of young women's bodies, the opposite was happening and the expected weight for women under age 30 was increasing at about the same rate that the average weight for the centrefolds was decreasing. So, just as "real" women looked nothing like the centrefolds, men were turning away from what was being put in front of them. It must be said that after a year, *Playboy* reintroduced pictures of nude women with the brand declaring itself shifting back to its former glory days.

Would an anorexic ballet dancer be anorexic if she wasn't a ballet dancer? Principle ballerina with the Kremlin Ballet, Joy Womack, admitted to being anorexic and bulimic for years. As a dancer she embodies the roles she takes on. She cannot ever imagine bits of her wobbling as she is lifted gracefully up into the air. She sees herself as an ethereal, weightless being, and as a woman who breaks barriers. We can turn to psychoanalyst Joyce McDougall's paper "The Artist and the Outer World" (1995) to think further about forms of creativity such as ballet that are unconsciously experienced as acts of transgression. McDougall writes:

> one has dared to play along through one's chosen medium of expression in order to fulfil secret libidinal, aggressive, and narcissistic aims; one has dared to display the resulting product to the outside world; one has dared to exploit pregenital sexuality with all its attendant ambivalence; and, finally, one has dared to steal the parents' generative organs and powers in order to make one's own creating offspring.
>
> (McDougall, 1995: 60)

We can turn to another psychoanalytic passage to see how sometimes this can be thwarted by an over-zealous mother and a disorientated daughter whose moves away from the maternal and pre-oedipal towards the paternal phallic order leaves her lacking and unfulfilled. In "Trauma of Language", Lucie Cantin introduces us to Myriam, a dancer who has been accepted into one of the finest schools in Paris. Her dreams of becoming a dancer are about to be realised. Myriam tells her therapist that she has discovered that her parents "wish her to be sick", with her hospitalisation at age 17 coinciding with her dancing ambitions taking off. Her father is presented as a child who needs looking after and her mother, preoccupied with her looks, flaunts her beauty. Myriam's elder sister is a top international model perpetuating her mother's youth and beauty, "but the mother never fulfilled the dream of her life, which was ... to be a dancer" (Cantin, 2002: 43).

Myriam is amenorrheic until the age of 25, which Cantin interprets as Myriam's unconscious response to her mother's demand that puts her "out of play". Myriam must not succeed where her mother did not, because this would mean a lack in the mother. At the same time, "the impossibility of becoming a woman, expressed by her amenorrhea, forced her to remain a little girl, both guardian and servant of her father" (Cantin, 2002: 44). Myriam's case also fits into the model of thinking about the symbiotic unions forged through familial narratives presented earlier. To round up this section, disordered eating can be seen as symbolic of that which defies the demands put on a woman by other women, just as much as it is a stand against "the rights and prerogatives of male society" (Chermin, 1986: 19).

Can her own everyday battles, both with herself and with those around her, take centre stage (not too much that it self-perpetuates a narcissistic retreat)? She must not be swallowed up in the socio-cultural discussions. Each and every one of these patients have their won story and this is the point – too long ascribed the role of narrator in other people's lives, she must now have the right to tell, to tell it her way and to live her own tale. This is quite contentious, as many patients want to find themselves within the context of a social narrative or they find it helpful to speak about issues of gender and sexuality on a broad scale when thinking about their own selves.

Menstrual irregularities, disordered eating and autism

The results of a global study published in July 2019 showed that metabolic abnormalities can be seen to contribute to the development of anorexia. In other words, anorexia can be viewed in part as a metabolic and not a wholly psychiatric disorder (Watson et al., 2019).

Contemporary research has found links between menstrual irregularities, autism spectrum disorder (ASD) and eating disorders. If we start first with autistic traits in women with menstrual irregularities, a 2016 case-control study of 70 females with primary dysmenorrhea (cramping pain in the lower abdomen just before or during menstruation, not linked to other diseases such as endometriosis) and 70 females without primary dysmenorrhea showed an association between autistic traits and dysmenorrhea in typically developing females (Toy et al., 2016: 2319). One explanation is the androgen theory that links elevated prenatal androgens as a precursor for autistic traits. Women with ASD are more vulnerable to medical conditions associated with elevated androgens and excessive androgens are typical in menstrual problems including amenorrhea, dysmenorrhea (painful periods) and irregular cycles.

ASD is characterised by "deficits in social communication and social interaction across contexts as well as restricted and repetitive patterns of behaviour, interests or activities" (Toy et al., 2016: 2320).

The prism of autism reflects similar patterns characteristic of eating disorders. Restriction in both, notably, encompasses SA, which as we know is a long-term restriction of menses. The results of "Exploring Autistic Traits in Anorexia: A Clinical Study" revealed links between anorexia and autism spectrum condition. This was uncovered "in socio-emotional and cognitive domains; this includes difficulties with empathy, set-shifting and global processing" (Tchanturia et al., 2013: 44).

In this study, 66 participants with AN and 66 in a control group completed self-report questionnaires, including the Sort Version Autism Spectrum Quotient and the Eating Disorder Examination Questionnaire. The results showed that in the AN group, autistic traits correlated to levels of anxiety and depression greater than in the control group with a greater difficulty in maintaining close relationships. Importantly, the association between symptoms of eating disorders and autistic traits was subtle:

> Women with anorexia possess a greater number of autistic traits than typical women. AQ-10 items that discriminated between groups related to "bigger picture" (global) thinking, inflexibility of thinking and problems with social interactions, suggesting that autistic traits may exacerbate factors that maintain the eating disorder rather than cause the eating disorder directly.
>
> (Tchanturia et al., 2013: 44)

The prevalence of eating problems is higher in those with ASD or ADHD and some researchers suggest that anorexia be included on the autistic spectrum based on the literature that draws parallels in the cognitive, behavioural and pathological features of both. They might both be on the same "neurodevelopmental trajectory" (Allely, 2013: 658) in which case it is worth comparing their therapeutic treatment. Simon Baron-Cohen writes in "Do Girls with Anorexia Nervosa Have Elevated Autistic Traits" (2013):

> There are several reasons for considering anorexia and autistic traits may be linked. First anorexia involves rigid attitudes and behaviour, which can be seen as resembling the unusually narrow interests and rigid and repetitive behaviour in autism but in anorexia happen to focus on food and weight. Secondly, patients with anorexia are often extremely self-preoccupied (about their own weight, or their right to do what they want) and the word "autism" literally means an exclusive focus on the self.
>
> (Baron-Cohen et al., 2013)

More recently, in "Clinical Evaluation of Autistic Symptoms in Women with Anorexia Nervosa" (2017) the researchers found that of the 60 women recruited for the study from specialist eating disorder services, 14 (23.3%) scored above the suggested clinical cut-off for ASD, suggesting the presence of elevated ASD symptoms: "These symptoms appeared to be associated with other psychiatric symptoms but not specific ED pathology. Autistic symptoms co-occur with a range of mental health problems which warrant further investigation and consideration for treatment" (Westwood et al., 2017).

As more studies reveal eating disorders in adult women with investigations linking neural mechanisms to the stubbornly entrenched habits that are difficult to treat (Foerde et al., 2015), it is understood that treatments such as antidepressants and cognitive therapy don't work well. The anxiety, long term, is not alleviated. If we consider this alongside new research that links selective eating in young children with psychopathological symptoms such as anxiety, depression and attention hyperactivity disorders both concurrently and prospectively, then again we must take seriously what it is that the patient is trying to communicate through food. Zucker's study "Psychological and Psychosocial Impairment in Pre-Schoolers with Selective Eating" (2015) revealed that as the selective eating became more severe so too did the severity of the psychopathological symptoms. Picky eating is now more fully understood as avoidant/restrictive food intake disorders (new to the *DSM-5* (American Psychiatric Association, 2013)).

From a psychoanalytic perspective, food might symbolise parts of the self and the symptoms of an eating disorder are used by the person to seek out affective self- regulation through dissociation amidst a war between self-states: it is impossible to eat with disgust and pleasure at the same time" (Breuer & Freud, 1893–1895: 89).

Object relation theorists write extensively about the passage from the normal autistic phase to the symbiotic phase to the separation individuation phase. If the transition between phases is compromised, the individual might revolt or retreat, seeking out clarity and rigidity through other means. Secondary amenorrhea might be thought of as symbolic of non-transition, which overrides passages between childhood, adulthood, womanhood and motherhood. It overrides gender, too. Intra-psychically, the cessation of menses might contain psychosexual conflict and associative emotions such as desire, revenge, shame, fear, etc., offering an alternative system of regulation in which all variables, ebbs and flow are wiped out. It allows for a reality that sits comfortably with the patient's sense of self that is dependent on what is understood as

> isomorphism between inner and outer reality, mind and body. The patient demonstrates a closeness, a more or less immediate connection between physical and psychological realities; for example restrictive control of food represents psychological self-control. The "as if" of mental representation is turned into an "is".
>
> (Skårderud, 2007: 324)

Secondary amenorrhea represents "is" and much more. It is not only a body-boundary signifier with its eradication of menstrual flow; it also signifies the threshold of both the benign and the malignant aspects of the self. It is perhaps both friend and foe. The problem in therapy is that often menses can return unexpectedly which precedes a breakdown. We shall see examples of this in the next chapter. We can understand it as the patient's sense of self, already tenuous with an "as is" reality created into "is" now weakened by change, as consciously experienced in the regaining of periods. If these patients are already deficient in their capacity to self-regulate, then clumsy work by the therapist creates destruction to this very system without providing a viable and secure alternative. The very practice of psychoanalysis might be experienced as a path made up of crazy paving stones beyond which lies famine, isolation and dissociation. Yet this is often a well-worn path, one that has been travelled too many a time for our patients. If we want to reach them and hold them, we must illuminate our thinking about the boundaries that intersect all of our lives. One way is through poetry, prose and myths. This is where we are heading.

Bibliography

Allely, C. (2013) "Anorexia Nervosa – On the Autistic Spectrum?" *The Psychologist*, 26 [online].

American Psychiatric Association. (2013) *Diagnostic and Statistical Manual of Mental Disorders*. 5th edition. Washington, DC: American Psychiatric Association Publishers.

Arcelus, J., Mitchell, A.J. & Nielsen, S. (2011) "Mortality Rates in Patients with Anorexia Nervosa and Other Eating Disorders. A Meta-Analysis of 36 Studies", *Archives of General Psychiatry*, 68(7): 724–731.

Baron-Cohen, S., Jaffa, T., Davies, S., Auyeung, B., Allison, C. & Wheelwright, S. (2013) "Do Girls with Anorexia Nervosa Have Elevated Autistic Traits?" *Molecular Autism*, 4(1): 24.

Becker, P. in Taylor, K. (2008) *Going Hungry: Writers on Desire, Self-Denial and Overcoming Anorexia*. New York: Anchor.

Bleger, J. (1967 [2013]) *Simbiosis y Ambiguedad: Estudio Psicoanalítico*. Buenos Aires: Editorial Paidós. (Symbiosis and Ambiguity: A Psychoanalytic Study. J. Churcher and L. Bleger (eds.), tr, S. Rogers et al. Hove: Routledge, pp. 245–283).

Breuer, J. & Freud, S. (1893–1895) *Studies on Hysteria*. *Standard Edition*, 2: 1–335. London: Hogarth Press.

Bruch, H. (1973) *Eating Disorders: Obesity, Anorexia Nervosa and the Person Within*. New York: Basic Books.

Butler, J. (1993) *Bodies That Matter*. New York: Routledge.

Cantin, L. (2002) "Trauma of Language", in W. Apollon, D. Bergeron & L. Cantin (eds.), *After Lacan: Clinical Practice and the Subject of the Unconscious*. New York: SUNY Press, 35–48.

Caslini, M., Crocamo, C., Dakanalis, A., Tremolada, M., Clerici, M. & Carrà, G. (2016) "Stigmatizing Attitudes and Beliefs about Anorexia and Bulimia among Italian Undergraduates", *Journal of Nervous and Mental Disease*, 204(12): 916–924.

Chernin, K. (1986) *The Hungry Self: Women, Eating and Identity*. London: Virago Press.

Chrisler, J.C., Marván, M.L., Gorman, J.A. & Rossihi, M. (2015) "Body Appreciation and Attitudes to Menstruation", *Body Image*, 12: 78–81.

Crisp, A.H. (1980) *Anorexia Nervosa: Let Me Be*. London: Academic Press.

Dalle Gave, R., Calugi, S. & Marchesini, G. (2008) "Is Amenorrhea a Clinically Useful Criterion for the Diagnosis of Anorexia Nervosa?", *Behaviour Research and Therapy*, 46(12): 1290–1294.

Derrida, J. (1981) "Deconstruction and the Other", in R. Kearney (ed.), (1984) *Dialogues with Contemporary Continental Thinkers*. Manchester: Manchester University Press, 107–125.

Doughty, M. (2014) *The Bath*. Bennington, VT: Plain China [online].

Eli, K. (2014) "An Embodied Belonging: Amenorrhea and Anorexic Subjectivities", *Medicine Anthropology Theory*, 1: 53–80.

Fairbairn, W.R.D. (1952) *Psychoanalytic Studies of the Personality*. London: Routledge & Kegan Paul.

Falstein, E., Feinstein, S.C. & Judas, I. (1956) "Anorexia Nervosa in the Male Child", *American Journal of Orthopsychiatry*, 26(4): 751–770.

Foerde, K., Steinglass, J.E., Shohamy, D. & Walsh, B.T. (2015) "Neural Mechanisms Supporting Maladaptive Food Choices in Anorexia Nervosa", *Nature Neuroscience*, 18: 1571–1573.

Freud, S. (1918) *From the History of an Infantile Neurosis*. *SE*, XVII: 1–124. London: Hogarth Press.

Fries, H. (1977) "Studies on Secondary Amenorrhea, Anorectic Behaviour and Body Image Perception: Importance for the Early Recognition of Anorexia Nervosa", in R.A. Vigersky (ed.), *Anorexia Nervosa*. New York: Raven Press, 163–176.

Garner, D.M., Garfinkel, P.E., Schwartz, D. & Thompson, M. (1980) "Cultural Expectations of Thinness in Women", *Psychological Reports*, 47: 483–491.

Glück, L. (1990) *Ararat*. Hopewell, NJ: The Ecco Press.

Grosz, E. (1994) *Volatile Bodies: Toward a Corporeal Feminism*. Bloomington, IN: Indiana University Press.

Guntrip, H. (1969 [2011]) *Schizoid Phenomena, Object Relations and the Self*. London: Karnac.

Hart, L.M. (2011) "Unmet Need for Treatment in the Eating Disorders: A Systematic Review of Eating Disorders Specific Treatment Seeking among Community Cases", *Clinical Psychology Review*, 31(5): 727–735.

Hauke, C. (2000). *Jung and the Postmodern: Interpretation of Realities*. London: Routledge.

Hauke, C. (2005) *Human Being Human: Culture and the Soul*. East Sussex & New York: Routledge.

Hay, P. (2013) "A Systematic Review of Evidence for Psychological Treatments in Eating Disorders, 2005–2012", *International Journal of Eating Disorders*, 46: 462–469.

Hsu, L.K.G. (1984) "The Aetiology of Anorexia Nervosa", *Annual Progress in Child Psychiatry and Child Development, Part VII: Eating Disorders*, 26: 407–419.

Kearney, R. (1984) *Dialogues With Contemporary Continental Thinkers*. Manchester: Manchester University Press.

Levin, R.W. (1992) "Somatic Symptoms, Psychoanalytic Treatment, Emotional Growth", in E.V. Siegal (ed.), *Psychoanalytic Perspectives on Women*. New York: Brunner/Mazel Publishers, 44–62.

Lichtenberg, J. (1978) "The Testing of Reality from the Standpoint of the Body Self", *Journal of American Psychoanalytic Association*, 26(2): 357–385.

Loftus, T.A. (1962) "Psychogenic Factors in Anovulatory Women. III. Behavioral and Psychoanalytic Aspects of Anovulatory Amenorrhea", *Fertility Sterility*, 13(1): 20–28.

McDougall, J. (1995) "The Artist and the Outer World", *Journal of Contemporary Psychoanalysis*, 31(2): 247–262.

Micali, N., Martini, M.G., Thomas, J.J., Eddy, K.T., Kothari, R., Russell, E., Bulik, C. M. & Treasure, T. (2017) "Lifetime and 12 Month Prevalence of Eating Disorders amongst Women in Midlife: A Population-Based Study of Diagnoses and Risk Factors", *BMC Medicine*, 15(12) [online].

Minuchin, S., Rosman, B.L. & Baker, L. (1978) *Psychosomatic Families: Anorexia Nervosa in Context*. Cambridge, MA: Harvard University Press.

Orbach, S. (1982 [2016]) *Fat Is a Feminist Issue Book One: The Anti-Diet Guide & Book Two: Conquering Compulsive Eating*. London: Arrow Books.

Orlandi, E., Guaraldi, G.P. & Facchinetti, F. (1997) "Body Image in Secondary Amenorrhea", *Journal of Psychosomatic Obstetrics & Gynaecology*, 18(1): 45–52.

Owen, D. (1995) *Nietzsche, Politics and Modernity*. London: Sage.

Rizzuto, A.M. (1988) "Transference, Language and Affect in the Treatment of Bulimarexia", *International Journal of Psychoanalysis*, 69: 369–387.

Roberto, C.A., Steinglass, J., Mayer, L.E., Attia, E. & Walsh, B.T. (2008) "The Clinical Significance of Amenorrhea as a Diagnostic Criterion for Anorexia Nervosa", *International Journal of Eating Disorders*, 41(6): 559–563.

Rothenberg, A. (1990) "Adolescence and Eating Disorder: The Obsessive Compulsive Syndrome", *Psychiatric Clinics of North America*, 3(3): 469–488.

Schwartz, H.J. (1986) "Bulimia: Psychoanalytic Perspectives", *Journal of American Psychoanalytic Association*, 34(2): 439–462.

Shepherdson, C. (2000) *Vital Signs: Nature, Culture, Psychoanalysis*. New York & London: Routledge.

Shoenberg, J. (1975) "The Symptom as Stigma or Communication in Hysteria", *International Journal of Psychotherapy*, 4: 507–517.

Siegal, S.J. (1985–1986) "The Effect of Culture on How Women Experience Menstruation: Jewish Women and Mikvah", *Women & Health*, 10(4): 63–74.

Skårderud, F. (2007) "Eating One's Words Part III. Mentalisation-Based Psychotherapy for Anorexia Nervosa – An Outline for a Treatment and Training Manual", *European Eating Disorders Review*, 15(5): 323–329.

Sperling, M. (1978) *Psychosomatic Disorders in Childhood*. New York: Jason Aronson.

Swanson, S.A., Crow, S.J., Le Grange, D., Swendsen, J. & Merikangas, K.R. (2011) "Prevalence and Correlates of Eating Disorders in Adolescents: Results from the National Comorbidity Survey Replication Adolescent Supplement", *Archives of General Psychiatry*, 68(7): 714–723.

Tchanturia, K., Smith, E., Weineck, F., El., F., Kern, N., Treasure, J. & Baron-Cohen, S. (2013) "Exploring Autistic Traits in Anorexia: A Clinical Study", *Molecular Autism*, 4: 44.

The Lancet. (2016) "Trends in Adult Body-Mass Index in 200 Countries from 1975 to 2014: A Pooled Analysis of 1698 Population-Based Measurement Studies with 19.2 Million Participants", 267(10026): 1377–1396. [online].

Thomä, T. (1967) *Anorexia Nervosa*. New York: International Universities Press.

Toy, H., Hergüner, A., Simsek, S. & Hergüner, S. (2016) "Autistic Traits in Women with Primary Dysmenorrhea: A Case Control Study", *Neuropsychiatric Disease and Treatment*, 12: 2319–2325.

Tuval-Maschiach, R., Hasson-Ohayon, I. & Ilan, A. (2014) "Attacks on Linking: Stressor and Identity Challenges for Mothers of Daughters with Long Lasting Anorexia Nervosa", *Psychology & Health*, 29(6): 613–631.

Watson, H.J., Yilmaz, Z., Thornton, L.M., Hübel, C., Coleman, J.R., Gaspar, H.A., Bryois, J., Hinney, A., Leppä, V.M., Mattheisen, M. & Medland, S.E. (2019). "Genome-wide Association Study Identifies Eight Risk Loci and Implicates Metabo-psychiatric Origins for Anorexia Nervosa", *Nature Genetics*, 51(8): 1207–1214.

Westwood, H., Mandy, W. & Tchanturia, K. (2017) "Clinical Evaluation of Autistic Symptoms in Women with Anorexia Nervosa", *Molecular Autism Brain, Cognition and Behavior*, 8(12).

Wilson, C.P. (1988) "The Psychoanalytic Treatment of Anorexia Nervosa and Bulimia", in B.J. Blinder, B.F. Chaitin & R. Goldstein (eds.), *The Eating Disorders: Medical and Psychological Bases of Diagnosis and Treatment*. New York: PMA Publishing Corp, 433–446.

Wolf, N. (1991) *The Beauty Myth: How Images of Beauty are Used against Women*. New York: William Morrow and Company.

Zucker, N., Copeland, W., Franz, L., Carpenter, K., Keeling, L., Angold, A. & Egger, H. (2015) "Psychological and Psychosocial Impairment in Pre-Schoolers with Selective Eating", *Pediatrics*, 135: E582–590.

5 Metamorphosis – the story of Pygmalion and the process of change in the psychoanalysis and treatment of secondary amenorrhea

Ovid's *Metamorphosis* Book X The Pygmalion Verse

Pygmalion had seen these women spend
Their days in wickedness, and horrified
At all the countless vices nature gives
To womankind lived celibate and long
Lacked the companionship of married love.
As shame retreated and their cheeks grew hard,
They turned with little change to stones of flint.
Meanwhile he carved his snow-white ivory
With marvellous triumphant artistry
And gave it perfect shape, more beautiful
Than ever woman born. His masterwork
Fired him with love. It seemed to be alive,
Its face to be a real girl's, a girl
Who wished to move – but modesty forbade.
Such art his art concealed. In admiration
His heart desired the body he had formed.
With many a touch he tries it – is it flesh
Or ivory? Not ivory still, he's sure!
Kisses he gives and thinks they are returned;
He speaks to it, caresses it, believes
The firm new flesh beneath his fingers yields,
And fears the limbs may darken with a bruise.
And now fond words he whispers, now brings gifts
That girls delight in – shells and polished stones,
And little birds and flowers of every hue,
Lilies and coloured balls and beads of amber,
The tear-drops of the daughters of the Sun.
He decks her limbs with robes and on her fingers
Sets splendid rings, a necklace round her neck,
Pearls in her ears, a pendant on her breast;
Lovely she looked, yet unadorned she seemed
In nakedness no white less beautiful.

He laid her a couch of purple silk,
Called her his darling, cushioning her head,
As if she relished it, on softest down.
Venus' day came, the holiest festival
All Cyprus celebrates; incense rose high
And heifers, with their wide horns gilded, fell
Beneath the blade that struck their snowy necks.
Pygmalion, his offering given, prayed
Before the altar, half afraid, "Vouchsafe,
O Gods, if all things you can grant, my bride
Shall be" he dared not say my ivory girl –
"The living likeness of my ivory girl."
And golden Venus (for her presence graced
Her feast) knew well the purpose of his prayer;
And, as an omen of her favouring power,
Thrice did his flame burn bright and leap up high.
And he went home, home to his heart's delight,
And he kissed her as she lay, and she seemed warm;
Again he kissed her and with marvelling touch
Caressed her breast; beneath his touch the flesh
Grew soft, its ivory hardness vanishing.
And yielding to his hands, as in the sun
Wax of Hymettus softens and is shaped
By practiced fingers in to many forms,
And usefulness acquires by being used.
His heart was torn with wonder and misgiving,
Delight and terror that it was not true!
Again and yet again he tried his hopes –
She was alive! The pulse beat in her veins!
And then indeed in words that overflowed
He poured his thanks to Venus, and at last
His lips pressed real lips, and she, his girl,
Felt every kiss, and blushed, and shyly raised
Her eyes to his and saw the world and him.
The goddess graced the union she had made,
And when nine times the crescent moon had filled
Her silver orb, an infant girl was born,
Paphos, from whom the island takes its name.

(trans. A.D. Melville, 1986)

Introduction

Having considered what secondary amenorrhea is, both as a concrete and symbolic entity, its relevance within historical, cultural and social contexts and what it represents for women, both menstruating and non-menstruating, we can now go on to explore and examine it through the particular lens of psychoanalysis. The purpose of this is to discern the characters, communications, structures, organisational patterns, divisions and bonds within the psyche that have sought solace and respite in the settlements of the State of Amenorrhea. I want to do this through the application of psychoanalytic thinking into the reading and interpretation of the story of Pygmalion. My research into patients with SA through the psychoanalytic model has led me to themes of transformation, identification, separation, alienation and loss, both consciously and unconsciously experienced. These are prevalent themes in the narrative – themes shared in the story of Pygmalion and we shall look at them in detail as we go on.

I shall be using first Ovid's version and then George Bernard Shaw's retelling of the classical myth. I hope to demonstrate how we can interpret Ovid's work as a presentation of a pre-oedipal, pre-verbal world in which the ambiguity between what is illusionary and what is real is at its most heightened. Unconscious phantasy is communicated and defended against through the body and through the gaze. The creation of Pygmalion's mute statue in some ways enables the creator to live in a society that he does not feel part of. So too, Eliza Doolittle, in George Bernard Shaw's play feels alienated from those around her but in stark contrast to Pygmalion, she enters into a linguistic process attempting at some level to resolve internal and external conflict. She can see strangeness is in part from within and she does not project it all onto the outside world like Pygmalion does. Eliza wants to find out who she really is and who she could be and she seeks help from Higgins and others to realise this. Shaw's play, from a developmental point of view, is analogous to an oedipal/post-oedipal set-up in which ambivalence, conflict, individuation and inter-subjectivity are communicated and, to a degree, worked through. We shall unpack this carefully as we go through the texts making links with the bodily text of SA through the presentation of clinical overviews including case study material and analysis.

Why Pygmalion?

Why choose Ovid's tale of Pygmalion, the man, when my enquiry is essentially about women? The answer is four-fold. Firstly, I think in the preceding chapters I have given plenty of examples of amenorrheic women: Lilith, Lady Macbeth, Joan of Arc and so on. The quintessentially bombastic and powerful warrior narratives are rich and evocative, but their omnipotent impotent split leaves only the slightest of awkward wriggle room for empathy. In contrast to these narratives, which are encumbered by societal and cultural pressures, Pygmalion is a more solitary affair. It takes place in the privacy of Pygmalion's own living quarters, concretely as in his home, and allegorically in that the house stands for the mind. The reader as voyeur has the chance to engage directly with the text and has the chance to process in his/her own way Pygmalion's own processing of events as they unravel. It is, for many people, a bizarre tale; indeed Pygmalion behaves bizarrely at times but

I certainly can't help but feel for him. In fact I can't help but feel that he wants me, even needs me to feel all that he can't reach in himself, to feel empathy for him. Feeling is welcome. In our line of work, we can't just think and do, we must feel.

Secondly, gendering the work limits our thinking. Instead, we can apply the themes from the tale not only to different gendered identities but we can also think about these themes at a time even before issues of gender creep in to the shaping of one's identity. Psychoanalytically speaking, Pygmalion personifies a construct of psychic organisation and psychic fragmentation which affords the subject, whether he/she be male or female, a certain way of coming into being, of being and of relating to self and to other. One could read it as quite an autistic way of relating, richly creative on the one hand and narrow in field on the other. High spec, we are at a time when normal limits are challenged and "the laws of life and matter" (Segal, 1996: 11) are suspended. Through his artistry, Pygmalion creates a new reality for himself so that he can go on living in the world that he rejects and experiences as rejecting. He doesn't understand the world around him. The realities of life are unpleasant but Pygmalion creates an illusionary world that corresponds to his needs. And, as Freud would write of artists, like magicians, a new reality is created that satisfies the subject's unconscious need for magical omnipotence (Freud, 1913: 10). As we have seen in earlier chapters, SA is an art form that assists women who want to transfigure reality. Pygmalion protests against all that he is surrounded by, but is he delusional? So too, as SA embodies both the illusionary and the real, to what extent are we dealing with protest and with delusion?

Thirdly, I see it that all this magical thinking shows Pygmalion to be at a stage in his psychic development similar to that of a very young infant at the very beginnings of life; "the psychological birth of the human infant" (Mahler, 1974). We know that many studies of SA find the subject in a place of arrested development, paralysed at the point of maturation, rooted in between two stages of development. If we think about the baby, at the outset, it does not see the difference between I and not-I. Pygmalion symbolically represents the infant who resides in a state of total fusion with mother, symbiotically tied to her and to this stage of development, wrapped up in an embodiment of illusion and magical omnipotence. The developmental stages of separation–individuation, differentiation and rapprochement (Mahler, 1974) are frightening and dangerous prospects, placed far away from Pygmalion and his statue. His artist's studio is a safe house, representing sanity in what appears to be a mad world on the outside. I think that SA also provides the safe house, a body that affords relief. It manages frustration and tension like a mother who presents herself to her baby to offer comfort. Pygmalion seeks this out and finds relief in the creation of his statue. In his case, his fetishism and tendency to re-seek pleasure from his caressing of the statue represents a psychosexual infantilism. He behaves like a young masturbator, needing no one but himself and his tools. It's not erotic, more eroticised. The more he keeps at it, the more he seems frustrated. Yes he created it, clever boy, but she is after all just a lump of ivory. The coming-to-life of the statue propels him into having to make a developmental shift. Now that she is real, he will be required to be a "real man". Similarly, SA can represent the paralysis of a maturing body, menses arrested, allowing the subject to avoid the pressures of womanhood and motherhood and all that society demands of its "real" women.

Fourthly, what of the statue? Is it an object with which Pygmalion identifies, representing an internalised aspect of himself? Jungians might describe this as Pygmalion finding the anima, the internal female part of "soul" of the psyche, to partner his animus, the masculine. Pygmalion goes one step further and creates his anima into a "form", shaping it from ivory. We could read this as Pygmalion attempting to find wholeness of self. It is up to the reader to decide whether he is creating on the outside all the things he loves about himself, or whether he is evacuating and splitting off his feminine side that he can't bear to house within. If he were to have allowed himself to unify the two more fluidly and less concretely, he would have made a wonderful precursor to Dustin Hoffman's character in the 1982 film *Tootsie*! We can understand that statue in Winnicottian terms, as a transitional object, separate and outside of Pygmalion but in part belonging to him, part of him. He needs it. He is incomplete without it. So too with SA:, it meets a woman's unconscious need and as we see in the analyses, when it goes and is replaced with menses some can feel lost without it, left now dangling in a middle space without a safety net. The container for holding the tension between opposite states of omnipotence and impotence, defiance and delusion, the illusionary and the real is gone, like the puff of smoke at the end of a magic trick.

Why myths and storytelling?

Pygmalion's story has been reincarnated and reinterpreted many times in literature, art, film and music. From Shakespeare's *A Winter's Tale* to Shelley's *Frankenstein*, from the films "Blade Runner" to "Pretty Woman", Disney's "Pinocchio", Coppélia the ballet and paintings by Gérôme and Goya, its cultural legacy lives on, deservedly so. But in the field of psychoanalysis, Pygmalion hardly features. In fact, it is not even an Echo to the infamous Narcissus, whose tale is resplendent across the field. Similarly, the psychoanalytic work of the subject of amenorrhea, both primary and secondary, is thin and scantily clad whilst that on menstruation continues to evolve and take shape. I hope to redress this imbalance by using the Pygmalion myth as a way to elucidate further thinking and understanding of the way we engage analytically with patients who present with SA, for whom menses has been interrupted or has stopped.

A hallmark of Ovidian poetry is that Ovid himself sought to transcend and transgress boundaries in his writing. The genius of Ovid's *Metamorphosis* in which Pygmalion features is that

> [it] creates an analogous freedom, releasing creative energy in which new forms are continually coming into being and normal limits are suspended. Human and bestial, animate and inanimate, male and female can flow into one another ... this suspension of the laws of life and matter can produce a golden age or a nightmare, miracle or monster.
>
> (Segal, 1996: 11–12)

The artistry of Pygmalion the sculptor, whose statue comes to life, and the technical accuracy of Professor Higgins the linguist who transforms a girl from the gutter into a duchess, demonstrates how in art, philosophy and language, as opposed to science, we can make "real" the fantasies of omnipotence. And as psychoanalyst Sandor Ferenczi writes in his 1913 paper "Stages in the Development of the Sense of Reality", it is in fairy tales that "man has wings, his eyes pierce the walls, his magic wand opens all doors ... in the fairy-tale a magic cap enables every transformation" (Ferenczi, 1913: 80–81).

Bruno Bettelheim (1976) mirrors Ferenczi's understanding of the fairy tale "motifs":

> experienced as wondrous because the child feels understood and appreciated deep down in his feelings, hopes and anxieties without these all having to be dragged up and investigated in the harsh light of a rationality that is till beyond him.
>
> (Bettelheim, 1976: 19)

Whilst we might view the rational world as being driven by a dominant consciousness, the world of myths and fairy tales can offer us a legitimate route to transcend and transgress boundaries. As described by Zipes (1991), they can be used as templates for social and cultural codes of conduct. If we look at how many ways the Pygmalion myth has been reinvented to reflect the needs and wishes of mankind at certain periods of time, we see how it has its own magical capabilities. With each transformation, with each retelling of the story and in our interaction with it, we can pursue a deeper understanding of our own unconscious and internal psychic processes. Challenged and hopefully enriched by this, we can learn more about ourselves and each other. The myth of Pygmalion is a great example of how, according to the psychology of Jung, it is precisely through the mythical, symbolic tales that we can approach and express our psychic reality. As understood by Guggenbühl-Craig, "it is not ruled by causes and does not follow the law of cause and effect ... To put it in extreme terms; all psychology is mythology or; psychology is modern mythology" (Guggenbühl-Craig, 1995: 65).

Whether you agree with this or not, we find ourselves suspending belief when we read the Pygmalion myth which allows us to question and perhaps reformulate certain truths. After all, we go along with the fact that the statue really does come to life. It is an emblem for one of Freud's earlier thoughts, expressed in a letter to Wilhelm Fliess written February 1899: "reality-wish fulfilment. It is from these opposites that our mental life springs" (Freud, 1899 cited in Masson, 1985: 345).

Ovid's Pygmalion and the pleasure principle

Ovid's Pygmalion features in Book 10 of *Metamorphosis*. It tells the tale of a sculptor who creates the most perfect statue of a woman out of snow-white ivory. Enamoured by her beauty, and by his own artistic mastery, he adorns the statue with clothes and jewels and he relates to her as if she were real. He prays to Venus for a wife *just like her* and the goddess grants him a wish and brings the statue to life: it's not exactly what he wished for. We shall explore this later on.

The mythical character of Pygmalion can be used as a representation for all that is navigated and negotiated in the very early stages of life, with much investiture in the realms of the Pleasure Principle (Freud, 1920). How Pygmalion views himself and the world around him is comparable to the infant who turns his back on the actual reality of things and through insistent wishing magically creates what he needs. In doing so, he can preserve his feelings of omnipotence. He can fulfil his wishes and think himself to really be in possession of magic capabilities. Shut away from everyone and everything, Pygmalion chooses to engage with his inanimate statue in a way that symbolises sexuality as being independent of the outside world, chiefly because man can satisfy himself auto-erotically. The period of unconditional omnipotence with regards to sexuality can last, so long as one does not give up on the auto-erotic means of satisfaction. In other words, it can last a lifetime. With regards to narcissism, if we confine ourselves to self-love, we can retain the illusion of omnipotence throughout life. We do not need another to be our love object. When the statue comes to life, Pygmalion is forced to renegotiate the way in which he relates to this new other, thus marking a developmental shift away from the Pleasure Principle towards the Reality Principle. Furthermore, as the statue transforms into a human being, a "she" who is now separate from him and who we imagine will have needs and wants of her own replaces an "it". We shall consider their new relationship later on in the chapter.

In Ovid's Pygmalion, we have raw, unedited, instinctual life pulsating throughout. Eroticism bleeds across the margins into the previous and following lines and verses. We have symbols of the unruly id and the way in which the ego defends against it. We also witness, at times, an overwhelmed Pygmalion. To assist in our thinking about Pygmalion's ego functioning, psyche and bodily processes and in consideration of the links made to amenorrhea, we can turn to Freud's formulation of the ego. He wrote that the ego is derived from bodily sensation and is always a body ego: "The ego is first and foremost a bodily ego; it is not merely a surface entity, but is itself the projection of a surface" (Freud, 1923, *SE*, XIX: 26). Freud leads up to this statement with:

> A person's own body, and above all its surface, is a place from which both external and internal perceptions may spring. It is seen like any other object, but to touch it yields kinds of sensations one of which may be equivalent to an internal perception.
>
> (Freud, 1923, *SE*, XIX: 25)

The amenorrheic can use her body in two ways. Her female outer bodily form, whose zones are sensitive to touch and yield sensations, allows that she makes herself available to her own libidinal strivings and the libidinal searching of another. At the same time, her inner bodily form that is non-menstruation and non-procreative yields not to the touch of another's external seed and contains some of her "internal precepts" that she wishes not to externalise onto the outer contours of her body.

Drawing on the work of Freud, Melanie Klein correlated the body to the instinct, with the instinct essentially being a biological entity. As psychoanalyst Thomas Ogden explains in his 1984 paper "Instinct, Phantasy, and Psychological Deep Structure – A Reinterpretation of Aspects of the Work of Melanie Klein":

> From the perspective of the concept of inherited codes, or templates, by which actual experience is organised, the Kleinian concept of inborn "knowledge ... inherent in bodily impulses" (Isaacs, 1952: 94) can be understood not as inherited thoughts, but as a biological code that is an integral part of the instinct.
>
> (Ogden, 1984: 501)

For me, these definitions are containers and boundaries akin to the mast that Odysseus ties himself to whilst looking at and listening to the Sirens. In Book 12 of Homer's *Odyssey*, the Sirens and their songs are so enchanting that they can drive a man mad, causing him to jump perilously into the sea. To avoid this, Odysseus ties himself to the mast of his ship thus allowing him to experience their beauty whilst at the same time narrowly avoiding both a physical and psychic death. For Pygmalion, this concrete and symbolic holding in the face of internal and external positions untamed, comes in the form of the hard, white, ivory substance. It allows him to work on

> the project of the body and knowing through the body, essentially by way of erotic experience, since eroticism makes the body most fully sentient and also most "intellectual," the most aware of what it is doing and what is being done to it.
>
> (Brooks, 1993: 278)

The pendulum of activity carried out by Pygmalion is narrow. We are constantly moving within a short range between asceticism and self-gratification and as we travel along the body of work, we find ourselves stone-stepping between what is real and what is illusionary, what is present and what is absent, what is tragic and what is comic. One is constantly oscillating between them. We have here an allegory for the sexual configurations of early infantile, adolescent and adult life, and we have a template of entanglement that often dominates the clinical work between the analyst and the analysand of those who present with SA. It remains imperative for the analyst to distinguish between his/her needs and wants and those of the patient.

We shall now look at the Ovid text in sections. A.D. Melville's translation (1986) I have used at the front of the chapter; a translation rightly applauded for its quality. Here though I will be using an older translation by Brookes More (1859–1942). Written in 1922, this version, spun in patriarchy, is useful in that it shows how words and experiences give themselves over to one another. Bear in mind too that Shaw's *Pygmalion* was published in 1916, Shaw being a rebel against traditional views of the time.

The promiscuity of the Propoetides and the paranoid schizoid position

> *Pygmalion saw these women waste their lives in wretched shame, and critical of faults which nature had so deeply planted through their female hearts, he lived in preference, for many years unmarried.* [243; NB: verse numbers are approximate]

These, the first line of the Pygmalion verse, refer to the Propoetides, the daughters of Propetus, with whose narrative Ovid ends the previous verse. We could say that what we have here, carried over, is unfinished business with women and with Pygmalion's attitude towards them. In finding their actions abhorrent, he retreats into celibacy and misogyny. But things are not that straightforward. The Propoetides are prostitutes because the goddess Venus forced them into it. They had once denied her divinity and Venus, enraged, declared them impious and subsequently punished them with a life of impiety. If a life of prostitution was the punishment and not the crime, what then was the crime? Non-conformity? Celibacy even?! The final outcome of their transgression is that they are turned to stone and thus rendered impotent. I would interpret this as Pygmalion's aversion to his own state of impotence, unconsciously and unapologetically projected far from him and onto the whole of the female sex. The Propoetides have become both physically and mentally deadened from what has become an intolerable state of being; one full of helplessness, anxiety, shame and mourning; "and so blushing shame was lost, white blood, in their bad faces grew so fast, so hard, it was no wonder they were turned with small change into hard and lifeless stones" [238]: they have died. As readers are we being asked to turn a blind eye to all of this? After all, their story trails at the end of the previous verse and can be easily overlooked. What is it we are not supposed to see? We could interpret this as Pygmalion in the paranoid schizoid position; a position in which man, as psychoanalyst Ronald Britton describes, "has buried his unacknowledged thoughts in others, in his actions or in his perceptions, and though they are symbolic in form they are treated as things" (Britton, 1998: 35). In describing the treatment of such patients in his book *Belief and Imagination: Explorations in Psychoanalysis* (1998), Britton goes on to refer to psychoanalyst Betty Joseph:

> As Betty Joseph pointed out in her paper on "Different Types of Anxiety and Their Handling in the Analytic Situation", analysis in such cases is likely to be a scene of action rather than thought (Joseph, 1989). It is then the analyst's task to reclaim for thought what may otherwise be dispersed in action and reaction.
>
> (Britton, 1998: 35)

In Pygmalion's case, the disgust that he shows the Propoetides perhaps disguises self-disgust which is in conflict with an unruly and insatiable id from within. Perhaps his idea of a perfect wife is one who is a whore in the bedroom, thus legalising prostitution through the order of marriage. Pygmalion goes about creating a statue of his perfect woman. Clearly, there is a split between what is hated and what is idealised. The Propoetides are bad as are the bad parts in Pygmalion's psyche that register the experience as bad and which must be got rid of in the face of "a dread of imminent annihilation" (Bion, 1967 [1984]: 37). Frustration and anxiety are intolerable concepts and reality is to hate which "as Freud pointed out, is extended to all aspects of the psyche that make for awareness of it" (Bion, 1967 [1984]: 37).

The further Pygmalion moves away from the Propoetides and the closer he moves towards his perfect statue, the more he seems to lose the capacity to live in the real world. Pygmalion exemplifies a man unable to think. He has been unable to, as Bion describes it, start with a "preconception" which is not an idea but a potential for an idea of something dangerous and fuse it with the actual "realisation" of what is experienced as dangerous. It is from this that a conception or thought will come about (O'Shaughnessy, 1992: 89–91). Bypassing this, we have Pygmalion with his immaculately conceived statue: she who has no name. By way of summary we can cite Jung:

> The effect of projection is to isolate the subject from his environment, since instead of a real relation to it there is now only an illusionary one. Projections change the world into the replica of one's own unknown face. In the last analysis, therefore, they lead to an autoerotic, autistic condition in which one dreams a world whose reality remains forever unattainable. The resultant sentiment d'incomplétude and the still worse feeling of sterility are in the return explained by projection as the malevolence of the environment, and by means of this vicious circle the isolation is intensified.
>
> (Jung, 1951, *CW* 9ii: para. 17)

The castrating sense of the Propoetides makes me wonder about the impotent penis and perhaps this is what is at the root of Pygmalion's celibacy. Did the eroticism of the Propoetides prove just too overwhelming for him, forcing his hands into that of an artistic (masturbatory?) project? Masturbation can be viewed as an ersatz and a replacement for intercourse. However, the act of masturbation often comes with persecutory thoughts and feelings. Perhaps Pygmalion was inhibited by the prohibition, fantasy and guilt associate with masturbation and he found relief in his artistry. The ivory white substance he used for his statue might have made up for the insufficient discharge. He might be lacking in actual semen but with the artist's materials he still creates life itself, one of an immaculate conception. And he does so without the need or use of a woman or a womb.

There are dynamic links between the systems that Pygmalion implements and the state of amenorrhea and anorexia that circumvent the subject away from procreation, into a state of self-containment and singularity. Pygmalion found creative, imaginative ways via his statue to circumvent both external tension and internal psycho-sexual conflict. Amenorrhea, as a different sort of artistic expression, does the same.

Subject and object in the artistry of Pygmalion

> But while he was single, with consummate skill, he carved a statue out of snow-white ivory, and gave to it exquisite beauty, which no woman of the world had ever equalled: she was so beautiful, he fell in love with his creation. It appeared in truth a perfect virgin with the grace of life, but in the expression of such modesty all motion was restrained – and so his art concealed his art. Pygmalion gazed, inflamed with love and admiration for the form, in semblance of a woman, he had carved. He lifts up both his hands to feel the work, and wonders if it can be ivory, because it seems to him more truly flesh – his mind refusing to conceive of it as ivory [380].

Pygmalion's statue is a masterpiece of both technical and visual virtues, which we might expect from a man who came from a sculpting dynasty that, according to Homer, made Agamemnon's shield. His statue is that of "Womanufacture" (Sharrock, 1991), representing an art-object moulded by the ideas and reflections of women as perceived by a man. But this is not just about Pygmalion's love for his art-object, that which is the product of his own imaginations; he is smitten "with his own creative and erotic process. Such are the erotics of the art-text. As 'reader' of his own art-text, Pygmalion is seduced by it and enticed to penetrate its meaning" (Elsner & Sharrock, 1991: 169).

I would agree with this and suggest that we have the continuation of a masturbatory process of part-object rather than whole-object relating. The statue mesmerises Pygmalion. We too as reader can become mesmerised by

Ovid's text and by Pygmalion's handling of his statue. Even Goethe, who said that only a "brute" would take sexual interest in a material object, went to church one day and got an erection whilst looking at a nude body of Christ gazing down towards one of his saints (Hersey, 2009: 6). The pose of kneeling towards the onlooker was copied many times.

Freud only once refers to Pygmalion in all of his writings: "We should hardly call it uncanny when Pygmalion's beautiful statue comes to life" (Freud, 1919, *SE*, XVII: 246). This quote is from Freud's paper "The Uncanny". Borrowing from Ernst Jentsch's 1906 paper "On the Psychology of the Uncanny", Freud wondered about the power of wax figures, dolls and automata. Of dolls that appear alive, Freud writes: "Jentsch believes that a particular favourable condition for awakening uncanny sensations is created when there is intellectual uncertainty whether an object is alive or not, and when an inanimate object becomes too much like an animate one" (Freud, 1919, *SE*, XVII: 233). He remarks that for many children, "the idea of a 'living' doll excites no fear at all; the child had no fear of its doll coming to life, it may even have desired it" (Freud, 1919, *SE*, XVII: 233).

Feminist writers have been critical of the way in which Freud swiftly moved from an incomplete exploration of the female "doll" on to analysing male characters from Hoffman's story "The Sandman", thus replacing the female, the female body and even the maternal body, in favour of a more masculine symbol. Hélène Cixous accuses Freud of discarding the doll: "The doll is however, relegated to some more profound place than that of a note [footnote], a typographical metaphor of repression which is always too near but nevertheless negligible" (Cixous, 1976: 537).

"The Sandman" was first published in an 1817 collection of stories called *Nachstücke* (Night Pieces). It tells the story of a university student called Nathanael who becomes infatuated with a beautiful, young woman called Olympia. He does not realise, or consciously cannot acknowledge, that she is in fact a wooden doll. She moves and she talks but whereas other people notice that she is "strangely stiff and lacking in animation" he does not. His friends describe her as "cold and prosaic" but Nathanael refuses to accept this, preferring the blank screen that she offers him with her lifeless eyes, onto which he can project his own self. She is his ideal woman, "a perfect listener" unlike his fiancée Clara whose intellect and opinion results in him calling her a "lifeless automaton". When Nathanael eventually "sees" the truth about Olympia, he goes mad. Freud's analysis of this story all but ignores this central plotline in favour of focusing on Nathanael's relationship with a man called Coppelius. Coppelius, whom Nathanael identifies with the monstrous Sandman, was thought to have been a cruel figure from Nathanael's childhood, complicit in the death of the young boy's father. Freud, interpreting the interplay between these men uses the story to symbolise male castration fears. Interestingly, Freud overlooks Clara as a figure who has the potential to castrate with her superior intellect and discriminating mind. I am reminded here of Freud's psychoanalytic work with one of his early hysterical female patients Dora. His "Dora", for that is the name he gave to his leading lady in "Fragments of An Analysis of a Case of Hysteria" (Freud, 1901 [1905]), lay on the coach and presented her narrative and her own thoughts and ideas about her situation. It appears that they were nullified or at best reconfigured to fit in and to accommodate Freud's own hypothesis about her situation. He designed a new reality for Dora, penetrating her with his interpretations. He wrote:

> I can only repeat over and over again – for I never find it otherwise – that sexuality is the key to the problem of the psychoneuroses and of the neuroses in general. No one who disdains the key will ever be able to unlock the door.
>
> (Freud, 1901 [1905]: 15)

Jane Gallop asks in her own analysis of Dora's Case:

> Is this not the worst sort of vulgar, predictable "Freudian" interpretation? The predictability of Freud's line about keys offends Dora by denying the specificity of her signifiers (by not attending to her but by merely applying general formulas) ... What woman wants to be opened by a skeleton key?
>
> (Gallop cited in Bernheimer & Kahane, 1990: 206)

Poignantly, Dora eventually walked out on Freud and their analytic relationship abruptly ended. Challenging the prerogatives of his male gaze and voice, this woman killed off the analysis. We might even say she castrated him, the thing he feared most. Freud wrote about Dora and continued to reflect on her case during his lifetime, perhaps by way of sublimatory redemption and retribution and perhaps as a means to feel in control. For, as Madelon Sprengnether writes:

> Freud's attempt to enforce an oedipal interpretation on Dora's desire coupled with his repeated attempts to achieve narrative closure point finally to a fear associated with that of castration, although not identified with it: that of not being in control ... Finally, however, he does not even have the power of a Pygmalion to make a woman who will love him. She is more like Spenser's False Florimell, a seductive but empty image, composed literally of dead metaphors.
>
> (Sprengnether cited in Bernheimer & Kahane, 1990: 270–271)

Pygmalion with his inanimate statue need not concern himself with the issues that come with relating to women like Clara or Dora (or even to men like Freud!). He has found a solution to avoid issues of separateness, individualisation and autonomy. He is in control, more so than Nathanael from "The Sandman" whose doll moves and speaks. Pygmalion has total power over the desired object and all of his omnipotent wishes can be fulfilled. We can contrast this with Winnicott's model of the transitional object, where the subject assumes rights over his object, let's say a doll, but at the same time, this doll will often represent an "Other", in that "it must seem to the infant to give warmth, or to move, or to have texture, or to do something that seems to show it has vitality or reality of its own" (Winnicott, 1971: 4).

Playing with the transitional object provides the infant with a paradoxical experience in that the infant can believe he magically creates this object and at the same time he can discover the object, thus acknowledging its separate existence. In the realm between the "me" and the "not me", the infant negotiates between the concept of having and losing and reclaiming what is both part of the self and separate from the self. When the child fixates on the object as a pacifier or when, translated into adulthood, the object becomes one that satisfies fetish tendencies, we have a way of relating that is exemplified by Pygmalion's caressing and adorning of his statue:

> he kisses it and feels his kisses are returned. And speaking love, caresses it with loving hands that seem to make an impress, on the parts they touch, so real that he fears he then may bruise her by his eager pressing. Softest tones are used each time he speaks to her. He brings to her such presents as are surely prized by sweet girls; such as smooth round pebbles, shells, and birds, and fragrant flowers of thousand tints, lillies, and painted balls, and amber tears of Helliads, which distill from far off trees – he drapes her in rich clothing and in gems: rings on her fingers, a rich necklace round her neck, pearl pendants on her graceful ears; and golden ornaments adorn her breast. All these are beautiful – and she appears most lovable, if carefully attired – or perfect as a statue, unadorned. He lays her on a bed luxurious, spread with coverlets of Tyrian purple dye, and naming her the consort of his couch, lays her reclining head on the most soft and downy pillows, trusting she could feel. [250]

The eroticisation of the prose mirrors the eroticisation of the libidinal impulses. The non-verbal cues, the sensory processing and the rituals can be decoded within the framework of all that has sexual meaning, as they can be for early infantile experiences. But it appears as if there has been a break or a fixation in Pygmalion's development resulting in fetish tendencies. Fetishistic scopophilia "builds up the physical beauty of the object, transforming it into something satisfying in itself" (Mulvey, 1975: 14). Laura Mulvey, writer of feminist film theory, explains in her paper "Visual Pleasure and Narrative Cinema" (1975) that, in psychoanalytic terms, the female figure with her lack of penis implies a castration threat. Fetish tendencies provide the male's unconscious relief or even "complete disavowal of castration by the substitution of a fetish object or turning the represented figure itself into a fetish so that it becomes reassuring rather than dangerous (hence over-valuation, the cult of the female star)" (Mulvey, 1975: 21).

We can also interpret Pygmalion decoration of his statue with excess visible adornments as a way not only to alleviate castration anxiety but also to compensate, replace, or eradicate an imaginary lack, embodied in the statue's female form. In *The Trauma of Birth* (Rank, 1924 [1952], early psychoanalytic pioneer Otto Rank had explained the mechanism

> of which Freud long ago described as a partial repression with compensatory substitute formations: the Repression quite regularly concerns the mother's genitals in the meaning of the traumatic anxiety-cathexis, and the genitals are replaced by a pleasure-invested part of the body or its aesthetically still more acceptable covering – dresses, shoes, corsets, etc.
>
> (Rank, 1924 [1952]: 34)

By turning her into a figure of fetishism, the risk of annihilation can be done away with, just as it was with the Propoetides. We are not told if the statue has been crafted with genitalia. Her gesture implies sexual availability and we know that she is beautiful, a concept which has its roots in sexual excitation: "This is related to the fact that we never regard the genitals themselves, which produced the strongest sexual excitation, as really 'beautiful'." Freud added this statement as a footnote in 1915 to his 1905 paper "Three Essays on the Theory of Sexuality". If the inanimate statue has genitals, their artificiality would be non-threatening to Pygmalion. As Freud writes:

> It often happens that neurotic men declare that they feel there is something uncanny about the female genital organs. This unhomely [*unheimlich*] place, however, is the entrance to the former home [*Heim*] of all human beings, to the place where each one of us lived once upon a time and in the beginning. There is a joking saying that 'Love is homesickness' and whenever a man dreams of a place or a country and says to himself, while he is still dreaming: 'this place is familiar to me, I've been here before', we may interpret the place as being his mother's genitals or her body.
>
> (Freud, 1919, *SE*, XVII: 244)

In other words, if Pygmalion's statue has new, ready-made genitals, they are non-threatening in terms of their potential to annihilate man because they are not of where man first originated. We could say that Pygmalion represents the man who objectifies and sexualises women as a way to render their genitalia impotent. We have the artificial concrete, non-changing ivory in contrast to human flesh that changes in between soft and hard, moist and dry. And sometimes these spontaneous changes, notably the erection of the man's penis and the lubrication of the woman's vagina, are beyond our control. In a way, the feminine statue can be turned into a masculine version with these signifiers. Similarly turning away from the menstruating female form and embracing the way of a woman who like a man does not bleed menses, the amenorrheic creates the space to avoid issues of femininity: those seen, experienced and commented on through the eyes of both the female and male gaze. This we can link to the idea that a young girl transforming into a tomboy allows her the chance to escape both the clutches of her mother, father and their combined already conceptualised ideas of what it means to be a woman and/or a man.

Another way of looking at Pygmalion is to suggest that he is sublimating his envy of woman and of her potential as child bearer. Thus, as Kaplan explores in "Is the Gaze Male?" (1983), man's gaze might not be as pleasurable as he would first have us believe. For Freud, man endeavours to find the penis in the woman because he fears his own castration. For Karen Horney, this is because he wishes to deny the existence of female genitalia, which are threatening and so, if we apply this "logic" to the story, Pygmalion's idealised beautiful creation conceals a "dread that through her he might die and be undone" (Horney, 1932: 134).

Interestingly, the reader of the Pygmalion verse is not given any details about the statue's face, her figure, hair, the shape of her breasts, her height, etc. As we are not supplied with conscious images drawn through the male gaze of Ovid, we can fill her body out with our own unconscious projections just as Pygmalion (and Nathanael) do. We shall see in the section on Shaw's play *Pygmalion* how we as the reader have the chance to imagine what Eliza Doolittle looks like when she views herself in a full-length mirror for the first time. As readers, we can negotiate some space for ourselves in terms of putting authorship to one side and imagining what we each suppose she looks like and in what way we might imagine relating to her. This process of "visualisation" (phantasia) by which images are transformed by the mind's eye was very popular in the philosophy and literature of antiquity. Ovid's talent for this was greatly admired by his peers. As Quintilian writes,

> By them, images of things absent are represented to the mind so that we seem to see them with our own eyes and have them with our presence. Whoever has the mastery of them will have a powerful effect on the emotions.
> (Quintilian, Inst. Or. 6.2.29 in Butler, 1921: 433–435)[1]

And what then of the female gaze? In mythology the forecast is not good, as best exemplified by the fate of Medusa. According to Ovid, she was ravishingly beautiful. Raped by Poseidon in the temple of Athena, the goddess punished her and made her repellent. The snakes in her hair represented castration and her gaze acquired the power and the power of female genitalia. Freud's interesting account of the decapitated head of Medusa is as follows:

> To decapitate = to castrate. The terror of Medusa is thus a terror of castration that is linked to the sight of something. Numerous analyses have made us familiar with the occasion for this: It occurs when a boy, who has hitherto been unwilling to believe the threat of castration, catches sight of the female genitals, probably those of an adult, surrounded by hair, and essentially those of his mother. The hair upon Medusa's head is frequently represented in

works of art in the form of snakes, and these once again are derived from the castration complex. It is a remarkable fact that, however frightening they may be in themselves, they nevertheless serve actually as a mitigation of the horror, for they replace the penis, the absence of which is the cause of the horror. This is a confirmation of the technical rule according to which a multiplication of penis symbols signifies castration. This sight of Medusa's head makes the spectator stiff with terror, turns him to stone. Observe that we have here once again the same origin from the castration complex and the same transformation of affect! For becoming stiff means an erection. Thus in the original situation it offers consolation to the spectator: he is still in possession of a penis, and the stiffening reassures him of that fact. This symbol of horror is worn upon her dress by the virgin goddess Athena. And rightly so, for thus she becomes a woman who is unapproachable and repels all sexual desire – since she displays the terrifying genitals of the Mother. Since the Greeks were in the main strongly homosexual, it was inevitable that we should find among them a representation of woman as a being who frightens and repels because she is castrated.

(Freud, 1922 [1940], *SE*, XVIII: 273)

Freud goes on to write that for a man to display the erect penis, he is essentially declaring his fearlessness. Let us presume that Pygmalion is impotent, already castrated by internal and external forces – what better way to regain control than by creating an inanimate female figure whose artificial genitals, if she has any at all, cannot threaten him? He can split off the potential for harm from the capacity for pleasure in the same way that Freud describes Medusa's head which "takes the place of a representation of the female genitals, or rather if it isolates their horrifying effects from the pleasure-giving ones" (Freud, 1922, *SE*, XVIII: 273–274).

Pygmalion is having a hard time (or so he wishes!). If we can look more favourably at what Pygmalion does achieve, we can return to one of Freud's more desired and most perfect vicissitudes of the sexual drive; the art of sublimation. In the context of the pleasure ego and the reality ego, Freud states in "Formulation of the Two Principles of Mental Functioning":

Art brings about a reconciliation between the two principles in a peculiar way. An artist is originally a man who turns away from reality because he cannot come to terms with the renunciation of instinctual satisfaction which it at first demands, and who allows his erotic and ambitious wishes full play in the life of phantasy ... Thus in a certain fashion he actually becomes the author, the king, the creator, or the favourite he desired to be, without following the long roundabout path of making real alterations in the external world.

(Freud, 1911: 41–42)

Many find it difficult to stay with Pygmalion's commitment with his statue. This is why sometimes it's described as comical. With the Pygmalion text, it

feels as if the art of sublimation is unable to adequately contain the unconscious emotions repressed within. I think respite is indicated in the use of the
lilies that we normally associate with death and commemoration. We know
though that they soon will wither and die. What's to be done? Well, if this
was a tale of our time, we would anticipate the intervention of the all-
knowing psychiatrist/psychoanalyst. Cue the entrance and intervention of
Venus into Ovid's story.

In third space

> The festal day of Venus, known throughout Cyprus, now had come, and
> throngs were there to celebrate. Heifers with spreading horns, all gold-
> tipped, fell when given the stroke of death upon their snow-white necks;
> and frankincense was smoking on the altars. There, intent, Pygmalion
> stood before an altar, when his offering had been made; and although he
> feared the result, he prayed: "If it is true, O Gods, that you can give all
> things, I pray to have as my wife" – but, he did not dare to add "my
> ivory statue-maid," and said "One like my ivory —. Golden Venus
> heard, for she was present at her festival, and she knew clearly what the
> prayer had meant. She gave a sign that her Divinity favored his plea:
> three times the flame leaped high and brightly in the air. [270]

The fact that Pygmalion is asking for a living girl shows that he is at least attempting to engage with the external world and its associated realities. Perhaps through
lack of experience and insight he has not fully anticipated and thought through all
that this might involve. In granting his wish, Venus is forcing Pygmalion to abandon his concrete ideal in favour of a real woman with whom he must learn a new
way of relating. What is important here is the fact that Venus does listen to the
prayers of Pygmalion but she grants them with a twist. He asks for a woman *like*
his statue and Venus brings the actual statue to life. We are told that he did not
dare ask such a specific request and most scholars interpret this as him showing
respect and timidity in the face of the gods. Pygmalion would not have dared
incur their wrath. I propose something altogether different, in that unconsciously
he did not dare himself to ask that it be turned into a real woman for that would
result in a complete overhaul of his comfortable, uninterrupted narcissistic set-up.
As a statue, she can be used as a mirror image or a double through which he can
gain an "I" whilst at the same time retaining his own self-being. He can circumvent any castration anxieties and he can use her as a representation of immortality,
which will protect him against any thoughts about the realities of death and indeed
death itself. But as Freud warns us in reference to Otto Rank's 1914 work:

> The "double" was originally an insurance against the destruction to the ego,
> an "energetic denial of the power of death" as Rank says; and probably the
> "immortal" soul was the first "double" of the body … Such ideas … have
> sprung from the solid of unbounded self-love, from the primary narcissism

which holds sway in the mind of the child as in that of primitive man; and when this stage has been left behind the double takes on a different aspect. From having been an assurance of immortality, he becomes the ghastly harbinger of death.

(Freud, 1919, *SE*, XVII: 235)

Just as the statue's coming to life will jolt Pygmalion out of a state of primary narcissism, with a real mortal woman in front of him, he will now have to rewrite a more complicated, reality-orientated destiny for himself and for the two of them. It will include his witnessing of her ageing process, and of his own. Plus, this Other person will be seeking out her own mirror image and in doing so will never be completely available to him. And so what Pygmalion might be faced with now is a relationship between viewer and scene which "is no longer a relationship of plenitude but one of fracture, partial identification, pleasure and distrust" (Rose, 1986 [2005]: 227).

I think what Pygmalion had in mind was to have a real woman to marry, who would share in his day-to-day ordinary life whilst at the same time keeping his inanimate statue hidden behind closed doors. Hidden from view, he could continue to engage with it in a way that a real woman might take offence. Or she might not – and that is precisely the point I want to make. Up till now, Pygmalion has viewed her and related to her in a specific, ritualistic way that suits and works for him. What if it doesn't suit or work for her? What if she has needs of her own, different to his, and she desires to be gratified in different ways? To what extent will they influence each other's choices? Thus they are propelled into the stuff of relationships, the matter and composition of which is in constant flux and flow, unlike the hard ivory substance. (We can refer analogously to the waxing and waning of the physiology of the menstrual cycle as opposed to the amenorrheic phenomena that is constant, consistent and still.)

Once Venus brings the statue to life, presumably it has no traces of memory but Pygmalion does. Should he continue to have ownership and authorship of her? Will he continue to use her as a canvas for his projections? I believe that Venus will have granted this "living girl" a psychology of her own with the necessary cognitive tools required to live as a human. If she chooses to remain solely as a machine for sexual activity, then let's hope it's her choice. She might develop a creative mind of her own in which case she might ironically become for Pygmalion what Clara was for Nathanael in "The Sandman", a "lifeless automaton".

We don't have the answers, which allows for our minds to wander. We must though have sympathy and empathy for Pygmalion who has to restart from the position that requires a new way of thinking and relating. Similarly, the analyst must have compassion and remain attuned to the route that his patient takes, especially the patient who presents with SA. Her coming-to-life via a return of her bodily menses comes not only with the threat of the analysis breaking down but also with the threat of her own psychological breakdown (and who knows, perhaps the analyst's too).

I would like to end this section with a note on symbolisation. Many see Venus as the "third" without whom there would be no advancement. But perhaps the third space has and will always belong to Pygmalion's own artistry and what Venus represents is the potential for growth from creative doing to creative thinking through the process of symbolisation. I want to quote one of Winnicott's skilfully observed and documented patient encounters, to highlight the coalition of the illusionary and the real in bodily terms and to suggest the level of difficulty I suspect Pygmalion might have with his newly animated companion. Winnicott writes:

> it seems that symbolisation can only be properly studied in the process of the growth of an individual, and that it has at the very best a variable meaning. For instance, if we consider the wafer of the Blessed Sacrament, which is symbolic of the body of Christ, I think I am right in saying that for the Roman Catholic community it is the body and for the Protestant community it is a substitute, a reminder, and is essentially not, in fact, actually the body itself. Yet in both cases it is a symbol. A schizoid patient asked me, after Christmas, had I enjoyed eating her at the feast. And then, had I really eaten her or only in fantasy. I knew that she could not be satisfied with either alternative. Her split needed the double answer.
>
> (Winnicott, 1975 [1992]: 234)

We can conclude here that Pygmalion had wanted both his concrete, idealised statue along with a real woman. He had wished for "the double answer" but Venus sees fit to accommodate him differently. As an addendum, might I suggest that Venus be used as a representation and a reminder to clinicians of how important it is that we have our own third other; by this, I mean to have the presence and use of our own analyst and/or supervisor. When analyst and patient are in danger of merging, when during the mirror phase it is difficult to extrapolate for whom the double is serving, self-analysis just won't do!

True love's something or other – self-efficacy and the unknown

> When he returned, he went directly to his image-maid, bent over her, and kissed her many times, while she was on her couch; and as he kissed, she seemed to gather some warmth from his lips. Again he kissed her; and he felt her breast; the ivory seemed to soften at the touch, and its firm texture yielded to his hand, as honey-wax of Mount Hymettus turns to many shapes when handled in the sun, and surely softens from each gentle touch. He is amazed; but stands rejoicing in his doubt; while fearful there is some mistake, again and yet again, gives trial to his hopes by touching with his hand. It must be flesh! The veins pulsate beneath the careful test of his directed finger. Then, indeed, the astonished hero poured out lavish thanks to Venus; pressing with his raptured lips his statue's lips. [270]

We have here the shift from a fused state to the beginnings of a relationship ushering in a lost state of wholeness. We might see Pygmalion as representing the mother who must re-surface from a fantasised emotional fusion which Helene Deutsch called the "psychic umbilical cord" (Deutsch, 1945: 278). Through this cord, the mother can simultaneously regress in fantasy to the early conditions in life where she was lovingly identified with her own mother. However, as far as Pygmalion is concerned, it seems that a rupture is on the horizon as he displays a "heightened sensitivity" (Winnicott, 1956 [1958]: 302) and a schizoid rambling in response to the emerging other. Both Freud and Lacan wrote that a search for a reunion is symbolised in substitution and displacement. At birth, we are cast out and we endlessly search to recover this lost state of wholeness. The repetition of themes in Ovid's *Metamorphosis* symbolises the repetition of the displaced desire. As Virgil wrote:

> For the hope is that the first can be put out by the same body that is the source of the burning. Nature protests that entirely the opposite is the case: this is the one thing, the more of which we have the more our breasts burn with terrible desire.
>
> (Virgil, *Aen.*, 1086–1090)

The statue embodies Pygmalion's desire but something transformative happens when she changes from inanimate to animate:

> Now real, true to life – the maiden felt the kisses given to her, and blushing, lifted up her timid eyes, so that she saw the light and sky above, as well as her rapt lover while he leaned gazing beside her. [270]

She sees the world around him. In that moment, I see the first stages of separateness and autonomy as she looks beyond him to the skies, the unknown. Their eyes meet but one senses the urge in her, indicated by the libidinally driven blush, to move away from a state of magnetic narcissism and away from the trappings of what might become mutually gratifying perversion. She is much more than this. Yes, she has no voice and yes she appears malleable, but I would argue that she has the potential to be more than a symbol for Pygmalion's lost paradise of an original unity:

> and all this at once – the goddess graced the marriage she had willed, and when nine times the crescent moon had changed, increasing to the full, the statue-bride gave birth to her dear daughter Paphos. From which famed event the island takes its name. [298]

It is interesting how Ovid's tale delivers a conventional ending with a pregnancy of nine months resulting in the successful birth of a child. The moon is often linked to the periodicity of the menstrual cycle. At the same time, we are a million "crescent moon[s]" away from the unconventionality of where this story began. From this point on, we move to motherhood and we cannot deny the patriarchal slant of a romantic and idealised state as portrayed here which has continued down the centuries, "everything in woman hath one solution – it is called pregnancy" (Nietzsche, 1885: ch. 18).

When considering Galatea's new position (she was later given this name), we could take Freud's pessimistic view that a baby is the substitute for a woman's lack of a penis or, as Jung would propose, the child as a mythical symbol is the saviour. But we could also consider a developmental process of change from initial symbiosis linked to narcissism (as portrayed in the fetish stage) to a new arena that includes a reality dose of individuation, separateness, mortality and loss. It is she that symbolises the capacity for change through a capacity for reverie. This is all speculation of course but how interesting that in these last lines of the verse Pygmalion is not mentioned. He has been frozen out and it is he who is now immobile. In his absence, she becomes present. What will he do in the face of a stark new reality? How will he feel as he watches her age? How will they both negotiate the introduction of a third, which we can call female sexuality? What will happen once her childbearing days are over? Will her fate be that as described by psychoanalytic theorist Helene Deutsch when analysing the way in which society views its women?

> At the moment when expulsion of ova from the ovary ceases, all organic processes devoted to the service of the species stop. Woman has ended her existence as bearer of a new future, and has reached her natural end – her partial death – as servant of the species. She is now engaged in an active struggle against her decline ... Woman's biological fate manifests itself in the disappearance of her individual feminine qualities at the same time that her service to the species ceases. As we have said, everything she acquired during puberty is now lost piece by piece.
>
> (Deutsch, 1945: 460–461)

We might consider here how a woman with SA is above and beyond all of this emotional upheaval. With her clean lines, she is more aligned with the immortal Venus than with ordinary womenfolk and menstrual matters. She will not necessarily be tortured by the sense of loss associated with each menstrual cycle and ultimately the menopause. She need not suffer the same fate of her menstruating counterpart who "with the lapse of the reproductive service, her beauty vanishes, and usually the warm, vital flow of her feminine emotional life as well" (Deutsch, 1945: 461). Perhaps Pygmalion will welcome a menopausal wife so that she might serve him solely once again as a servant to him rather than "as a servant of the species".

Galatea's immediate pregnancy recapitulates an immaculate conception and postpones the development of more developed interrelations between woman and man. Their dynastic line continues impressively but there are no happy endings for what began with a union between creator and creation. What follows is Ovid's tale of a girl called Myrrha, who is the great-granddaughter of Galatea and Pygmalion. It is a tragic and evocative tale of incest.

Incest and exile – the story of Myrrha

Unlike Pygmalion who asked for something similar to his statue to be bought to life, Myrrha, the "dutiful" daughter, is deeply in love with her father and only he will do as the love object. Her father is the Great Cinyras who is the grandson of Pygmalion and Galatea. Myrrha is obsessed with the fantasy of having sexual relations with him. Absolutely no one else comes close. Her wishes are accompanied by a psychological conflict that torments her. She laments:

> All animals will mate as they desire – a heifer may endure her sire, and who condemns it? And the happy stud is not refused by his mare-daughters; the he-goat consorts unthought-of with the flock of which he is the father, and the birds conceive of those from whom they were themselves begot. Happy are they who have such privilege! Malignant men have given spiteful laws; and what is right to Nature is decreed unnatural, by jealous laws of men. [319]

These questions precede Freud's in his work *Civilisation and its Discontents*, in which he writes:

> The tendency on the part of civilisation to restrict sexual life is no less clear than its other tendency to expand the cultural unit. Its first, totemic phase already brings with it the prohibition against an incestuous choice of object, and this is perhaps the most drastic mutilation which man's erotic life had in all time experienced. Taboos, laws and customs impose further restrictions, which affect both men and women.
>
> (Freud, 1930, *SE*, XXI: 51)

Myrrha also makes available the thinking behind Freud's Oedipal theory. She asks of herself if she will become her father's concubine, her mother's rival? All she can do is vehemently call herself wicked as she endlessly revisits, in her mind, this most tragic of loops: "because he is mine he is never mine; because near to me he is far from me" [319]. The only way she envisages escaping from this trap, caught between desire and taboo, is through death. It is her nurse who snatches the noose away from Myrrha's neck thus preventing the young girl's suicide. The nurse, like Venus in the Pygmalion verse, can be seen as symbolising the triangulation. She comforts her mistress and arranges that Myrrha and Cinyras lie together in the dark so that Myrrha's identity remains hidden from him. She leaves the pair doomed in their crime – the father to pollute his own flesh in his own bed; where he tries first to encourage her from maiden fears, by gently talking to the timid girl. He chanced to call her "daughter" as a name best suited to her age; and she in turn, endearing, called him "father," so no names might be omitted to complete their guilt. [446]

As reader, one's own moral preconceptions become discombobulated. Interestingly A.D. Melville's translation (1986) translates it as "fate sealed the crime", which softens the blow (the guilt), but either way it's troubling. Myrrha's inability to accept social constraints case as law through the incest taboo, and the way in which she and her father related to one another, reflecting her fantasy wishes, is poignant. In her father lying with her, he facilitates an exit out of a torturous loop that until this point was infinite and unrelenting. Did he truly not know who she was? The same question can be asked of Lot when his daughters got him drunk and seduced him so that they could bear his children and continue the ancestral line (Genesis 19). Many rabbinical scholars say that on one level Lot knew. In Myrrha's case, we have a young girl who can conceptualise her wishes and ideas but for them to be realised, a third agent is required. The nurse partners the two of them together and then it is the father who brings her wishes to fruition. It is he who is the key development third, who moves on the plot line.

We have the "real" father and we have the father as lover and incest object. When he discovers who she is, he comes after her with his sword. A sword used against the skin brings forth blood. Here we can consider the menstrual taboo alongside the incest taboo. In psychoanalyst C.D. Daly's paper "The Role of Menstruation in Human Phylogenesis and Ontogenesis" (1943), Daly writes about man's ambivalence towards a menstruating woman. On the one hand, man is repulsed by what he sees and yet at the same time he lusts after it. For Daly, this goes back to the time when the infant witnesses his mother's menstruation, which causes him great anxiety; – an anxiety that precedes the castration anxiety associated with father later on. Daly cites Freud's work "Taboo and Virginity" (1918) to show how Freud linked sadistic menstrual taboos with man's fear of blood, but for Daly, Freud does not go anywhere near far enough in acknowledging the power of the symbol of the menstruating woman. For Daly, the blood that flows from the *vagina dentata* means that the mother is an active force in shaping the human psyche. If we apply this to King Cinyras, we have a man who wants to master his ambivalence. On the one hand, repulsed by their incestuous act he wants to strike Myrrha with his sword, but I would suggest that unconsciously he also wants to penetrate her a second time round with the erect phallic object. In fear of her life, Myrrha flees into exile. It's as if it's too much for her to witness her father's transformation from a familiar loved one into a foreign being and the place of exile represents a middle space and a sanctuary. Where now and who now is her father?

We can view Cinyras in a dual role as being similar to that of the hunts-man/father that we read about in so many folk and fairy tales such as "Snow White" and "Sleeping Beauty" (Bettelheim, 1976). In both these tales, it is true love's kiss that breaks the spell and allows for the child's interrupted development to restart. In "Beauty and the Beast", we have Belle's father as the cause of her exile to the Beast. Belle indeed thrives in his new kingdom where her curiosity can be satisfied. In "The Handless Maiden", the first part of the story tells of a miller who is tricked into giving his daughter to the devil: fearing that the devil will take him instead, the miller complies with the devil's request. The devil is unable to become the girl's master and she wanders into a new kingdom. British Jungian Coline Covington analyses:

> the concept of hero and heroine – and their different struggles – cannot be applied exclusively and respectively to men and women. Men can be under the influence of the heroine just as the women can follow the path of the hero. The anatomical difference between hero and heroine does not indicate a basic difference in the psychology of men and women; it is simply a metaphor of otherness.
>
> (Covington, 1989: 252)

The essential question for all of us is what does the child/patient feel when her wishes are fulfilled; when the symbolic has a life of its own? In view of a psychic breakdown following the fulfilment of her wishes, Myrrha asks the gods "but now because my life offends the living, and dying I offend the dead, drive me from both conditions; change me, and refuse my flesh both life and death!" [469].Again we have the idea that salvation is provided in the middle space. Following her wandering in exile, the gods turn Myrrha into a tree and in mute pain she gives birth to a baby boy, of her father's seed. It is she who is burdened by the guilt. But whose guilt is it? If we use Freud's early investigations into hysteria, where there is a low threshold between the conscious and unconscious worlds, we can question the location of uncon-scious motivation. Freud states in his letter to Wilhelm Fliess that "hysteria is not repudiated sexuality but rather perversion" (Freud, 1896 in Neu, 1991: 26).

He goes on to write that it is the father who is the seducer and the child/patient does not wholly repudiate the act of incest but has in her mind a pace that yearns for this seducer, "the prehistoric unforgettable other person who is never equalled to anyone later" (Freud, 1896 in Neu, 1991: 27).

This is like Myrrha who cannot contemplate being with anyone other than her father. We shall consider this in more detail in the clinical discussion of the amenorrheic patient and in a review of Freud's treatment of Emma Eck-stein, during which Freud moved from his seduction theory to a language of seduction and wishes and the interplay of reality and fantasy. These of course are emblems of the Pygmalion tale. Just as Freud formulae were in transition stimulated by his clinical work on hysteria, Ovid's work was written and inspired by a transition between pagan antiquity and emerging Christianity. This phase symbolised a psychological interplay between aestheticism and gratification. Ovid wrote *Metamorphosis* whilst in exile (circa 8 AD), mourning a lost love and desiring a return to Rome. It is believed he was exiled because he witnessed either an affair or a crime committed by Caesar. This is a nice analogy for Freud's theoretical move away from an actual committed crime of seduction to a middle ground where perhaps the child witnessed or overheard something she shouldn't have, which brought about later fantasies that offered self-relief in that they acted as sublimations, embellishments and protective structures (Freud, 2 May 1897, in Masson, 1985: 239). We have in Ovid's sequential stories inherited narratives in which "past, present and future are strung together, as it were, on the thread of the wish that runs through them" (Freud, 1908, *SE*, IX: 147–148).

What is lost can be found in what is present. All routes lead back to the idealised love object as exemplified by Pygmalion's creation. But his story is itself a textual wish fulfilment of another artist: Orpheus.

Orpheus and the underworld

Orpheus tells the tale of Pygmalion as a way to conjure up the presence of his dead wife Eurydice. In mourning the loss of his beloved, he is unable to partake in ordinary life, just as Pygmalion does. He abstains from the company of women, choosing to spend his days alone. A group of women, enraged by his scorn towards them, kill him and throw his dismembered body and his lyre into the river. The Muses find him and give him a proper burial. It is said that his soul returned to Hades and he was reunited with Eurydice. But this is not the first time he had met her in Hades. When Eurydice died, Orpheus mourned her loss with such grief that he was allowed into the Underworld. There he played his lyre so beautifully that he enchanted the wardens who then consented to her release. They told Orpheus that when escorting Eurydice out of the Underworld he should not glance back to look at her until they are both out. He does not heed their warning and as he turns back to look at her she is lost to him a second time. Why does he turn round? Is it that he is troubled by the unorthodoxy of rewriting fate? Is his turning back an indication of his humanness and of his mortal uncertainty in contrast to godly omnipotence? Could he not trust that she would follow him? Will mother's gaze be there should the infant chance it and look away? (Stern, 1985). Perhaps what is represented is a shift from a psychotic ego's attempt at a cure through magic to one in which the idea of permanently possessing the love object is recognised as a doomed cure because "reality testing has shown that the love object no longer exists and it proceeds to demand that all libido shall be withdrawn from its attachments to that object" (Freud, 1917, SE. XIV: 244).

It is *"near the margin, near the upper land"* that Orpheus turned round. The margins between the Underworld and the Upper World is perhaps the place where time stands still, freeze frames: the blood does not run through yet the body is still alive, as for the amenorrheic. Psychologically too there is a freeze frame, where the amenorrheic is unable to "go with the flow". Instead, in this realm, we have someone who is neither fully alive nor fully dead: a Myrrha, a Galatea, a Eurydice, an Orpheus, a Pygmalion. To move between these worlds one needs bridges, a healthy dose of narcissism and a third space to think. We shall see in the following clinical examples how important these ingredients are to the anorexic on the cusp of puberty, to the female who neatly avoids border crossing at the intersections of sexuality by becoming pregnant, and to the secondary amenorrheic who denies herself a passport to an onward analytic journey by remaining in a transference neurosis with hysterical tendencies. It is hoped that the Ovidian themes presented in this chapter are discerned and bought to life in the following case studies.

Case study "Mary" – a clinical overview

The transitional point between death and life is a middle space where time stands still and yet life goes on. Myrrha befriended death because she could not wholly trust life. Eurydice inhabited the secure margins in between the Underworld and Upper World. Each resides in between states. I ask that the analyst seriously consider in whose best interest it is to bring the patient across the margins and into the Upper World, a place imbued with developmental markers, variables in a four-dimensional frame. What happens when the analyst finds himself enchanted in her world and questioning his own capacity for separateness? In the analytic encounter, much is entwined and projective identification is a most powerful tool by which the analyst can become enslaved. As analyst, interpreter and reader of her narrative, he can become entangled in between past and future lines of prose. What those wishes are can become enshrined in a transference love or transference neurosis. As Balint describes it, it takes over the analysis and the patient becomes preoccupied with the motives of her analyst and her expectations of him become unrealistic: "To condense this situation into one sentence, one might say that the importance of the past is well-nigh lost for this patient; only the analytic present matters" (Balint, 1968 [1986]: 85). It is no easy task to extrapolate the unconscious wishes of the patient when she asks for both symbiosis and separateness, when she fills the consulting room with both life and death forces and when she keeps the treatment alive by terminating it. Identification, separation and transformation are matters of life and (or) death.

"Mary" – a clinical case of transference neurosis

The analysis of Mary, a patient with prolonged SA is published here for the first time with Mary's consent. Mary's menses returned during her treatment, during most of which she was in the throes of a transference neurosis. Just as Balint and Freud had described in their work on transference neurosis, she focused only on what was going on, or not going on, between her and her analyst. The outside world was split off. She found absence in the presence and presence in the absence. There was hardly any narrative other than a discussion about the two of them. She wasn't interested in third-party displaying pre-oedipal tendencies. She was preoccupied with knowing the degree to which her analyst found their work important. She would persistently ask how often he thought of her when they were not together. She would rebuke her therapist's attempts at interpretations that hinted at envy or greed. For her, it was about creative love and everything was resolutely in the here-and-now. For Mary's male analyst, central to the work was the idea that as her hysterical symptoms in the consulting room abated, the transference neurosis restarted. The backdrop to this was the fact that her menses had returned during her analysis and thus the background of the safety of amenorrhea was no longer available to her. She became increasingly paranoid that something in their union was not quite right. She described herself as the mute Galatea and told her analyst that it was his voice alone that created her therapy and that she felt increasingly and unjustly powerless. She started to suggest that the treatment was making her ill and she recognised the dangerous degree to which she could not break out of the cycle. Her analyst used the image of the see-saw to describe how perilous a state of being this felt for each of them, and for them as an analytic couple. This perhaps intimated his acknowledgement of the risk and dangers involved in the mechanism of psychoanalytic technique. She was angry that he appeared to her more and more like Rapunzel. In his second- floor consulting room, he was stuck in the tower, resistant to change. And what was the point of having magic if he were never going to cross the other side of the transference and take them into the real world? Unable to articulate her thoughts and exasperated by the idea that he was not listening, she wrote them down and gave them to him. She said the piece of paper represented the masturbatory object which he could touch and play with and which he could engage with through reading over and over again. In her own private thoughts, she considered the following:

> I want to talk about the intruder. I want space for my free associations and thoughts. When I don't get it I sense a gap and I alleviate the anxiety by feeding you with the life force. Who is seduced? Who is abandoned? Who is dependent? Who will be castrated? Who will end this therapy? To hear the words "Don't tell anyone, let's keep this between ourselves" is the stuff of madness.
>
> (pers. comm., 2014)

Around the fifth year of therapy, Mary fell down five stairs in her home. Her husband found her at the bottom of the stairs "hysterical". Mary felt that her analyst had invaded and taken over her psychic home, with the work becoming more about his narcissism and self-preservation and less about hers. The fall represented a sudden jolt out of an impasse/stalemate. He was a stale mate. Her analyst suggested that through the reception and the creation of meaning, they might begin the process of finding her voice and outlining the parameters of her space. He was in a double bind as he felt the need to sign-post a route to each of their self-efficacy, but he felt he could not deny separateness for fear that she would fall or jump off the see-saw into the gap. Would he become Orpheus in leading her out of the transference neurosis? Would he fail or would it be that she would choose not to go with him? What would fate have in store for them? It was a failed treatment.

The analyst is like a mother who needs to be able to intuitively sense where the infant is. Just as the balance on the see-saw needs to be securely maintained, the analyst also like the mother can help the patient develop creatively if she feels he is attuned to her. A premature or quick movement will startle her and cause anxiety. For Mary, when she believed that her analyst had chosen to move away from her in his mind, she withdrew and left with an angry rejection of him. She felt that she had become damaged goods because of him, but the damage could not withstand another fresh wound. Until this point, she had left and been called back but each repetition, rather than bringing clarity to the cause, made things worse. What she saw in the mirror was unreliable. The truth was unreliable. With a mirror image that is hypnotic and magnetic in its narcissism, who is Pygmalion and who is Galatea? Who is the subject and object of the transference love? In the face of these questions I have argued that it is essential that the analyst must not rely on self-analysis and he must seek supervision as a way to maintain distance and provide a third space. As Thomas Ogden brilliantly writes:

> Human beings have a need as deep as hunger and thirst to establish intersubjective constructions (including projective identifications) in order to find an exit from unending, futile wanderings in their own internal object world. It is in part of this reason that consultation with colleagues and supervisors – even [our own] analysts post analysis – is so important in our work.
>
> (Ogden, 1999: 105)

Many analyses pervaded by transference neurosis both erotic and eroticised result in failure. The ending of treatment for some patients who present with SA is never truly terminated. Instead, both patient and analyst are left in a state of limbo, a middle space. The air is rife with both human uncertainty and ghostly omnipotence. I am suggesting that both patient and analyst maintain this state of limbo unconsciously by going into their own narcissistic retreat. It might appear that the discontinuation of treatment provides space and time to remember and to mourn but it also enables them to deny its creation, existence and termination. Fixated at this point, they cannot accept the reality of a permanent ending or accept the uncertainties of continuing. What is being acted out is what the body in a state of SA does, which itself provides a mirror image of the patient's psychic organisation in which life and death, the inanimate and the animate can coexist infinitely, compatibly and equally.

Case study "Sylvia" – a clinical overview

To understand the psychological artistry of amenorrhea, one needs to bear in mind that the Immaculate Conception of Jesus to Mary stands alongside the incestuous rawness of Jocasta and Oedipus. Whilst the body envelops and contains, the unconscious mind is afforded a space to roam. One must acknowledge the bodily urges and the tension between the instinct libido and the ego libido. All that is present in the absence at the outset of treatment is steeped in omnipotence, but towards the end the patient comes to realise that it is through her vulnerability that she acquires knowledge and power. After all, the sexual instinct is linked to the instinct for knowledge. The analyst must be brave enough to enter into this no man's land and "the analyst must expend libido on his patient" (Freud to Ferenczi, 23 June 1912, in Haynal, 1994).

What of amenorrheic women who sidestep the acquisition of knowledge gleaned through the process of menstruation and become pregnant during the analysis? As a menstruating woman in analysis, the patient could have explored issues surrounding female sexuality and what it means to be a woman. Becoming pregnant, she can preoccupy herself with the role and demands of motherhood thus avoiding possibly more difficult conversations.

"Sylvia" – a clinical case of immaculate conception

Marie Langer in her book *Motherhood and Sexuality* (Langer, 1951) recounts the case of Sylvia, a patient of Edith Jacobson (Langer, 1951: 164–169). Aged 35, Sylvia came for treatment for depression, which she identified with her infertility. She had been amenorrheic since the age of 16 and along with hormonal disorders, she was physically weak and lacked appetite for food or life. She and her husband had adopted a baby, but unable to adequately care for him, she gave the baby back to the adoption agency. This bought on a severe depression in Sylvia. When she entered psychoanalytic treatment, her analyst asked that she be re-examined medically. The gynaecologist advised against any future hormonal treatment and saw no chance of her conceiving. But from the outset of analysis, her body changed: she put on weight, her breasts developed and in the eighth month of her analysis, she became pregnant without her menses ever returning.

Sylvia was the child of poor Jewish immigrants. Sharing her parent's bedroom, she would witness them having sexual intercourse and she believed that it was her mother eating a part of her father's penis that resulted in pregnancy. Orally fixated, when one of her brothers died young, she repressed her relief that his death meant there was one less mouth to feed. This guilt translated into sadness. In the analysis, it became clear that as a young girl she had envied the penis of her living brother and its associated powers. She decided she would emulate this masculinity and become successful and she planned to go to university. She met and fell in love with a Christian boy, but her perception of her family's judgement of her resulted in her not eating, which also acted as a vehicle to repress and prohibit her passion. She felt she had no choice but to break off her relationship with him and by this point she had stopped menstruating completely. She later married a man who was kind and who looked after her, "but her old desires of having a penis or a profession – in order to win her mother's love – or of being a mother – in order to conquer her mother through an identification with her – remained alive within her" (Langer, 1951: 167).

Jacobson interprets Sylvia's loss of appetite as self-punishment for oral envy and as a repression of the desire to eat something unorthodox. Her thin, shapeless body was that of a young boy, but at the same time she was a woman. She had hated and envied her pregnant mother but when she wanted a child of her own, she was afraid that she would be punished for wishing her mother dead:

> The ingenious solution that she found to this anguishing conflict was her amenorrhea which signified both an escape from her femininity and the realization in phantasy of her wish to become pregnant. Moreover, not to menstruate was to be like a man. Later, during her marriage, more regressive desires emerged and Sylvia renounced her pseudo-virility. She then utilized amenorrhea, lack of appetite, and her entire precarious physical state in order to be able to be a little girl, loved by her husband-mother.
>
> (Langer, 1951: 167–168)

Eight months into her analysis Sylvia became pregnant and she gave birth to a baby girl. She menstruated regularly after that and despite using contraception she soon became pregnant again, which she terminated with curettage. Again she became pregnant and she had another curettage. Jacobson hypothesised that her infertility transforming into hyper-fertility communicated the extent to which her basic conflicts had not been resolved. Eventually, rather than using extreme measures of curettage or sterilisation, her body put itself back into an amenorrheic state. We can also think about the pull and the push, the rejection and the invitation for boundaries and containers. Artificial, man-made boundaries – the laws of paternity, medicine, analysis, voices of reason – are those upon which we rely but they are also impositions and interferences in what should be a natural continuum. After all, "All boundaries are artificial interruptions to what is naturally continuous" (Leach, 1976: 34).

Caught up in the bounce between both, we are neither fully in nor fully out, neither captive nor free: And if we consider what is being communicated in terms of the maternal body, we have here what Bronfen describes as "the maternal body in her traumatizing intimacy" (Bronfen, 1998: 24). Bronfen has Montrelay in mind who writes of "time when nothing was thinkable: then, the body and the world were confounded in one chaotic intimacy which was too present, too immediate – one continuous expanse of proximity or unbearable plenitude. What was lacking was lack" (Montrelay, 1977 cited in Moi, 1987: 233).

Case study "Kirsty" – a clinical overview

There are clinical cases of anorexic female patients (with associated amenorrhea), whose family history includes the death of a loved one which the parents have been unable to adequately mourn. The "replacement" child can represent reincarnation of the deceased, and her anorexia stops her from asserting her own identity and individuation because unconsciously she is afraid of betraying her parents by growing up. Adolescence and the acquisition of a new sexual body represents individuation at its most threatening, when up until this point the child is entangled in the parental identifications. Analysis provides a separate space and as Henri Rey writes in *Universals of Psychoanalysis in The Treatment of Psychotic and Borderline States* (1994), it is hoped that the patient will glance away from her own image and project her feelings into a separate space that is not inhabited by her parents. Then the patient's well-being can improve. Paradoxically, I have found that parents of anorexic children often say they feel that they are forced into the role of the mirror, or that they experience their child as taking up the space carved out for their own shadow. It is hoped that family therapy will provide the arena for them to think about their own projections that the child is receiving. Parenting workshops help them to see the importance of creating not only distance but also a triangular space where the child can feel safe enough to relinquish her own omnipotence as she trusts in the vital dualism and potential of the parental couple.

"Kirsty" – a clinical case of mourning

Sarah Huline-Dickens, a child and adolescent psychiatrist, presents the clinical case of a 14-year-old anorexic patient "Kirsty" in her paper "Becoming Anorexic: On Loss, Death and Identification and the Emergence of Anorexia Nervosa" (2005). Kirsty came for treatment because she was having seizure-like movements. When Kirsty was four, her mother gave birth to a baby girl who was unwell with seizures and who nearly died. Her mother spent a lot of time nursing this infant. Kirsty's seizure-like symptoms were perhaps a form of communication through identification with the sister, as a means to reach out for assistance and care. However, during the therapy sessions in which family members attended together, it appeared to Huline-Dickens that the patient in the room was in fact the mother who was inconsolable over her divorce from Kirsty's father, and she was also displaying unresolved emotions about the death of her own father. It became clear that Kirsty was using her illness as a way to bring the family back together. She was also finding ways to identify with family members and in doing so she was searching erratically for her own sense of self. The anorexic model, with its clearly defined and uncomplicated parameters, was a new identity she embraced. It bought simplicity and it bought relief.

When Kirsty came for treatment, she would bring with her a laminated photograph of a pop star. He looked like her father. She would often hold it close to her body or place it carefully next to her. We can refer to Sontag's *On Photography* (1977), which describes a photograph as

> something directly stencilled of the real, like a footprint or a death-mask ... not only like its subject, a homage to the subject. It is part of, an extension of that subject; a potent means of acquiring it, or gaining control over it.
>
> (Sontag, 1977: 154–155)

As Kirsty became thinner and thinner, she would hug herself around the middle as if to provide a layer that would hold her in. At the same time, by disappearing through the act of not eating, she could avoid being unconsciously consumed by a dominant needy mother and a father whose love she craved:

> In weighing Kirsty I was aware of the parental significance of this act, and that for her there must have been feelings about her approval being in the balance. To meet with my approval she would need to gain weight, but to meet with her own, she would have to have lost weight.
>
> (Huline-Dickens, 2005: 320)

Kirsty had dreams about "ghosts and spooks" and at times she was sure she would die:

> It seemed to me that Kirsty was haunted by death, and her struggle to was to find some wholesome identity for herself before being overcome by feelings of grief and guilt about the illnesses and deaths in her parents' past which had not been dealt with.
>
> (Huline-Dickens, 2005: 325)

Anorexia and its associated symptoms allow for time to stand still, like the father in the photograph and like her mother who was unable to accept the losses in her life and move on. Kirsty wanted to maintain a link with the original external and internal losses. She would be death's nemesis. After several months of treatment, Kirsty was able to maintain a weight that both she and the clinic were satisfied with and as a result of her therapy she was able to see herself as a separate person. She started to talk about how others might view her as different and she showed a capacity to self-reflect as she stepped away from the mirror.

Conclusion

It is hoped that the study of Ovid's Pygmalion and the associated clinical material will allow for further creative thinking about SA as a state rich in symbolism and meaning, and as a bodily representation of a psychic state that is far from lacking. A patient with SA, similar to the hysterics of Freud's early work can be the patient that a male analyst dreams of treating, with the opportunity for him to display his artistry and embellish her treatment with all his pearls of wisdom. But as with many of the classical myths and with Pygmalion had Ovid continued, the analyst might reach a place where the id, ego and superego chant like a Greek chorus of antiquity: BE CAREFUL WHAT YOU WISH FOR!

A little goes a long way – Eliza Doolittle's transformation from a psychoanalytic perspective

This part of the chapter focuses on George Bernard Shaw's play *Pygmalion* (1916) and the process of change undergone by Eliza Doolittle. The aim is to show how elements in Shaw's play represent a developed, multi-dimensional way of intra-psychic relating aligned to the depressive position as opposed to the more paranoid schizoid state that we encountered in Ovid's version. There is much movement in Shaw's work allowing for creativity and growth. How Eliza manages change and how she balances all that she acquires with all that she loses demonstrates the precariousness of the process of transformation. Whilst we are all at risk of being exposed to this, it is with particular reference to patients in psychotherapy who present with SA that this section directs its focus. The reflections on Eliza Doolittle from a psychoanalytic perspective will be followed by a clinical case study and discussion of an amenorrheic patient in treatment.

Eliza – a twentieth-century Galatea

> Galatea never does quite like her Pygmalion; his relation to her is too godlike to be altogether agreeable.
>
> (Shaw, 1916 [2003]: 119)

With these words Bernard Shaw ends the 1916 publication of his stage play *Pygmalion*, as an addendum to his contemporary take on the myth. As readers of Shaw's work, we are invited to explore what it is that the female lead Eliza Doolittle wants. This is different to Ovid's model, in which one can become preoccupied with the needs and wants of Pygmalion. And in Shaw's version, there is a transformation that is different from its classical counterpart. Shaw's is aligned with independence, emancipation and freedom. It is the process of transformation itself that is as important, if not more so, than he who is the transformer and she who is transformed. Of course in Shaw's play, we have Professor Higgins whose linguistic mastery is to be applauded and we have Eliza Doolittle who capably absorbs and incorporates all that she is taught. But we do not start off nor do we end up with a Pygmalion and his Galatea. Firstly, Higgins is not the romantic hero, nor lover. He is devoted to his science and to improving the world and he is no Prince Charming, nor is Eliza a clone of the classical sultry heroine waiting for true love's kiss.:

> In his quest the modern hero does not always want to or need the fulfil-ment of marriage, and the modern maiden, more independent than her classical counterparts, may ignore the savior whose ideals she does not share. In the mythical retelling, then, Eliza may leave Higgins and marry Freddy, and Higgins, having freed his Andromeda from a living death, can move on to further adventures.
>
> (Vesonder, 1977: 43)

Myths enable us to cast aside the details and "truths" in terms of class and gender division of the Victorian age and afford ourselves the chance to become enraptured and curious about the encounter between Higgins and Eliza. Their collaborative work supported by the other characters legitimises Eliza's transformation. There is always a flow of discourse in which characters play, negotiate, agree and, importantly, challenge one another. It is precisely this inter-relating that results in a realistic and viable metamorphosis able to withstand the test of time. Eliza's outward transformation from a common flower seller into a duchess is not at the expense of her very essence, her spirit and her drive. The process is one of incorporation and of self-realisation. In contrast, once the perfect inanimate statue in the Ovidian ver-sion transforms and comes to life, the cracks start to appear. The splits between omnipotence and impotence, between perfection and denigration appear too wide. Subject and object are never really anything more than just that. Pygmalion and Galatea are endlessly inextricably linked. In Shaw's work, there is interplay between attachment and autonomy and an intra-psychic and interpersonal relating between Higgins and Eliza. This perhaps offers itself up as a new working model for Eliza to internalise. Notably, her outward and inward transformation might enable her to be alone in a way that is contrary to what she is used to, aloneness having been thrust upon her. As Anthony Storr writes on this state of mind: "The capacity to be alone thus becomes linked with self-discovery and self realization; with becoming aware of one's deepest needs, feelings and impulses" (Storr, 1988: 21).

We shall examine later on what it is that Eliza truly needs and desires. For now though, individualisation and separateness in Shaw's play are born out of Eliza's ability to leave Higgins, a choice that Higgins supports. And it is not

Eliza marrying her mentor Higgins that will define her womanhood. It is not this that will emancipate her. Galatea, on the other hand, is to marry her creator and her womanhood is to be defined by her beauty and by motherhood. Her fate is written in the stars. Eliza's beauty is from within: She is enchantingly blemished. She has a fiery nature, just like Higgins, with a rebellious streak and a drive to assert her individuality. Of course, through Higgins's skill, Eliza becomes more able and equipped to pursue her goals. She recognises how alike the two of them are but it is in leaving him that she can become whole. This liberates her, transforms her and defines her womanhood. The fact that her fate can be viewed as unsettled is testimony to the deep truths that reside in the id. Her instinctual life grabs our affections.

We are introduced to Eliza the flower seller at the start of the play. Had she not been allowed to sell flowers on the street, it is likely that she would have been selling her body as a prostitute. This situation was mirrored in Vienna during Freud's time, with a huge trade in prostitution servicing the sexual demands of men whilst nice girls remained chaste until marriage (Mitchell, 1974). Shaw was fighting for a society in which women like Eliza could be freed from this *in situ* and Eliza is offered a way out through her tutelage by Higgins. We can contrast her fate with that of Nancy, the prostitute in Charles Dickens's (1837) novel *Oliver Twist*. Nancy, like most women in nineteenth-century literature with a colourful sexual past, did not survive. There is no chance for Nancy to emerge triumphant as a non-confirming heroine. Eliza on the other hand carries the beacon of hope. Importantly though, she does not trade her common roots for a new middle-class milieu. There is no split or trade-off. This is very different to the split between the godlike Galatea who is protected to the point of being enslaved by her creator, and the Propoetides, the prostitutes, who, enslaved by their situation, must be done away with. So, Shaw's play demonstrates more fully developed ego integration on the side of whole-object rather than part-object relating. For me however, the most crucial ingredient to this is the non-repression of Eliza's instinctual life and the fact that she has found in Higgins a sparring partner who can bear and tolerate some of her "hysterical" tendencies and primitive anxieties. They often mirror one another, giving back as good as they get, but they are both committed to the process, to the talking cure, which acts as a third other, a framework that contains and metabolises.

Language – that which is acquired

Having never met before, Eliza and Higgins go on a journey in which words are central to the experience. The beginning and subsequent developments are like that of mother and infant:

> Just as the being-with experience of intersubjective relatedness require the sense of two subjectivities in alignment – a sharing of inner

experience of state – so too, at his new level of verbal relatedness, the infant and mother create a being-with experience using verbal symbols – a sharing of mutually created meanings about personal experience.

(Stern, 1985: 172)

If we go further back to the very earliest of days of the infant and mother inter-relating we can look to Didier Arizieu (1989) who writes about the child's acquisition of her own skin ego when there has been a successful psychic internalisation of the common skin of mother and child alongside a good mothering environment. The skin ego is protected by a second skin, that of the mother's. The threat is that the mother will reclaim the second skin and in doing so the infant's skin ego and thus the question of ownership is never decided. This appears in Shaw's play when Eliza asks what has happened to the set of clothes she arrived with at Wimpole Street. She asks this when deciding on whether to leave Higgins or not. She insists on knowing if the clothes she has been given by Higgins and Pickering now belong to her. The clothes represent the second skin. As Lacanian psychoanalyst Eugenie Lemoine-Luccioni writes in *La Robe* (1983): "the garment is always stolen ... she parades it and displays the maternal skin and embodies it in front of the man" (Lemoine-Luccioni & Courrèges, 1983: 97).Through this, the man can unconsciously identify with the woman who possesses it. Eliza shows her strength in that she is able in gesture to borrow the clothes and give them back. But we all know that now they belong to her. We could say that together, Higgins and Eliza work to create a maternal frame with paternal boundaries, an analogy for psychoanalysis.

Characterisation and the analytic encounter

What Eliza and Higgins have together can be thought about in the context of analysis, with the analyst recognising how important the patient is to him:

> Patient and analyst need one another. The patient comes to the analyst because of internal conflicts that prevent him from enjoying life and he begins to use the analyst not only to resolve them but increasingly as a receptacle for his pent-up feeling. But the analyst also needs the patient in order to crystalize and communicate his own thoughts, including some of his inmost thoughts on intimate human problems, which can only grow organically in the context of this relationship. They cannot be shared and experienced in the same immediate way with a colleague, or even with a husband or wife.

(Klauber, 1976: 46)

We must however not be misguided that all is rosy in the Garden of Wimpole Street. We have a strong pull/push relationship between the two and "the attraction of opposites is held in suspension by the stubborn independence of each and the play ends in tension, not resolution" (Berst, 1995: 200).

There are many immediate metaphorical references in Shaw's play to the analytic encounter. For example, Higgins says to Pickering about Eliza:

HIGGINS: You know Pickering, that woman has the most extraordinary ideas about me. Here I am, a shy, diffident sort of man. I've never been able to feel really grown-up and tremendous like other chaps. And yet she's firmly persuaded that I'm an arbitrary overbearing bossing kind of person. I can't account for it. (Shaw, 1916 [2003]: 40–41).

We also have in Higgins what psychoanalyst Adam Philips calls the "free listening analyst" (Philips, 2002: 31). When Pickering tells Higgins he can't hear a difference between most of the letter sounds Higgins replies

HIGGINS: [*chuckling and going over to the piano to eat sweets*] Oh that comes with practice. You hear no difference at first; but you keep on listening, and presently you find they're all as different as A from B. (Shaw, 1916 [2003]: 24)

And from Shaw, we have an Eliza who thinks of Higgins as follows:

She is immensely interested in him. She has even secret mischievous moments in which she wishes she could get him alone, on a desert island, away from all ties and with nobody else in the world to consider and just drag him off his pedestal and see him make love like any common man.
(Shaw, 1916 [2003]: 119)

Shaw wrote this in a sequel to the original play as an angry demonstration to his audience and to his actors who kept insisting that there be a romantic union between Higgins and Eliza at the end of the play. At the 1914 London theatre premiere, Herbert Beerbohm, the actor playing Higgins, threw flowers to Mrs Patrick Campbell, the actress playing Eliza Doolittle. He had ignored Shaw's ending replacing it with his own version, giving the audiences what they wanted. In his *Collected Letters*, Shaw is clearly a man on a mission: "Don't talk to me of romances; I was sent into the world to dance on them with thick boots-to-shatter, stab, and murder them" (Shaw, 1965: 163).

This resistance might have been born out of his refusal to fantasise about the relationship between his mother and her voice coach, whom she followed to London taking her two daughters with her and leaving Shaw behind with his father. Shaw emphasised that his play was designed to be an anti-romantic social satire about class and independence and although he did describe it as a romance, it was meant in the sense that the story was unlikely. In the sequel, a union between Freddy and Eliza is formed. Whilst Eliza can have her "private imaginations" about Higgins, marrying Freddy symbolises that "when it comes to business, to the life that she really leads as distinguished from the life of dreams and fancies, she likes Freddy and she likes the Colonel; and she does not like Higgins and Mr Doolittle" (Shaw, 1916 [2003]: 119).

This actually serves as a creative outlet for unconscious incestuous impulses without the resultant damage that we witness in Ovid's *Metamorphosis*. In Arnold Silver's book *Bernard Shaw The Darker Side* (1982), Silver discusses the issue of incest in Shaw's play from a Freudian perspective:

> Shaw knew that in longing for the union between Eliza and Higgins we ignore the secrete appeal of the Pygmalion legend … For, after all, the sculptor would be committing incest in marrying the woman he fathered parthenogenetically. And if the obvious appeal of the Pygmalion story lies in its adolescent fantasizing of the ideal woman, its hidden and concomitant appeal lies in incest, initially between father and daughter but also between son and mother, for deep within the male fantasy of the ideal woman are memories of the most fulfilling of ideal women, the mother. Galatea is thus daughter and mother simultaneously, as Pygmalion is father and son.
>
> (Silver, 1982: 198–199)

If Eliza is to inherit Higgins' legacy then she must as the legitimate heir, as "my creation of a Duchess Eliza". Does this play then offer us a successful example of sublimation in terms of a social value being the results of the artistry as described by Freud in "New Introductory Lectures on Psychoanalysis"? Freud describes, "A certain kind of modification of the aim and a change of object, in which our social valuation is taken into account, is described by us as 'sublimation'" (Freud, 1933, *SE*, XXII: 97). We can link this to Freud's earlier work, "Three Essays on the Theory of Sexuality" in which he writes that "sexual curiosity can be diverted ('sublimated') in the direction of art" (Freud, 1905, *SE*, VII: 156). In terms of the 18-year old Eliza, it might very well be that the creative act she partakes in with Professor Higgins is "an attempt to avoid a desired relationship with an object as well as to satisfy it; a developmental conflict that characterizes adolescence" (Levine, 2009: 10).

Let us bear in mind that Shaw was an adolescent 15-year-old when his mother left him and the family home for London. We might then suggest that the writing of this play was an act of sublimation for Shaw, offering him textual retribution and redemption from his feelings towards his parents. Shaw indeed admits to an Oedipus complex prior to writing the play and Erik Erikson explains in *Identity: Youth and Crisis* (1968) how Shaw used creativity to help contain an identity crisis and to resist identification with an impotent father, one who drank and was behaviourally dishevelled.

Higgins need not leave the comfort of his consulting room to feel that he has conquered the world and he congratulates himself on having transformed a gutter girl into a duchess. Shaw, through his own literary skill and artistry, can manage his own internal battle of omnipotence versus impotence and can become ruler supreme. But we do not have a sanitised play, nor do we have something that offers us the illusion of cohesion and reparation. Instead we have mess, guts and gore, visual and verbal. We have ambivalence and uncertainty and we experience the way in which preconceptions and perceptions are challenged.

The discourse of the other

The more articulate we become and the more we master this interlocution the further away we are from our true selves. So we start at the beginning with Eliza, who sounds out letters into a phonograph, over and over again. These sounds represent something raw and instinctual. As she becomes more proficient in the task of learning to talk like a duchess, and as she displays the capacity to replicate and mirror those around her, we can see that the addition of language and text to those primitive letters symbolises the unification of the id, ego and superego in the art of socialisation. But, Eliza, in her resistance to the seductive powers of a new order symbolised by her acquisition of language, never renounces those early days and she does not become a slave to the discourse of others. For me, she is a true heroine. In Act II of the play Shaw shows us how determined Eliza's drive is to be unrepressed. Higgins is testing her out on a trip to his mother's house. The conversation between Eliza, Mrs Higgins and a visiting friend Mrs Eynsford Hill unravels:

LIZA: *[darkly]* My aunt died of influenza: so they said.

MRS. EYNSFORD HILL: *[clicks her tongue sympathetically.]*

LIZA: *[in the same tragic tone]* But it is my belief they done the old woman in.

MRS. HIGGINS: *[puzzled]* Done her in?

LIZA: Y-e-e-e-es Lord love you! Why should she die of influenza? She come through diphtheria right enough the year before. I saw her with my own eyes. Fairly blue with it, she was. They all thought she was dead; but my father he kept ladling gin down her throat till she cam to so sudden that she bit the bowl off the spoon.

MRS. EYNSFORD HILL: *[startled]* Dear me!

LIZA: *[piling up the indictment]* What call would a woman with that strength in her have to die from influenza? What become of a new straw hat that should have come to me? Somebody pinched it; and what I say is, them as pinched it done her in.

MRS. EYNSFORD HILL: What does done her in mean?

HIGGINS: *[hastily]* Oh, that's the new small talk. To do a person in means to kill them. (Shaw, 1916 [2003]: 60)

We could say that this unravelling is an example of how Plato anticipated the lawless voice as a catalyst for a chaotic situation that would bring about a breakdown in social bonding. As Dolar describes in his book *A Voice and Nothing More*:

In order to forestall this truly apocalyptic vision – the end of civilisation, a return to chaos initiated by innocuous-looking changes in musical forms – one has to impose a firm regimentation of musical matters. The first rule, the prize antidote for combating the monster, is already known: 'The music and the rhythm must follow speech' (Plato, 1978 *Republic* III 398d. 400d.). For the core of the danger is the voice that sets itself loose from the word, the voice beyond logos, the lawless voice.

(Dolar, 2006: 45)

All parties at Mrs Higgins' house survive the ordeal and Eliza and Higgins return to Wimpole Street to continue to refine the model; the model being the transformation and not Eliza. At her next outing, the ambassador's ball, an arena for music, all the guests believe Eliza to be of middle- to upper-class status, of royal blood even. So we have a process of change, which to borrow Forrester's words is that of "speech which transforms the speaker in the very act of saying" (Forrester, 1990: 147).

Obviously we must accept the post-structuralist argument that language is more than a tool to communicate or to pass on information. It is an agent that can create and destroy and Eliza can never be the same again, nor for that matter can Higgins. But we are not left with an apocalyptic transformation. Eliza has undeniably changed, grown and matured out of an impoverished state but wonderfully, her unconscious realm was never going to be taken as a hostage to this new order. At the end of the play, during a heated and passionate display of emotional attachment, the question of "what is to become of her" comes up but this time a realistic solution, an emotional compromise is formalised in her mind. This is not a stalemate nor does it have the quality of a negative therapeutic reaction, testimony to Higgins' commitment to the process even it if means not giving Eliza what she thought she wanted. The process, the transformation has enabled her to claim:

LIZA: Aha! Now I know how to deal with you. What a fool I was not to think of it before! You can't take away the knowledge you gave me. You said I had a finer ear than you. And I can be civil and kind to people, which is more than you can. Aha! *[Purposely dropping her aitches to annoy him]* That's done you, Enry Iggins, it az. Now I don't care that *[snapping her fingers]* for your bullying and your big talk. I'll advertise it in the papers that your duchess is only a flower girl that you taught, and that she'll teach anybody to be a duchess just the same in six months for a thousand guineas. Oh when I think of myself crawling under your feet and being trampled on and called names, when all the time I had only to lift up my finger to be as good as you, I could just kick myself.

HIGGINS: *[wondering at her]* You damned impudent slut, you! But it's better than snivelling; better than fetching slippers and finding spectacles, isn't it? *[Rising]* By George, Eliza, I said I'd make a woman of you; and I have. I like you like this.

LIZA: Yes. You can turn round and make up to me now that I'm not afraid of you, and can do without you.

HIGGINS: Of course I do, you little fool. Five minutes ago you were like a millstone round my neck. Now you are a tower of strength: a consort battleship. You and I and Pickering will be three old bachelors instead of only two men and a silly girl. (Shaw, 1916 [2003]: 104–105)

Some feminists would regard this as a misogynist statement from Higgins. However, the route of the word "bachelor" comes from the Anglo-Norman word *bachelor*, which is linked to "*escolier*", meaning a young squire in training. They are all students in training, regardless of their gender, when it comes to relating to one another and navigating their way within this new dynamic that they find themselves in. Is this not a new way of revisiting the question of transformation that they tackled earlier with their linguistic endeavour? And is this not another attempt at something from much earlier; the re-enactment of the first image, that of "coming in by the mouth" where the mother and her infant are trying to attune themselves with "a breast, a movement of mouth seizing a breast … revivified" (Laplanche, 1976: 60). Higgins and Eliza both represent people outside of the institution, non-conformists. On a concrete level, he lacks a father. She lacks a mother. What they offer each other is a new setting that chimes with what Anna Freud and Dorothy Burlingham describe in their 1943 paper "War and Children":

> The ability to love … has to be learned and practiced. Wherever, though the absence of or the interruption of personal ties, this opportunity is missing in childhood, all later relationships will develop weakly, will remain shallow. The opposite of this ability to love is not hate but egoism.
>
> (Freud & Burlingham, 1943: 191)

Higgins and Eliza have their own defensive egoism, but they appear to acknowledge what each of them lacks as much as what each of them brings to the table. They are egalitarians yet each have conceptualised entitlement in their own individual way.

Do you see what I see?

I believe that Shaw's play symbolises the Lacanian idea that "man's desire finds its meaning in the desire of the other, not so much because the other holds the key to the object desired, as because the first object of desire is to be recognized by the other" (Lacan, 1959 [1977]: 58).

Higgins, like the analyst, perhaps can be a figure to be desired. He is seductive to Eliza. As he offers her chocolates from the bowl to entice her to stay, he takes from the same bowl an apple and munches on it, demonstrating that his life force, if not charged, can be easily replenished. All of Eliza's questions, notably what is to become of her, I believe is linked to Freud's understanding of the intrusion of the adult's unconscious fantasies into the psychic world of the child. Higgins might have mastered intellectual and technical erudition, but Eliza wants to know what it is he wants from her in the face of his own unconscious and un-mastered fantasies. She wonders why it is that he is interested in her and yet she tells him she has noticed that he does not notice her. For Freud, the child's questions are a series of displacements, circling around the one question she cannot ask: "why are you telling me this?" I think this is an important point in terms of the analytic technique that includes the analyst choosing self-disclosure and/or sharing his counter-transference. She wants to know if she is loved and in Lacanian terms, following his theory that the phallus is a signifier of the desire of the Other:

> it is in order to be the phallus, that is to say, the signifier of the desire of the Other, that a woman will reject an essential part of femininity, namely all her attributes in the masquerade. It is for that which she is not that she wishes to be desired as well as loved.
>
> (Lacan cited in Salecl, 1998: 25–26)

But this phallus is also a signifier equivalent to the lack of the other. In Stephen Heath's reading of Joan Riviere's "Womanliness as a Masquerade" (1929), Heath points to the phallus as "the supreme signifier of an impossible identity" (Heath cited in Burgin, Donald & Kaplan, 1986: 53).

What of Eliza's acquisition of the vagina? Freud writes about the displacement of the symbolised by the symbol and it could be suggested that the use of the slippers and the gloves at the end of two of Shaw's revisions tidies up any symbolic thinking with regards to Eliza acquiring the vagina. When Eliza first settles in to her new home at Wimpole Street, Mrs Pearce, Higgins's housekeeper, gives Liza her first bath, wanting to start the process of changing her from a "frowzy slut" into a "clean, respectable girl". Cleanliness is equal to self-esteem:

MRS PEARCE: You've got to make yourself as clean as the room then you won't be afraid of it. (Shaw, 1916 [2003]: 35)

What a perfect metaphor for the amenorrheic body! Mrs Pearce continues:

MRS PEARCE: Well, don't you want to be clean and sweet and decent, like a lady? You know you can't be a nice girl inside if you're a dirty girl outside. (Shaw, 1916 [2003]: 36)

Mrs Pearce proceeds to scrub Eliza with a phallic-shaped brush. In this scene, Eliza sees herself naked in a full-length mirror for the first time. Shaw does not give us much description of this scene and so we are open to use our imagination. One could theorise that Eliza's desire and approach to master the pronunciation of language is an attempt to "get" the phallus, but to what extent can her attempt be realised? Perhaps when looking in the mirror she sees for the first time Eliza the prostitute and she questions her potential to manipulate, seduce and acquire the phallus, maximising her potential as the objectified object. Does she become aware of those coquettish charms that she might posses and employ to redirect her narrative back to the Cinderellas and Galateas of this world? Earlier in the play when Higgins offers her a chocolate to entice her to stay she says:

LIZA: *[halting, tempted]* How do I know what might be in them? I've heard of girls being drugged by the likes of you. (Shaw, 1916 [2003]: 33)

Perhaps in looking at herself in the mirror she realises more fully how she, Higgins and their joint project have the capacity to intoxicate like chocolates. Higgins declares his allegiance by eating half and offering the other half of the chocolate in a "*Pledge of good faith*". Whilst this is a clear play in the erotic transference, we know that a play is all it is. When pressed by Pickering on the matter, Higgins consciously declares:

HIGGINS: I've taught scores of American millionairesses how to speak English: the best looking women in the world. I'm seasoned. They might as well be blocks of wood. I might as well be a block of wood. (Shaw, 1916 [2003]: 38)

No danger of acting out in the erotic transference then! Despite his boasting though, Eliza is afforded much space for her femininity to breathe. Returning to Eliza in the mirror, I think she is an example of someone who is defended against the Freudian notion of exhibitionism, which, as Pacteau (1994) describes in her book *Symptom of Beauty*,

> originates in the auto-erotic activity of looking at a part of one's own body – an activity that initially coincides with pleasurable bodily sensations which will later evolve into looking at someone else's body by a process of comparison...the pleasure afforded by self display arises from the subject's identification with the gaze of the other.
>
> (Pacteau, 1994: 148)

Pacteau also refers to Flügel's book *The Psychology of Clothes* (1930) in which is invoked

> the scene of the child prancing around naked, without any sense of shame, its pleasure sustained and heightened by the adoring gaze of the parents or adults standing by. He suggests that the pleasure afforded by sartorial display derives initially from such narcissistic investment in one's own body, which is later metonymically displaced onto the clothes and other decorations that the body wears.
>
> (Pacteau, 1994: 148)

Eliza has missed out on the vicissitude of the scopophilic drive which oscil-
lates between being looked at and looking at. Freud states that "anyone who
is an exhibitionist in his unconscious is at the same time a voyeur" (Freud,
1905, *SE*, VII: 167)

Taking this a step further, the drive to look facilitates a learned skill to
lose. For the daughter who is able to look kindly at herself in the mirror, she
is able to acknowledge that she is different from her mother. As Eliza does
not have an actual mother, perhaps it is a separation from her internalised
mother that will bring about a successful maturation. From this moment on,
Eliza demonstrates an increased, more authentic capacity and resilience.

Do you hear what I hear?

Whilst looks might kill, this is offset with Eliza's voice preserved in the
phonograph and it is Higgins who acts as the paternal presence, watching
her, listening to her, studying her and interpreting both as the gazing subject
and the gazed-at subject. This enables Eliza to hear herself speak:

> Voice and gaze relate to each other as life and death: voice vivifies,
> whereas gaze mortifies. For that reason, "hearing oneself speak" [*s'en-
> tendre-parler*], as Derrida has demonstrated, is the very kernel, the funda-
> mental matrix, of experiencing oneself as a living being while its
> counterpart at the level of the gaze, "seeing oneself looking" [*se voir
> voyant*] unmistakably stands for death: when the gaze qua object is no
> longer the elusive blind spot in the field of the visible but is included in
> this field this one meet's one's death.
>
> (Žižek, 1996: 94)

Shaw's play demonstrates how there need not be a split between voice and
gaze, living and dying, omnipotent and impotence as we saw in Ovid's tale:

> metaphysics stands for the illusion that in the antagonistic relationship
> between "seeing" and "hearing," it is possible to abolish the discord, the
> impossibility, that mediates between the two terms (one hears a thing
> because one cannot see it at all, and vice versa) and to conflate them in
> a unique experience of "seeing in the mode of hearing".
>
> (Žižek, 1996: 95)

This is facilitated in Higgins: As the linguist watching and interpreting, we
could say he represents the paternal. Importantly, Eliza does not idealise him.
She sees him as another human being, of flesh and blood like her. She in fact
gives him a project that ignites his raw instinctual life into the arena of creative sublimation. Surely this is true love? As Lacan describes it, true love is
always a love returned.

The Lacanian idea that language interrupts the imaginary relationship between mother and infant might explain why Eliza says to Colonel Pickering as she enters the banquet:

ELIZA: It is not the first time for me, Colonel. I have done this fifty times – hundreds of times – in my little piggery in Angel Court in my daydreams. I am in a dream now. Promise me not to let Professor Higgins wake me; for if he does I shall forget everything and talk as I used to in Drury Lane. (Shaw, 1916 [2003]: 70)

We have Eliza whose destiny looked likely to evolve into a life of prostitution now in the circle of a higher culture. Shaw describes Eliza's withstanding of her ordeal: "she walks like a somnambulist in a desert instead of a debutante in a fashionable crowd" (Shaw, 1916]2003]: 71). I am reminded of the somnambulistic state associated with hysteria (that of Lady Macbeth is an obvious one) and with disassociation. Eliza says she is in a dream but it is not: "Dreaming as a recreation for the brain which by day has to satisfy the stern demands of thought imposed by a higher culture" (Nietzche, 1878b: 24–27 cited in Hauke, 2000: 151).

It is more a fugue state, an awakened state that lacks awareness, and is imbued with a ghostly sense of self. This enables her to pass through the salon. People stop talking to look at her and to admire her dress and jewels. At this stage, we are closer to Galatea than we might wish to admit but there are very important differences. Eliza is not merely a product of one man's wish fulfilment. Higgins has worked with the raw materials that Eliza presented with and they each played their part in creating their shared vision of the ideal woman. Although at this stage there is this disconnect, Eliza is not mute nor in someone else's skin. In that moment, at the banquet, past, present and future flash before her eyes and she survives it – she's not paralysed by it. This play is not solely about Liza realising her own fantasies; it's about her acquiring a narrative of her own, that which seems a far-reaching fantasy for Galatea, reliant on hope more than anything. Eliza's successful transformation is in her autonomy. When she makes a mistake, she can correct herself. Akin to those patients who have internalised the analytic function, she now has a choice and it is this that is empowering.

Final thoughts

When Eliza arrives and agrees to stay with Higgins, her clothes are burnt and she is given a set of Japanese clothes. In her new attire, she represents sobriety but she reaches for her old hat that she arrived with, one with three ostrich feathers: orange, sky blue and red:

ELIZA: I shall look alright with my hat on. (Shaw, 1916 [2003]: 48)

This offers her a psychic equilibrium and a defence against fragility, now further compounded by the fact that her father has turned up searching for money. Her father likes a drink, as did Shaw's. In this scene, I am reminded of the synthesis between the unconscious and conscious landscape of the hysterics that Charcot treated. Elaine Showalter (1997: 32) described how Charcot, at a public session during which he planned to discuss hysterical tremors, bought in three women wearing hats with long feathers each of which trembled in a way that was characteristic of the disease. The slightest movement by the patient was picked up in the shaking feathers. Furthermore, the exact ways in which the feathers shook demarked the particular movement associated with the particular disease in the nervous system.

When Higgins presents Eliza on her first public outing to show how the "common idiot" can be "a consort to the king", Higgins's mother warns:

MRS HIGGINS: She is a triumph of your art and her dressmaker's but if you suppose for a moment that she doesn't give herself away in every sentence she utters, you must be perfectly cracked about her. (Shaw, 1916 [2003]: 64)

I am reminded of the clinician's early warning to parents whose daughters are on the cusp of developing anorexia and the associated amenorrheic symptoms. Parents are warned against being disillusioned by the idea that all is within a safe perimeter. The discrepancy between reality and illusion with regards to what the adolescent girl sees in the mirror is often reflected at the outset in the attitude of the parents who unconsciously act collusively into the myth, as they are unable to bear witness to the truth.

The truth of Eliza's predicament at the beginning of the play is that her father was narcissistically devoted to himself, her mother was absent from the outset and her psychic impoverishment and the nourishment it acquired was attached to her job as a flower seller. She demonstrates the capacity to thrive at Wimpole Street, despite the burden of what is lacking. Language is a transformative, saving third. It is as Jung explains the transcendent symbolic third that mediates between the opposites that consciousness cannot reconcile on its own. Creative expression and meaning add to the transcendent function and individuation and a greater psychic wholeness is possible (Jung, 1939 [1954], para. 780). We can turn to Foucault for added inspiration:

Before the imminence of death, language rushes forth, it also starts again, tells of itself … headed towards death, language turns back upon itself; it encounters something like a mirror; and to stop this death which would stop it, it possesses but a single power: that of giving birth to its own image in a play of mirrors that has no limits. From the depths of the mirror where it sets out to arrive a new at the point where it started (at death) but so as finally to escape death, another language can be heard – the image of actual language, but as a minuscule, interior, and virtual model.

(Foucault, 1963: 54)

So we have language as a transformative third alongside the thematic conceptual terms voiced by Higgins and the feelings and emotions expressed by Eliza. In other words, Higgins talks the talk and Eliza walks the walk. Is Higgins like Freud, who perhaps believed that he knew more than Dora did about herself and furthermore did he think that he knew more than Dora wished to know of herself? As Eliza insightfully tells her mentor:

ELIZA: I'm no preacher. I don't know things like that. I notice that you don't notice me. (Shaw, 1916 [2003]: 101)

A clinical case of amenorrhea showing psycho-hormonal interrelationships

The following case study is taken from psychotherapist Ruth Easser's paper "A Case of Amenorrhea Showing Psycho-Hormonal Interrelationships" that she presented to the Association for Psychoanalytic Medicine in April 1954. At this time, Easser's research into SA was part of a more general study of the psychodynamics and psycho-physiological links in patients with long-standing amenorrhea. The study, under the direction of Dr George E. Daniels observed 26 unselected cases, which had been referred to his Endocrine Clinic. Easser's research was with those patients who were seen for psychotherapy and she investigated the possible relationship between emotional attitudes and hormone levels. Would changes in the patient's "adaptive functioning" influence the hormone levels that would in turn impact on menstruation?

Easser presents a patient, a 23-year-old attractive woman, who was amenorrheic from the age of 18. Her menarche occurred around the age of 13 and until the age of 18 she menstruated regularly. Easser describes the patient's family environment. She was the sixth child in a family of seven, of which there were five girls and two boys. The family was very poor. Her father did not work until the patient was 16. His wife often mocked him and the children copied this. The parents would argue a lot. The mother was domineering and would often play the martyr, denying herself food to feed the children. She often displayed hysterical outbursts with threats to leave or commit suicide. When the patient was born, her mother was hospitalised. The patient was told it was because she had scratched her mother's breast causing blood poisoning.

Whenever the patient recalls her mother's menses, it is always linked to her mother visiting the hospital. She grew up believing that anyone who went to hospital, male or female, could have a baby. When she was about eight years old, a boy kissed her and she was so ashamed she wanted to throw herself off the roof of the house. She wanted her genitals to be bandaged, seeing them as a wound. At the age of ten, her 17-year-old brother played with her sexually and she kept quiet about it, ashamed. Her older sisters, who competed with one another for the title of best mother surrogate, looked after her. They were keen to delay the patient's initiation into womanhood, so as to prolong their role as caregiver. The patient recalled a family outing to the swimming pool when she proudly announced that like her sisters she couldn't go swimming because she was menstruating. They examined her knickers, laughed at her and made her go into the water. When boys would ask her out on dates, her sisters made fun of her and became hostile. All of her dreams of being in the sisterhood were shattered. Menses went from something to boast about as a newly acquired symbol of femininity to something dangerous and indeed her last two bleeds she associated with shameful traumas. The first incident was when her female dance teacher told her she was mannish. The second incident involved a married teacher who told her he would leave his wife to marry her. During her last menstrual period, they went away for the weekend. They "petted" but they did not have intercourse. Despairing of the whole affair, the patient's menses abruptly stopped. Easser writes:

> She reacted to her amenorrhea with mixed feelings. She broke off the affair and confessed to an older sister, experiencing some emotional relief, but at the same time she developed the fear of pregnancy and the fear of defeminisation, both partially induced by the statements of a physician who was consulted. After the artificial induction of menses, the patient refused to continue therapy because she felt it was not going to help make her normal. For a time she became obsessed with the fear that she was changing sex. She would frequently examine her clitoris and look for evidence of physical change.
>
> (Easser, 1954: 429)

The patient was in effect identifying with her martyr-suffering mother and competing with the mother (both real and internalised) signified a death struggle. The idea that she could take a man from another woman entailed a fate that included a fear of retaliation from her sisters. She broke off the affair and gave up her desire to be beautiful and feminine, experiencing this as too dangerous a position. To control her menses meant she could control her sexual desires. I am reminded of Eliza Doolittle repeating "I am a good girl, I am", despite Higgins insisting she is from "the gutter".

During the patient's time in psychotherapy, her hormone levels were recorded. At the outset, her estrogen level was below the normal physiological range corresponding to pre-menarche functioning levels. This low level prevailed throughout most of the treatment with the exception of two occurrences when there was a marked increase, taking the estrogen level to that of a "normal" adult female. The first increase was at eight weeks into the study, at a time when she was able to speak about the hostility towards her sisters and towards her female boss. But with the sense of independence came feelings and expressions of confusion. She had started the treatment anxious that the therapist would make her menstruate and this would mean her sisters would withdraw their protection from her. The patient's anxiety became heightened and one week she returned to her therapy reporting that she had attacked her husband for being weak and unambitious. She had impending menstrual symptoms such as a tingling sensation in her breasts and abdominal cramping. Her eyes felt weak and she felt her teeth were shifting. She told her therapist that as a child she had been told that childbirth had caused her mother to have no teeth. This experience "appeared to be the beginning of a psychotic decomposition" (Easser, 1954: 430).

The therapist endeavoured to stabilise the patient's emotions and correspondingly her hormone level returned to the previous low and the menstrual symptoms ceased. During this time of reflection, the patient gained insight into the nature of her fear towards her retaliatory sisters and felt more independent. In the 18th week, her hormone level rose markedly again. She had a nightmare and believed that if she were to become a parent she would mutilate her children. The focus of the work was now on her unmet needs and her competition with her mother, with the therapist becoming the surrogate mother:

> The patient's desire to complete herself as a woman by bearing a child evoked early memories of her oral destructive fantasies towards her own mother, which were then projected onto the fantasied child. The patient's understanding of the nature of her hostility and of its ramifications enabled her to re-establish her equilibrium.
>
> (Easser, 1954: 430)

When the anxiety subsided, her estrogen levels resumed to their low levels. We are told that soon after, the patient left therapy because she had got a summer job in another city and the project had discontinued before her return. Easser uses this case study to confirm "In the majority of the cases studied in the 'amenorrhea project' adaptive decompensation, actual or threatened, did occur with either a return of the menses or an increase in the hormone level" (Easser, 1954: 431).

A hormonal rise in this particular patient occurred when she felt independent and most able to compete with her sisters. But with a glance towards mature femininity, sexuality and maternity came also a mental confusion, emotional stress and a threat to her "ego integration". Thus, Easser stressed the need for practitioners to think carefully before a patient with SA embarks on psychotherapy, as most will start out with a weak ego and treatment might result in an emotional disruption that threatens the ego's very existence.

Further reflections

This patient's menses were of the model studied by anthropologists in which the rich blood can symbolise both the fertile provider and the powerful destroyer. Her actual mother was both ally and enemy, so too the sisters. Her father was mocked for his powerlessness and yet had enough life force in him to argue vociferously with his wife. The omnipotent/impotent split runs deep. Amenorrhea frees the psyche of the burdens associated with such a schism and split. It overrides the struggle between the life and death forces. That is why the treatment of SA should always be treated with caution because a potential return to menses could become a matter of life and (or) death. The thought of bringing together the internalised omnipotence (and the repressed rage) with the internalised impotence (and the repressed rage!) is hard for the patient to conceptualise as something that represents "normal" viable growth. Many women with SA are not concerned with growth. Their energies are honed towards mastering the art of survival.

Easser tells us that her patient masturbates for the first time when she is a married woman and intercourse with her husband, although pleasurable, is always first anticipated with terror. Clitoral stimulation by her husband makes her believe she is being injured. Being caught between desire and repulsion is linked to the child witnessing the primal scene (an act of aggression by the father in a sadomasochistic relationship, according to Freud), unable to make sense of what she sees. The unconscious fears she might one day replace the mother and invite her wrath. During the time of the affair, the patient was horrified her lover might leave his wife for her and she feared her sisters' retribution: "At this point she withdrew from the struggle, broke up the affair, ceased to menstruate and withdrew from the dangerous feminine position. She overtly feared but unconsciously desired the defeminised 'hermaphroditic status'" (Easser, 1954: 429).

When I left my first analysis I remember so many times I would look in the mirror and "wish" my face to change into that of a man's. Out of the damage of the analysis, as part of my own reparation, I looked for my masculine, handsome face. This was my desired feminine state, the heroic heroine. Needing to incorporate rather than deny my menses, I though of myself as a new revision – of man and of woman with gender becoming an out-dated marker of difference. I was to be my own person. The failings of my analyst had both hardened me and weakened me. He was no man and no match for the task of my ego rebuild. When I left my analyst, I identified with Eliza Doolittle, freed from "the prison of her former existence" (Reynolds, 1994: 212).

For many women with SA who menstruate again, there is a struggle to come to terms with the fact that things can never be the same again. Eliza Doolittle articulates how a transformation represents a place of no return:

LIZA: You told me, you know, that when a child is brought to a foreign country, it picks up the language in a few weeks, and forgets its own. Well, I am a child in your country. I have forgotten my own language, and can speak nothing but yours. (Shaw, 1916 [2003]: 96)

Her outburst and her attack signpost the fragility of too soon a rebirth. The research by Ruth Easser confirms that those who experience a return to menstrual activity from analytic intervention are prone to suffering break-downs. I believe it is because the menses is too readily celebrated and the lost amenorrheic state too soon renounced and forgotten. The patient needs to mourn the loss. So-called progression and advancement of one's psychic homeland cannot exist without thought for the motherland:

LIZA: I sold flowers. I didn't sell myself. Now you've made a lady of me I'm not fit to sell anything else. I wish you'd left me where you found me. (Shaw, 1916 [2003]: 78)

The messy business of menses and non-menses and the process of transformation requires that the analysis continually holds in mind the Freudian symbols of the faeces, odour and phallus; so too the Kleinian breast and Lacanian symbols of the voice and the gaze. There is a kinaesthetic feel to it all that can overwhelm and intoxify the analyst. My analyst would often declare that I filled him with the Life Force! Looking back, I could (should?) have killed him with it!

Each patient tells their own story and their treatment requires that they not be typecast. A woman with secondary amenorrhea is elusive to all generalisations. Is she not therefore the Eliza of psychoanalysis?

Note

1 See Ovid's love elegy "Corinnae Concubitus" from *Amores 1.5* for an example of love poetry which is of its time and yet is unique in that it describes a successful sexual encounter between a man and a woman, a rarity in ancient works.

Bibliography

Anzieu, D. (1989) *The Skin Ego – A Psychoanalytic Approach to the Self.* trans. C. Turner. London & New Haven, CT: Yale University Press.

Balint, M. (1968 [1986]) *The Basic Fault – Therapeutic Aspects of Regression.* London & New York: Routledge.

Bernheimer, C. & Kahane, C. (eds.), (1990) *In Dora's Case: Freud-Hysteria-Feminism.* 2nd edition. New York & Chichester: Columbia University Press.

Berst, C.A. (1995) *Pygmalion – Shaw's Spin on Myth and Cinderella.* New York: Twayne Publishers Inc.

Bettelheim, B. (1976) *The Uses of Enchantment: The Meaning and Important of Fairy Tales.* New York: Knopf.

Bion, W.R. (1967) *Second Thoughts: Selected Papers on Psychoanalysis.* London & New York: Karnac Books.

Blade Runner. (1982) motion picture, directed by Ridley Scott, distributed by Warner Bros.

Britton, R. (1998) *Belief and Imagination: Explorations in Psychoanalysis.* London: Routledge.

Bronfen, E. (1998) *The Knotted Subject, Hysteria and Its Discontents.* Princeton, NJ & Chichester: Princeton University Press.

Brooks, P. (1993) *Body Work: Objects of Desire in Modern Narrative*. Cambridge, MA & London: Harvard University Press.

Burgin, V., Donald, J & Kaplan, C. (1986) *Formations of Fantasy*. London & New York: Methuen.

Cixous, H. (1976) "Fictions and Its Phantoms: A Reading of Freud's *Das Unheimliche* ("The Uncanny")", *New Literary History*, 7(3): 525–548.

Covington, C. (1989) "In Search of the Heroine", *Journal of Analytic Psychology*, 34(3): 243–254.

Daly, C.D. (1943) "The Role of Menstruation in Human Phylogenesis and Ontogenesis", *International Journal of Psychoanalysis*, 24: 151–170.

Deutsch, H. (1945) *Psychology of Women, Volume 2: Motherhood*. New York: Grune & Stratton.

Dickens, C. (1837) *Oliver Twist*. reprint, ed. S. Connor (1994). London: Dent.

Dolar, M. (2006) *A Voice and Nothing More*. Cambridge, MA & London: The MIT Press.

Easser, R. (1954) "A Case of Amenorrhea Showing Psycho-Hormonal Interrelationships", *Psychosomatic Medicine*, 16: 426–432.

Elsner, J. (1995) *Art and the Roman Viewer: Transformation of Art from the Pagan World to Christianity*. Cambridge: Cambridge University Press.

Elsner, J. (1996b) "Naturalism and the Erotics of the Gaze: Intimations of Narcissus", in B. Kampen (ed.), *Sexuality in Ancient Art – Near East Egypt, Greece and Italy*. Cambridge & New York: Cambridge University Press.

Elsner, J. & Sharrock, A.R. (1991) "Re-Viewing Pygmalion – Visual Mimesis and the Myth of the Real: Ovid's Pygmalion as Viewer and the Love of Creation Including the Story of Myrrha", *Ramus: Critical Studies in Greek and Roman Literature*, 20(2): 149–182.

Erikson, E.H. (1968) *Identity: Youth and Crisis*. New York: W.W. Norton & Company Inc.

Ferenczi, S. (1913) "Stages in the Development of the Sense of Reality", in J. Borossa (ed.), (1999) *Selected Writings of Sandor Ferenczi*. London: Penguin Books, 67–81.

Flügel, J.C. (1930) *The Psychology of Clothes*. London: Institute of Psychoanalysis & Hogarth Press.

Forrester, J. (1990) *The Seductions of Psychoanalysis: Freud, Lacan and Derrida*. Cambridge: Cambridge University Press.

Foucault, M. (1963) *Naissance de la Clinique (The Birth of the Clinic)*. Presses Universitaires de France. trans. A. Sheridan (1973). London & New York: Tavistock Publications Ltd.

Frankel, H. (1945) *Ovid: A Poet Between Two Worlds*. Berkeley, CA & Los Angeles, CA: University of California Press.

Freud, A. & Burlingham, D.T. (1943) *War and Children*. New York: Medical War Books.

Freud, S. (1901 [1905]) *Fragment of an Analysis of a Case of Hysteria*. SE, VII. London: Hogarth Press.

Freud, S. (1905) *Three Essays on the Theory of Sexuality*. SE, VII: 125–245. London: Hogarth Press.

Freud, S. (1908) *Creative Writers and Day-Dreaming*. SE, IX: 143–153. London: Hogarth Press.

Freud, S. (1911) *Formulation of the Two Principles of Mental Functioning. SE*, VII. London: Hogarth Press.

Freud, S. (1913) *Totem and Taboo. SE*, XIII: 1–161. London: Hogarth Press.

Freud, S. (1915) *The Unconscious. SE*, XIV: 161–215. London: Hogarth Press.

Freud, S. (1917) *Mourning and Melancholia. SE*, XIV: 239–258. London: Hogarth Press.

Freud, S. (1918) *Taboo of Virginity (Contributions to the Psychology of Love). SE*, XI: 191–208. London: Hogarth Press.

Freud, S. (1919) *The Uncanny. SE*, XVII: 219–256. London: Hogarth Press.

Freud, S. (1920) *Beyond the Pleasure Principle. SE*, XVIII: 7–64. London: Hogarth Press.

Freud, S. (1923) *The Ego and the Id. SE*, XIX: 3–66. London: Hogarth Press.

Freud, S. (1930) *Civilisations and Its Discontents. SE*, XXI: 59–145. London: Hogarth Press.

Freud, S. (1933) *New Introductory Lectures on Psychoanalysis. SE*, XXII: 3–182. London: Hogarth Press.

Freud, S. (1922 [1940]) *Medusa's Head. SE*, XVIII: 273–274. London: Hogarth Press.

Gallop, J. (1985) *Reading Lacan*. Ithaca, NY & London: Cornell University Press.

Guggenbühl-Craig, A. (1995) "Reality and Mythology of Sexual Child Abuse", *The Journal of Analytic Psychology*, 40(1): 63–75.

Hardie, P. (2002a) *Ovid's Poetics of Illusion*. Cambridge & New York: Cambridge University Press.

Hardie, P. (2002b) *The Cambridge Companion to Ovid*. New York & Cambridge: Cambridge University Press.

Hauke, C. (2000) *Jung and the Postmodern: The Interpretation of Realities*. East Sussex & New York: Routledge.

Haynal, A. (1994) "Introduction", in E. Brabant, E. Falzeder, & P. Giampieri-Deutsch (eds.), *The Correspondence of Sigmund Freud and Sandor Ferenczi, Vol. 1, 1908–1914*. trans. P.T. Hoffer. Cambridge, MA: Harvard University Press.

Heath, P. (2013) "Joan Riviere and the Masquerade", in V. Burgin, J. Donald & C. Kaplan (eds.), *Formations of Fantasy*. London: Methuen, 45–61.

Hersey, G.L. (2009) *Falling in Love with Statues: Artificial Humans from Pygmalion to the Present*. London: University of Chicago Press.

Hoffman, E.T.A. (1817) "The Sandman", in R.J. Hollingdale (ed.), (1982) *Tales of Hoffmann*. London & New York: Penguin Books, 85–125.

Homer, *The Odyssey*. trans. E.V. Rieu (1946). Harmondsworth: Penguin Books.

Horney, K. (1932) "The Dread of Women", in H. Kelman (ed.), (1973) *Feminine Psychology*. New York: W.W. Norton and Company, 133–146.

Huline-Dickens, S. (2005) "Becoming Anorexic: On Loss, Death and Identification and the Emergence of Anorexia Nervosa", *Psychoanalytic Psychotherapy*, 19(4): 310–329.

Jung, C.G. (1939 [1954]). "Psychological Commentary on the Tibetan Book of the Great Liberation", *CW* 11, paras. 759–830.

Isaacs, S. (1952) "The Nature and Function of Phantasy", in M. Klein, P. Heimann, S. Isaacs & J. Riviere (eds.), *Developments of Psychoanalysis*. London: Hogarth Press & The Institute of Psychoanalysis, 67–121.

Jentsch, E. (1906) "On the Psychology of the Uncanny", *Journal of the Theoretical Humanities*, 2(1): 7–16 (trans. A. Sellars [1995]).

Joseph, B. (1989) *Psychic Equilibrium and Psychic Change: Selected Papers of Betty Joseph*. ed. M. Feldman & E. Bott Spillius. London: Routledge.

Jung, C.G. (1951) "Aion: Researches into the Phenomenology of the Self", in G. Adler & R.F.C. Hull (eds.), *Collected Works*. Vol. 9ii. trans. (1969). Princeton, NJ: Princeton University Press.

Jung, C.G. (1963 [1983]) *Memories, Dreams and Reflections*. London: Flamingo/Fontana.

Kaplan, E.A. (1983) "Is the Gaze Male?" in A. Snitow, C. Standsell & S. Thompson (eds.), *Powers of Desire: The Politics of Sexuality*. New York: Monthly Review, 309–327.

Klauber, J. (1976) "Infrequently Described Elements of the Psychoanalytic Relationship and Their Therapeutic Implications", *Psyche (Stuttg.)*, 30(9): 813–826.

Lacan, (1959) *Écrits: A Selection*. trans. A. Sheridan (1977). New York: W.W. Norton & Company.

Langer, M. (1951) *Motherhood and Sexuality*. trans. N. Hollander (2000). New York: Other Press.

Laplanche, J. (1976) *Life and Death in Psychoanalysis*. trans. J. Mehlman. Baltimore, MD: Johns Hopkins University Press.

Leach, E. (1976) *Culture and Communication: The Logic by Which Symbols are Connected*. Cambridge: Cambridge University Press.

Lemoine-Luccioni, E. & Courrèges, A. (1983) *La Robe – Essai Psychoanalytique sur le Vêtement*. Paris: Le Seuil.

Levine, S. (2009) *Technique and Theory in the Therapeutic Relationship*. Plymouth: Jason Aronson.

Mahler, M.S. (1974) "Symbiosis and Individuation", *The Psychoanalytic Study of the Child*, 29(1): 89–106.

Masson, J.M. (ed. & trans.) (1985) *The Complete Letters of Sigmund Freud to Wilhelm Fliess, 1887–1904*. Cambridge, MA: Harvard University Press.

Mitchell, J. (1974) *Psychoanalysis and Feminism: A Radical Reassessment of Freudian Psychoanalysis*. New York: Pantheon.

Moi, T. (ed.), (1987) *French Feminist Thought: A Reader*. Oxford: Basil Blackwell.

Montrelay, M. (1978) "Inquiry into Femininity", *m/f*, 1(1): 83–101.

Mulvey, L. (1975) "Visual Pleasure and Narrative Cinema", *Screen*, 16(3): 6–18.

Neu, J. (ed.) (1991) *The Cambridge Companion to Freud*. Cambridge & New York: Cambridge University Press.

Nietzsche, F. (1885) *Thus Spoke Zarathustra (A Book for Everyone and No One)*. trans. R. J. Hollingdale (1974). Harmondsworth: Penguin Classics.

O'Shaughnessy, E. (1992) "Psychosis: Not Thinking in a Bizarre World", in R. Anderson (ed.), *Clinical Lectures on Klein and Bion*. London & New York: Tavistock, 89–101.

Ogden, T.H. (1984) "Instinct, Phantasy, and Psychological Deep Structure – A Reinterpretation of Aspects of the Work of Melanie Klein", *Contemporary Psychoanalysis*, 20: 500–525.

Ogden, T.H. (1999) *Subjects of Analysis*. Northvale, NJ: Jason Aronson Inc.

Ovid. *Amores*. trans. J. Alison (2014). Oxford: Oxford University Press.

Ovid. *Metamorphosis*. trans. A.D. Melville (1986). Oxford: Oxford University Press.

Ovid. *Metamorphosis*. trans. B. More (1922). Boston, MA: Cornhill Publishing Co.

Pacteau, F. (1994) *The Symptom of Beauty*. London: Reaktion Books Ltd.

Philips, A. (2002) *Equals*. London: Faber & Faber.

Plato. *Republic III*. trans. R. Waterfield (1993). Oxford & New York: Oxford University Press.

Quintilian. *The Institutio Oratoria of Quintilian in Four Volumes*. trans. H.E. Butler (1921). Cambridge, MA & London: Harvard University Press & William Heinemann Ltd.

Rank, O. (1924 [1952]) *The Trauma of Birth*. reprinted (2010). Mansfield Centre: Martino Publishing.

Rey, H. (1994) *Universals of Psychoanalysis in the Treatment of Psychotic and Borderline States – Factors of Space-Time and Language*. London: Free Association Books.

Reynolds, J. (1994) "Deconstructing Henry Higgins or Eliza as Derridean 'Text'", in B. F. Dukore (ed.), *1992 Shaw and The Last Hundred Years*, Vol 14. University Park, PA: Pennsylvania State University Press, 209–218.

Riviere, J. (1929) "Womanliness as a Masquerade", *International Journal of Psychoanalysis*, 10: 303–313.

Rose, J. (1986 [2005]) *Sexuality in the Field of Vision*. London & New York: Verso.

Salecl, R. (1998) "I Can't Love You Unless I Give You Up", in idem, *(Per)versions of Love and Hate*. London & New York: Verso.

Segal, L. (1996) "Freud and Feminism: A Century of Contradiction", *Feminism & Psychology*, 6(2): 290–297.

Sharrock, A. (1991) "Womanufacture", *Journal of Roman Studies*, 81: 36–49.

Shaw, G.B. (1916) *Pygmalion*. reprint, ed. D. H. Laurence (2003). London: Penguin Books.

Shaw, G.B. (1949) *Sixteen Self-Sketches*. London: Constable.

Shaw, B. (1965) *Collected Letters 1874–1897* ed. D.H. Laurence. London: Max Reinhardt.

Showalter, E. (1997) *Hystories: Hysterical Epidemics and Modern Culture*. New York: Columbia University Press.

Silver, A. (1982) *Bernard Shaw the Darker Side*. Stanford, CA: Stanford University Press.

Sontag, S. (1977) *On Photography*. London: Penguin Books.

Stern, D. (1985) *The Interpersonal World of the Infant*. New York: Basic Books.

Storr, A. (1988) *Solitude A Return to the Self*. New York: Ballantine Books.

Vesonder, T.G. (1977) "Eliza's Choice: Transformation Myth and the Ending of Pygmalion", in R. Weintraub (ed.), *Fabian Feminist – Bernard Shaw and Woman*. University Park, PA & London: Pennsylvania State University Press, 39–45.

Virgil. *The Aeneid*. reprint, ed. J. Griffin, trans. C. Day Lewis (1986). Oxford & New York: Oxford University Press.

Winckelmann, J.J. (1964) *History of Art of Antiquity*. trans. H. Mallgrave (1996). Los Angeles, CA: Getty Research Institute.

Winnicott, D.W. (1956 [1958]) "Primary Maternal Pre-Occupation", in idem, *Collected Papers: Through Paediatrics to Psycho-Analysis*. London: Tavistock, 300–306.

Winnicott, D.W. (1971) Playing & Reality. London: Psychology Press.

Winnicott, W.D. (1992) *Through Paediatrics to Psychoanalysis: Collected Papers*. London & New York: Routledge (originally published 1975 by Basic Books, New York).

Zipes, J. (1991) *Fairy Tales and the Art of Subversion – The Classical Genre for Children and the Process of Civilisation*. New York: Routledge.

Žižek, S. (1996) "'I Hear You with My Eyes', or 'The Invisible Master'", in R. Salecl & S. Žižek (eds.), *Gaze and Voice as Love Objects*. Durham, NC & London: Duke University Press, 90–126.

6 A bloody affair

The case of Emma Eckstein and Freud's Irma dream

An introduction by means of a Shavian textual transition

MRS HIGGINS: You certainly are a pretty pair of babies, playing with your live doll.

HIGGINS: Playing! The hardest job I ever tackled: make no mistake about that, mother. But you have no idea how frightfully interesting it is to take a human being and change her into a quite different human being by creating a new speech for her. It's filling up the deepest gulf that separates class from class and soul from soul.

PICKERING: Yes: It's enormously interesting. I assure you, Mrs Higgins, we take Eliza very seriously. Every week – every day almost – there is some new change. We keep records of every stage –dozens of gramophones disks and photographs –

HIGGINS: Yes, by George: it's the most absorbing experiment I ever tackled. She regularly fills our lives up: doesn't she, Pick?

PICKERING: We're always talking Eliza.

HIGGINS: Teaching Eliza.

PICKERING: Dressing Eliza.

MRS HIGGINS: What!

HIGGINS: Inventing new Elizas.
(Shaw, 1916, Act III, lines 179–187)

Twenty-one years earlier, in 1895, we similarly have two self-congratulatory collaborators, Sigmund Freud and Wilhelm Fliess, testing out, reviewing and revising techniques on *their* object of enquiry, Emma Eckstein. Theirs is a real-life case, the content of which is very much taken up with discerning truth from fiction, the illusionary from the real. Creating a tailor-made treatment for Eckstein, Freud and Fliess sought to cure Eckstein of menstrual irregularities and hysterical tendencies. Freud was testing out the effects of his "talking cure". Transformation, as it does in Shaw's work, takes place amidst a sea of wider social, cultural, philosophical, scientific and religious change, but the question of what was to become of Eckstein post–treatment was an oversight, just as it had been for Eliza Doolittle. Unlike Higgins, a stalwart practitioner of phonetics, Freud was at the start of his career as a psychoanalyst, young and inexperienced.

Psychoanalyst Ernest Jones, Freud's friend and biographer, writes of Freud's interest in the psychology of women, notably women like Eckstein who were of "a more intellectual and perhaps masculine cast" (Jones, 1955: 469). Emma is regarded as Freud's first patient in a "training analysis". She is sharp, challenging and bright. Emma's nephew, Albert Hirst, recalls in an interview with Dr Eissler how Freud relished his work with this beautiful, young woman, from a well-to-do family. Importantly, she at first seemed to be responding well to the treatment.

The end result though was a very different matter. Retrospectively, the treatment had failed dramatically and Emma was left psychically scarred and physically disfigured, with the left side of her face caved in.

When she first arrived at Freud's consulting room, the 27-year-old Eckstein presented with abdominal pain, and slight to moderate feelings of depression associated with menstrual discomfort and menstrual irregularity. Freud diagnosed dysmenorrhea and claimed it to be symptomatic of a nasal reflex neurosis, linked to masturbation. He consulted German laryngologist Dr Wilhelm Fliess, who performed a turbinectomy to treat the neurosis. Fliess unknowingly left surgical gauze in Eckstein's nose, which resulted in an infection. On 4 March 1895, Freud wrote to Fliess informing him that Emma had suffered a "massive haemorrhage" and that her condition was "still unsatisfactory". On 8 March 1895, he wrote again, this time reporting a near-fatal incident: A colleague, Dr Rosanes, is instructed to clean the area around Emma's bleeding nose: Freud writes that Rosanes

> removed some sticky blood clots and suddenly pulled at something like a thread, kept on pulling. Before either of us had time to think, at least half a meter of gauze had been removed from the cavity. The next moment came a flood of blood. The patient turned white, her eyes bulged, and she had no pulse. Immediately thereafter, however, he again packed the cavity with fresh iodoform gauze and the haemorrhage stopped. It lasted about half a minute, but this was enough to make the poor creature, whom by then we had lying flat, unrecognizable.
>
> (cited in Masson, 1985: 62–63)

Despite Freud admitting that Eckstein's nosebleed was near fatal, he puts all his energies into trying to exonerate himself and Fliess from the messy business of culpability. She is to blame for her own misfortune, after all: "She has always been a bleeder" (Freud, 1985 [Freud, 1985: 185–186]). Furthermore, she is a dangerous thing and a year after the event, Freud is convinced that Eckstein is delusional, recreating past traumas in present fictitious form. Her bleeding is an expression of wishes and thus "she is an agent of her own pathology" (Hartman, 2007: 24).

Freud goes to great lengths to exonerate Fliess of all responsibility, driven mainly by his need to renew his faith in Fliess, whom he refers to as

a magician. Fliess is in fact Freud's surgeon and so his life depends on him, quite literally. He had written on April 20, 1895:
Dearest Wilhelm,

> … I did of course immediately inform Rosanes of your recommendations concerning E … For me you remain the physician, the type of man into whose hands one confidently puts one's own life and that of one's family … With regard to my own ailment, I would like you to continue to be right … that the nose may have a large share in it and the heart a small one.

(cited in Masson, 1985: 125)

First thoughts

Although it seems implausible today, nasogenital medicine was de rigueur during Freud's time, having featured in many different cultural contexts for centuries beforehand. In Western medicine, the first recorded theory of naso-sexual medicine is Hippocratic. Hippocrates writes about the "hodos" or path that links the woman's nose and mouth with her genitals. At each end of the "hodos" is a "stormos" or mouth through which fluids including blood can leak out. Medicine can be administered through these paths, essential in curing many conditions, notably the wandering, displaced uterus that needs restoring to its natural place. In *Aphorisms V.28*, Hippocrates puts the ame-norrheic condition down to the wandering womb and suggests the best way to return menses is to return the uterus by enticing it back with sweet scents placed at each end of the "hodos". The theory evolved in that suppressed menses, causing a build-up of toxins, could cause hysteria if left too long. Circa 131 AD physicians such as Galen recommended sneezing the phlegm out of the nose to expel the corresponding uterine toxins, which would then restore a natural flow of blood around the uterine area. Galen observed that the link between hysteria and the retention of menses most likely affected widows and those who had to swap a life of sex and childbearing for one of celibacy. One case study was of a "long-time" widow whose hysteria was cured by the midwife applying medicine to the genital area "causing orgasm and the release of seed" (Mattern, 2008: 113).

The fashionable cure in the 1880s for dysmenorrhea and "menstrual mad-ness" was to remove the patient's ovaries. We know that many doctors in the second half of the nineteenth century believed that the way to cure hys-terical epilepsy and catalepsy was by removing the clitoris. Hysteria linked to habitual masturbation of girls was also commonly treated with "clitoris scarifi-cation or amputation" or "cauterization of the labia or of the entrance of the vagina" (Fleischmann, 1878: 49, trans. Bonomi, 2015).

The subject of masturbation became the focus of Eckstein's own work when she became a practicing psychoanalyst and she undisputedly regarded this bad habit as a hateful one. Many scholars agree that Freud went along with Fliess's plans to operate on Eckstein's turbinate bone (to create a larger opening of one of her sinuses) because, compared to an ovarectomy, this "must have appeared to Freud as innocuous" (Eissler, 1997: 1303 cited in Bonomi, 2015: 97).

By the time we get to Fliess's work around 1893, narogenital reflex theory is widely accepted in the fields of gynaecology and otolaryngology. Fliess was convinced that in terms of nasal and genital problems it worked both ways, in that whichever one was faulty it caused a fault-line in the other. Furthermore, there were two spots in the nose that correlated to the genital area. By working on the nose, he could cure the damaged "sex" of a woman. Nasal surgery was the operation of the day to cure dysmenorrhea. Working on a theory of periodicity Fliess wrote "the pathology of menstruation finds its reflection in birth: the same mechanisms and the same conditions that hold true for nasal dysmenorrhea also controls the pains of contraction" (Fliess, 1897: 19). Disturbances in the nose were linked to a faulty reproductive system and

> on the basis of the purported nasogenital link, Fliess went on to insist that Freud's category of the actual neurosis was frequently associated by virtue of its endogenous sexual origins, with the complicating systems of a nasal reflect neurosis. In clinical proof of this, Fliess cited, amongst other evidence, the phenomenon of visible swelling by the turbinate bone during menstruation, the occurrence of vicarious nose-bleeding during menstruation and pregnancy and the fact that cocaine application to the nose were capable of inducing accidental abortions.
>
> (Sulloway, 1992: 140)

Fliess and Freud are determined to overlay Eckstein's self-analysis with their own version of events. They behave in a way similar to Freud's mentor Charcot at the French hospital: "To many observers it was clear that the Salpêtrière was a carnival of unconscious suggestion and conscious simulation from which had emerged a 'hysteria' sui generis that was a product of one man's desire to classify run amok" (Shorter, 1992: 185). According to Charcot in his "Lectures on the Diseases of the Nervous System", that he delivered at the Salpêtrière in 1877, mental health was affected by the excitation of the vulva and clitoris. Eckstein fulfils many a doctor's stereotype of the hysterical patient who "will make the most of her dysmenorrhea as she will of any other gynaecological complaint" (Garrey et al., 1972: 117, cited in Laws, 1990: 169).

Freud hijacks Eckstein's analysis. It becomes more about him than her, just like the absent parent whose narcissism drives them to the forefront of the abandoned child's mind. He hinders and arrests the development of a healthy analysis, just as he wrote about mothers who hinder and arrest their daughter's sexual activity (Freud, 1915: 267). What develops is a web of secrecy and lies, part revealing and part hiding, with communication and dialogue between the three main players active and passive, moving and still. In this case, it is the unconscious that runs amok outwitting all of them and Eckstein is left in a very sorry state. But Freud won't even allow her that. Whilst in reality she is left with ghostly imprints of her former self, he implies that she has a witchlike potency, potentially ruinous to men. Influenced by sixteenth-century commentaries on witchcraft, Freud takes from these works the idea that witches are delusional, with even their stories deluding them (Swales, 1982). Their accounts of reality, like Eckstein's, should not be trusted for these women often "mistake the hallucinations of their fancy for truth" (Remy, 1585: 111).

Just as he couldn't take as truth the stories and events she retold to explain her condition, so too he manhandled the transference, overwhelmed and confused by the task of discerning conscious from unconscious narratives. In what he would describe in a letter to Fliess written on 21 September 1897 as grappling with a certain insight/discovery he retold in his *Interpretation of Dreams* (1900), "there are no indications of reality in the unconscious, so that one cannot distinguish between truth and fiction that is cathected with affect" (cited in Gay, 1995: 113).

And so emerged a new aetiology of hysteria, a condition spun out of the patient's fantasies of seduction. Eckstein was central to Freud relinquishing his seduction theory (which supported the patient's version of traumatic events as being real) in favour of a new line of enquiry that leads him to a place of uncertainty in that a patient's reality is always informed by the existence of a reality whose origins are from psychic fantasy life. All the meanwhile, Freud is also nurturing the Oedipus complex theory that becomes central to Freudian psychoanalysis. Essentially, this story of the male hero Oedipus supersedes stories and theories of female hysteria and the feminine.

In *An Autobiographical Study* (1925 [1963]), Freud reflects back to the technical errors made in his earlier work and regards them as near fatal. His first thought though is not necessarily for the patient but more for the future of psychoanalysis and his new theory of the mind:

> When I had pulled myself together, I was able to draw the right conclusions that from my discovery; namely, that the neurotic symptoms were not related directly to actual events but to wishful phantasies, that as far as the neurosis was concerned, psychical reality was of more importance that material reality. I do not believe even now that I forced the seduction-phantasies on my patients, that I "suggested" them. I had in fact stumbled for the first time upon the Oedipus complex which was later to assume such an overwhelming importance, but which I did not recognize as yet in its disguise of phantasy. Moreover, seduction during childhood retained a certain share, though a humbler one, in the aetiology of neuroses. But the seducers turned out as a rule to have been older children.
>
> (cited in Gay, 1995: 21)

Psychoanalytic orienteering through a patient's free associations, one of Freud's earliest speaking tools in the clinical work,[1] inevitably lead to uncharted territory, fraught and erratic, and not for the faint hearted. Indeed, Freud actually became faint on occasion with Emma, probably because his theoretical wanderings with Fliess were badly mapped out, causing all parties extreme physical and mental distress. Upon seeing Emma's haemorrhaging from her nose, Freud felt faint and he wrote afterwards that it was not the sight of her actual blood that overwhelmed him but the "storm of emotion" (Freud, 1925: 252).

His letters to Fliess show how he was flooded by thoughts and ideas based on multiple identities and narratives. Metaphorically, he was wandering through the woods of his own self-analysis whilst culling old theories and planting the seeds for new ones. In the early to mid-1890s, Freud was reassessing his formulations on hysteria that he had worked on with Joseph Breuer, developing a theory of psychic fantasy life and infantile sexuality, formulating the beginnings of the Oedipus complex and in the analytic encounter he was discovering the transference. Within the seas of change, "the storm of emotion", Fliess was proving to be an unreliable compass but one that Freud was having great difficulty giving up. Indeed, it was Eckstein who grounded Freud amidst the fragility of the whole disastrous episode. When he returned to the consulting room, having recovered from feeling sick at the sight of the blood, she declared "so this is the strong sex" (Freud to Fliess, 8 March 1895 [Freud, 1985]).

Irma's dream

Central to our understanding of this case is the examination of a dream that Freud had in 1895, five months after he finished "working" with Eckstein. The dream inaugurates Freud's methodology of dream interpretation that he goes on to present in his 1900 publication *The Interpretation of Dreams*. After his own 13 pages of self-analysis on Irma's dream, Freud writes in italics: *"After the work of interpretation has been completed, the dream reveals itself as a wish fulfilment"* (Freud, 1900 [1999]: 97). For the first time Freud was applying his technique of free association to each element of the manifest dream, making connections until a meaningful trend took shape. Furthermore, as Erik Erikson importantly explains, Freud as the dreamer

> in experimenting with traumatic reality, takes the outer world into the inner one, as the child takes it into his toy world. More deeply regressed and, of course, immobilized, the dreamer makes an autoplastic experiment of an alloplastic problem: his inner world and all the past contained in it becomes a laboratory for "wishful" rearrangements.
>
> (Erikson, 1954 cited in Schlein, 1995: 259)

Irma's dream has the residues of the bloody and traumatic reality of the Eckstein episode. Here is the dream in full, translated by Austrian-born American psychologist, Abraham Arden Brill (1874–1948).

Freud's Dream of 23–24 July 1895

> A great hall – many guests whom we are receiving – among them Irma, whom I immediately take aside, as though to answer her letter, to reproach her for not yet accepting the "solution." I say to her: "If you still have pains, it is really only your own fault." She answers: "If you only knew what pains I now have in the neck, stomach, and abdomen; I am drawn together." I am frightened and look at her. She looks pale and bloated; I think that after all I must be overlooking some organic affection. I take her to the window and look into her throat. She shows some resistance to this, like a woman who has a false set of teeth. I think anyway she does not need them. The mouth then really opens without difficulty and I find a large white spot to the right, and at another place I see extended grayish-white scabs attached to curious curling formations, which have obviously been formed like the turbinated bone – I quickly call Dr. M., who repeats the examination and confirms it. Dr. M.'s looks are altogether unusual; he is very pale, limps, and has no beard on his chin.. My friend Otto is now also standing next to her, and my friend Leopold percusses her small body and says: "She has some dulness on the left below," and also calls attention to an infiltrated portion of the skin on the left shoulder (something which I feel as he does, in spite of the dress).. M. says: "No doubt it is an infection, but it does not matter; dysentery will develop too, and the poison will be excreted.. We also have immediate knowledge of the origin of the infection. My friend Otto has recently given her an injection with a propyl preparation when she felt ill, propyls.. Propionic acid.. Trimethylamine (the formula of which I see printed before me in heavy type).. Such injections are not made so rashly.. Probably also the syringe was not clean.

Who was Irma?

Some commentators believe Irma to be Eckstein whilst others think it is the young widow Anna Lichteim who was the daughter of Freud's religious teacher Samuel Hammerschlag. She later became Anna Freud's godmother and was thought to be "one of Freud's favourite patients" (Gay, 2006: 83). Both women shared similar features in that they were diagnosed as suffering from hysteria, and were without a male companion; they were from the observant Jewish milieu, and their families were on friendly terms with Freud's.

We might also consider Irma to represent Freud himself. The throat material certainly links up with the throat and mouth cancer that gripped him. It was Fliess who was treating Freud at the time as well as treating Eckstein. So, as Freud witnessed Eckstein's health spiralling along a downward trajectory, he understandably became increasingly anxious about the patient/doctor relationship. Paranoia and panic fill both the dream and the treatment of Eckstein. As Schur observes:

here was a patient being treated by Freud for hysteria who did have an organic, largely "iatrogenic" illness; who had narrowly escaped death because a physician really had committed an error; whose pathology was located in the nasal cavity; whose case had confronted Freud with a number of emergencies requiring him urgently to call in several consultants, all of who had been helpless and confused; Emma's lesions had a foetid odor (propylamyl); Freud had had to look repeatedly into her nose and mouth.

(Schur, 1966)

Max Schur's quote was intended to be part of a complete edition of Freud's letters to Fliess that Schur was working on with Ernst Young. Schur was the author of "Some Additional 'Day Residues' of the Specimen Dream of Psychoanalysis" (1966), and in this paper many of the letters that Freud wrote about Eckstein were published for the first time. They had previously been censored in part by Anna Freud. Schur had acquired the letters from Marie Bonaparte. In a previously unpublished letter from Anna Freud to Ernest Jones, written 19 November 1953, Anna Freud writes: "Emma Eckstein was an early patient of my father's and there are many letters concerning her in the Fliess correspondence which we left out, since the story would be been incomplete and rather bewildering to the reader" (Masson, 1992: 55).

This letter was found by Masson in the Jones Archives, London Institute of Psychoanalysis. For Schur, what also links the Eckstein episode with the Irma Dream is Freud's relinquishing of his seduction theory in favour of the idea that fantasies lie at the heart of neurosis. He makes this analytic diversion in part to exonerate the incompetent male surgeon in favour of apportioning blame on to the female hysterical patient. Similarly in the Irma dream, the female patient, not the male doctors, is to blame for her misfortune. Schur concluded that the dream was a fulfilment of Freud's wish to exculpate Fliess and Freud of Emma's injuries. It was to serve as "a disclaimer that he had not been conscientious" (Schur, 1966 cited in Loewenstein et al., 1966: 70).

Freud was undeniably attached to Fliess. Shirley Nelson Garner interprets his regard as both homoerotic and homophobic. To lose Fliess at this time would send Freud into a state of "paranoia" that he later claimed he successfully avoided. In a letter to Ferenczi dated 6 October 1910, he wrote "A part of homosexual cathexis has been withdrawn and made use of to enlarge my own ego. I have succeeded where the paranoid fails" (Jones, 1955: 83).

Frank Hartman takes up the themes of self and co-dependency in his paper "A Reappraisal of the Emma Episode and the Specimen Dream" (1983). He links the treatment of Emma to early childhood memories Freud had of him as a 3-year-old boy, with his cousin John, teasing John's younger sister Pauline (Freud's letter 3 October 1897, Freud, 1985: 219). The two boys were both in love with Pauline and in stealing her flowers, fulfilled their wish to deflower her. Their tormenting treatment of her strengthened and reasserted their male bond. Hartman writes: "I speculate this is the importance of the Emma episode and the source of Freud's powerful affects. If so, we have understood, for the first time, the importance of the repetition of infantile conflict in the discovery of psychoanalysis" (Hartman, 1983: 559).

Prohibition

Hartman's paper also includes a draft from Freud to Fliess in which Freud speculates on how neurasthenia could be the outcome of either masturbation or "onanismus conjugalis – incomplete copulation in order to prevent conception" (Freud, Draft B 8 February 1893: 66–72 cited in Hartman, 1983: 578).

If we think about the backdrop to this draft, Jewish law prohibited men from masturbation, they were not allowed to touch their wives during certain times in the menstrual cycle and it was customary for husbands to abstain from having sex with their pregnant wife. Freud's wife was observant, coming from an orthodox family. Freud wished to renounce much of the Jewish customs. I am reminded here of the gauze accidentally left in Emma's nose. The link to the menstrual tampon is obvious along with the symbolism of repressing unclean thoughts. But we can think too of the piece of cloth that a Jewish woman inserts into her vagina once her bleeding has stopped during each menstrual cycle. For several days before she plans to visit the Mikvah, the gateway to purity, she checks to make sure there are absolutely no remnants of menstrual blood left over. This piece of cloth would pick them up. In Jewish tradition, she then visits the Mikvah and before immersing herself into this pool of rainwater she cleans her outer body. Upon leaving the site, she is available to resume marital, sexual relations with her husband. A bloodied white cloth or piece of gauze represents a woman unavailable for the intimacies of sex and the act of procreation. Thus, symbolically, Eckstein is rendered unavailable to either of the men thereby allowing for their duality to flourish undisturbed. The texts tell us that Freud was hopeful that Fliess's research into the menstrual cycle would offer a way in which coitus could take place without a contraceptive. At the time of the dream, Freud's wife Martha had become pregnant again. Anzieu (1975) suggests that Irma's open mouth represents the uterus of the mother and the dream is an expression of Freud's ambivalence about Martha's pregnancy and perhaps even an expression of his fantasies of abortion. So too, had she allowed him to perform cunnilingus, she would not have become pregnant. This is supported by the views of Erikson who wrote that the mouth opened wide represented the "woman's procreative inside which arouses horror and envy because it can produce new 'formations.' It is also the investigator's oral cavity, opened to medical inspection" (Erikson, 1954 cited in Schlein, 1995: 272).

The gynaecological investigation into Irma's mouth runs parallel to the analytic investigation that Freud was making, and the mouth might symbolise his entry into the realm of the unconscious, as yet a dark, hollow and unknown place. The foul-smelling solution in the dream and bleeding of Emma might be linked with trimethylamine, which is an organic compound that produces a strong "fishy" odour and can be linked with bacterial vaginitis. In other words, Eckstein and her menstrual issues were odious. If we consider this further, we can pick up Lotto's hypothesis that Freud was troubled by "the conflict between misogynistic thoughts and deeds and the guilt this generated as well as a reminder of those shameful parts of himself that he characterised as feminine, the passive castrated Jewish victim" (Lotto, 2001: 1310).

Castration

Healthy Jewish baby boys are circumcised when they are eight days old as part of a ritual service called the *bris milah*, meaning covenant of circumcision:

> Circumcision is such a basic element of Judaism that the child does not enter into account in his generation unless he is circumcised. Moreover the covenant of circumcision is considered as important as all the mitzvoth (commandments) in the Torah together.
>
> (Matzner–Bekerman, 1984: 44)

We know that Freud was traumatised when he witnessed his baby brother Julius's circumcision. Julius was always an unwell child and he died aged eight months old. Freud, who was jealous of his younger brother, was left with residues of guilt associated with his wishes that Julius disappear.

At the time of his writing, Freud would have been aware of some tribes amongst which the men would slit part of their penis to create a bloody discharge reminiscent of the physiological bloodletting of menstruation. Anthropologists recording this ritual bloodletting interpreted it as a way that men rid themselves of bad blood so as to be healthy like their women. Chris Knight explains how this might be if menstruating women are also seen as polluting. Knight writes that the philosophy underlying the male ritual of incising the penis came from the fact that women's menses made them powerful:

> The warriors who make sure to menstruate before setting out on a raid like the canoe-travellers and hunters who act likewise are cleansing themselves of the contamination which stems from an excess of marital life, performing artificially the spouse-repelling function which women perform with each menstrual flow.
>
> (Knight, 1985: 681)

Freud wanted to turn away from all of the trauma and conflict associated with bloodletting, passivity and female hysteria, so vividly bought to life by Eckstein, in search of a new theoretical realm in which a strong, male, active hero dominates the narrative; one with phallic potency. Freud turns to the story of Oedipus. This shift would also help Freud exorcise some of the ghosts of his past. One such ghostly impression left on Freud was the memory of him bathing in a pool of red bathwater when he was a young boy. It is believed that he was sharing the same water that his menstruating nanny had used. What impact would this have had on him? According to Daly, a deeply suppressed "hysterical amnesia" would be the long-lasting trauma for the male boy confronted by his mother's menstrual blood (Daly, 1943).

Not all psychoanalysts saw it this way, for example Groddeck

> believed he derived insight as a doctor from having bathed with his mother as a child when she was menstruating. He saw "the black and white, and the red", the pubic hair, the white skin, the red menstruation, and had no fear.
>
> (Shuttle & Redgrove, 1978: 259)

Shuttle and Redgrove also cite Jung as believing that the menstrual experience could be a transformative one in the minds of men. In *Wise Wounds* (1978), they write up one of Jung's dreams from his autobiography *Memories, Dreams and Reflections* (Jung, 1962). As a young boy of three or four, he dreams that he has discovered a rectangular chamber of hewn stone with an arched ceiling laying deep beneath a rectangular stone-lined hole in the ground. It was accessed by a stone stairway that he descends in fear:

> From the entrance across the flagstones runs a red carpet to a low platform on which is standing a rich gold throne "a real king's throne." There is perhaps a red cushion on the seat, but standing on that is something like a tree-trunk, huge, reaching almost to the ceiling, made of flesh with a rounded, faceless, hairless head. There is a single eye on the very top of the head unmovingly gazing upwards ... He is paralysed with terror. Then he hears from outside and above his mother's voice calling out: "Yes, just look at him. That is the man-eater!" He awakes sweating with terror, and for many nights after that is afraid to go to sleep.
>
> (Jung cited in Shuttle & Redgrove, 1978: 105–108)

For Jung this dream symbolised "the motif of cannibalism" and what he had seen was a "ritual phallus". Shuttle and Redgrove interpret Jung's dream journey as one in the womb where the phallic shape is the cervix of the womb, which during menstruation ejaculates blood like "a red carpet". They also suggest that the man-eater is in fact the woman and her menstrual bleed symbolises the moment when the potential for a baby to survive and grow is no more.

Many of Freud's dreams around the time of writing *The Interpretation of Dreams* were on hysterical impotency and castration fears. In Irma's dream, the solitary female patient, at the start of the dream, refuses the solution. She is replaced by a group of male doctors, pungent potions and a dirty, phallic-shaped syringe.

Cocaine

If we consider again that Irma represents Freud, we have a man alleviated of his ailments with a cocktail of drugs. So it is possible that this dream is about Freud's love and need of cocaine. We know that in 1884 Freud was enthusing about the curative powers of cocaine, which was prescribed in the treatment of morphine and alcohol addiction and was also used to alleviate stomach pains and indigestion:

> I have experienced personally how painful symptoms attendant upon large meals – viz., a feeling of pressure and fullness in the stomach, discomfort and a disinclination to work – disappear with eructation [i.e. burping] following small doses of cocaine (0.025–0.05g). Time and again I have brought such relief to my colleagues.
>
> (Freud, 1884 cited in Alexander & Shelton, 2014: 401)

By 1895, the time of the dream, Freud had stopped using the syringe and was instead applying "cocaine paste" into the nose. Four years earlier, he had witnessed the death of his friend Fleische-Marxow, addicted to injecting morphine and cocaine. Taken intra-nasally, cocaine can constrict blood flow to the septum causing a perforation to the nose. Perhaps upon seeing Eckstein's nasal damage, he questions the supposed wonder powder. Perhaps too he had even suggested to Eckstein that she take cocaine to alleviate her symptoms. He had written about a female patient whose use of the substance had caused "extensive necrosis of the nasal membrane" (Freud, 1900: 144).

Maybe the patient he was referring to was Eckstein? Did Eckstein's exposure to cocaine aggravate her symptoms? A report in 1997 "Cocaine's Effects on Neuroendocrine Systems: Clinical and Preclinical Studies" (Mello & Mendelson, 1997) concludes that whilst it is difficult to interpret the data because many of the participants in the study are polydrug users (opiates and alcohol misuse might also be associated with menstrual-cycle disorders such as amenorrhea and anovulation), it seems likely that cocaine disrupts the endocrine system, reproductive functions and the menstrual cycle in some women.

Irma's dream takes place in a large hall in which we can imagine a large, stomach-ingesting banquet prepared. The throat, stomach and abdomen pains experienced by Irma in this dream are an indication of Freud's own throat and stomach pains which are to be cured by the white lines of cocaine. Significantly on 24 January 1895, a few months before the dream, Freud writes to Fliess from Vienna:

> I must hurriedly write to you about something that greatly astonishes me; otherwise I would be truly ungrateful. In the last few days I have felt quite unbelievably well as though everything had been erased – a feeling which in spite of better times I have not known for ten months. Last time I wrote you, after a good period which immediately succeeded the

reaction, that a few viciously bad days had followed during which a cocainization of the left nostril had helped me to an amazing extent. I now continue my report. The next day I kept the nose under cocaine, which one should not really do; that is, I repeatedly painted it to prevent the renewed occurrence of swelling; during this time I discharged what in my experience is a copious amount of thick pus; and since then I have felt wonderful, as though there never had been anything wrong at all.

(cited in Masson, 1985: 106)

Freud continues to write to Fliess during this time on two key subjects, Eckstein's health and his own. As he reports Eckstein's demise to the point where a renewed haemorrhage nearly causes her to die, he also informs Fliess of his self-observations in relation to his dependency on cocaine. On 20 April 1895, following an improvement in Eckstein's case, Freud writes that in terms of his own health, cocaine, the wonder drug, has worked its magic easing him out of a "miserable attack". On 12 June 1895, Freud writes "I need a lot of cocaine."

One last note on cocaine: if Eckstein's hysteria was to be associated with masturbatory activity, a light dusting of cocaine might have been part of the cure. In those days, many people thought that cocaine when applied topically to a woman's vagina numbed the area and prevented masturbation (Grinspoon & Bakalar, 1976: 23–24). We could have witnessed a careful medical and analytic "touching" of the patient. What unfolded instead was a dangerous and intrusive method of treatment. Perhaps it was Freud and Fliess, mutually gratifying one another, whose excitation needed capping, not Eckstein's! Amidst the chaos and confusion, both external and internal in Freud's professional and personal life, the dream of Irma offers Freud a fortress of solitude and a space to reflect and to think whilst maintaining a semblance of being in possession of heroic, superman-esque powers for himself.

Per os

There is a certain sense of neurotic conflict related to masculine and feminine identities in this piece and so too a pull/push towards/against an "autarkic" state of mind (Chasseguet-Smirgel, 2005), one in which the system prioritises self-sufficiency whilst restricting any contact with neighbours. For me, Irma represents Freud and the move towards the dirty syringe is his wish, in part, to be in receipt of the penis in a pleasurable but guilt-ridden act of oral sex. Freud had this dream whilst his wife was pregnant, a conception that Freud openly bemoaned. Oral sex would dispose of the possibility of procreation. We know that discussions on the subject of oral sex came up during Freud's analysis of Dora in 1900. When Dora discusses the love affair between her father and Frau K., Dora declares that her father is impotent and Frau K. must be sexually gratifying him orally. As Freidman writes in his chapter "The Cigar":

This is Freud's eureka moment. When Dora has a coughing fit, she is acting out a sexual fantasy. Dora is imagining that it is she, not Frau K, who is giving "sexual gratification per os" (orally) to her father. This conclusion, Freud harrumphs, is "inevitable." Later, feminist analysts would raise the opposite possibility: that Dora's father was giving "sexual gratification per os" to Frau K., something that does not seem to have crossed Freud's phallo-centric mind at all. Rather, Freud is convinced that Dora's hatred for Frau K. is the hatred of a "jealous wife." Dora's cough and persistent hoarseness is a "hysterical conversion," symptoms of her repressed Oedipal desire to be penetrated by her father's penis. If not vaginally, orally.

(Friedman, 2001: 179)

Dora disagreed. In Freud's analytic excitement, failing to listen carefully to his patient, two became one. Dora cut the analytic chord and left. With the act of the analytic union only half-baked, partly consummated, Freud had no choice but to finish off the job himself. With a sort of masturbatory vigour and determination he writes prolifically about the case and it becomes one of his most famous and widely read. Significantly, oral sex can give a semblance of intimacy without either party having to be a servant to the continuation of the species. In the consulting room, oral engagement does not mean analyst and analysand will ever achieve true analytic intimacy. There are so many moving parts and those such patients are hardly ever truly reached. The analyst who thinks he has succeeded is misguided.

Hero/heroine

The reader's attention turns away from Irma to the gaggle of male doctors. The female symbols of the mouth and white patches are replaced with the phallic syringe which might be seen as unclean but might also be associated with bacteria or germs that are curative rather than deadly. Concurrently, whilst treating Eckstein, Freud renounces her and the seduction theory he's been working on in favour of Oedipus. As Martha Noel Evans describes:

at the centre of the seduction theory is a young girl seduced by the father; at the centre of the Oedipus Complex there is a young boy constructing erotic fantasies about his mother. In the new substitute theoretical formulation, then, the little boy takes the place of the victimized girl.

(Evans cited in Hunter, 1989: 80)

Eckstein is cast aside as a woman who is dangerous and who has only herself to blame for an ill-fated future. The future for Freud is in the masculine, which means he must render the "feminine" and his identification with Eckstein as impotent. That way he can alleviate his own fears of castration:

Maternal aggression, named but not explored in the concept of parental seduction, ceases to have meaning in the new Oedipal theory and slips to the margins of consideration. Eckstein's bleeding, deprived of its traumatic effect, is later reintegrated into the Oedipal paradigm through the concept of female castration, from which its author can safely dissociate himself by virtue of his aggressive masculinity.

(Sprengnether, 1990: 37)

Daniel Boyarin states, "The Oedipus Complex is Freud's family romance of escape from Jewish queerdom into gentile, phallic heterosexuality" (Boyarin in Geller, 2007: 27).

Hysteria is woman: Jew is woman (through her bloodline) and so Freud must forego his theories and his attendance on Emma and align himself with the masculine. Note too that at some point, he turns his attention to Jung, the Gentile, in front of whom he faints at a meeting in Munich, admitting homosexual feelings to be at the root of this turn.

Poet and literary critic Sprengnether, in her chapter "Freud, Fliess and Emma Eckstein" (1990), emphasises the castration fear but very usefully also suggests that in seeing Emma nearly bleed to death, Freud feared an identification with the victim of a sexual violation as analogous to being a woman, a subordinate. Sprengnether goes on to refer to Koestenbaum's interpretation of Freud's reaction to Emma's bleeding in terms of anxiety about anal penetration:

Blood results from male medical force: such blood would flow from Freud if Fliess fully influenced him, if their congress took place not merely in Freud's "lubricated temporal lobe" but in his anus. Male menstruation, in this context, seems a figure for the distressing anal bleeding that would have been the likely consequence of their intercourse – if we postulate the existence of a symbolic, anal hymen, broken upon first penetration.

(Koestenbaum, 1988 cited in Sprengnether, 1990: 31)

In support of this we have Faergeman who writes that "the chief organ of expression of the [male] fantasy of menstruation is usually the rectum" (Faergeman, 1955: 16).

White out

On 21 September 1897, Freud writes to Fliess announcing that he no longer believes in his theory of hysteria and neurosis, formatively built on the idea that seductions and traumas in childhood had actually taken place. He ends the letter with "A little story from my collection occurs to me: Rebecca, take off your gown, you are no longer a Kalle [bride]" (Freud 1897, quoted by Masson 1985: 108–109).

There is a double entendre in the use of the Yiddish word *Kalle* here in that it can mean bride or prostitute. In Jewish tradition, the groom wears

white on his wedding day, but Freud was psychically tied to Fliess and therefore Eckstein is both a bride and not a bride, left for half alive and half dead
;– a Myrrha of her day. During one session, she turns white, her eyes bul-
ging, her breath appearing as if it were to disappear. The white gauze, too,
that had up to this point intruded upon her nasal cavity to such an extent
that it swamped the area, was a deathly symbol of annihilation. Only through
bleeding is Emma released from the tension and signs of life emerge, but the
flow is so full of energy that it needs to be reined in so as not to kill her.
Equilibrium is a life-saver.

At this juncture, I would like to introduce the case study of "Belinda"
whose experiences were retold to me by her and her mother over a couple
of interviews in 2016. Thirteen years old, "Belinda" was referred to
a specialist eating disorders unit in the Child and Adolescent Mental Health
Services Department in a large UK NHS hospital. She was rapidly losing
weight, defiantly not eating, using her anorexic ideation to, in part, contain
marital disharmony and discord between her parents. The rows were loud
and intrusive in the shared family space. Belinda was trying to rescue her
parents by means of a diversion and a degree of friction was indeed dissem-
inated as they collectively pooled their resources into helping her. The
mother recalled how one afternoon she was sitting on her bed and her
daughter came in wearing her wedding dress and veil. Belinda asked her
mother if she looked pretty and she was told she looked beautiful. In fact
she looked like a dolly, like a mythical apparition "part ghost, part human
whose guts had not been totally ripped out". When the doorbell rang,
Belinda raced downstairs to open it for she knew it was her father. He
greeted her, trying not to look too alarmed, and he embraced her saying
she looked like a princess. The three of them regrouped in the parents'
bedroom and after a while, Belinda went off to her room to take the dress
and veil off. She had needed to internalise the parental couple as a creative
one and not a destructive one. Up until then she had a feeling of being
intruded upon and as Marilyn Lawrence suggests in her book *The Anorexic
Mind* (2008): "this fear of intrusion is linked with a very intrusive object in
the mind of the patient. I further suggest that this intrusive part is linked
with the patient's own intrusiveness, particularly with regard to the relationship between the parents" (Lawrence, 2008: 27). Belinda had to be seen in
the eyes of her parents as just a child, playing at being grown up. Her
mother remembers this scene as one that she reckons will haunt and inspire
her (pers. comm. 2016)

White, whether it be the wedding dress, or the "large white patch", den-
tures or spit referred to in Freud's dreams is an important symbol, for it can
represent an objectless world, perfect, pure and uncontaminated in quaran-
tine. The white wedding dress that Miss Havisham never takes off in Charles
Dickens's novel *Great Expectations* (1861) represents the internal world of
a woman for whom all life is annihilated, wiped out. Lawrence describes the
anorexic patient who talks of a "white out" as

a state of mind where the couple no longer exists. It is very significant that the state is white. It is felt by the anorexic to be "pure", "clean", and hence good. The murderous destructiveness that has been employed in order to bring about this state of affairs is entirely denied.

(Lawrence, 2008: 45)

Belinda's mother recalls discussing with her daughter how the wedding dress was grubby and grey, having been in a box for over twenty years. They discussed how it had potential – how a new underskirt could be made and sequins re-sewn whilst keeping the essence of the dress unchanged. The mother was aware that she was talking to Belinda about her daughter's (and to some degree her own) internal world and this conversation did mark the beginning of Belinda's turning her back on the eating disorder. The back of the wedding dress was backless, the side that awed the guests.

Post analysis

Fourteen years post treatment, Eckstein suffers a relapse which was perhaps caused by a Viennese architect, whom she loved, marrying another woman. Freud wrote that "she proved inaccessible to a further attempt at analysis" (Masson, 1992: 255–256) and according to Eckstein's nephew, Albert Hirst, there was a conflict between Eckstein and Freud. Hirst describes in an interview he gave to Dr. Eissler that "Dr Dora T." a female physician and friend of the family, called on Emma one day only to discover an abscess near her navel, which the doctor immediately drained. Dr T. claimed to have discovered the root of Emma's illness and cured it, dismissing Freud's theory that Emma was showing signs of an old neurosis revisiting on itself. Freud was furious and claimed the doctor's diagnosis to be "fake". Albert Hirst speculates that this provided Freud with the perfect opportunity to drop the case, to unburden himself once and for all of this sorry situation. Freud claimed unprofessional interference from a meddling doctor and excused himself from his duties. Hirst describes Eckstein as up and well for a short period of time before returning to her couch, surviving, unwell and as an invalid for several years thereafter.

We should bear in mind that Albert Hirst was also a patient of Freud and appears to have had a rather idealised transference towards his analyst and towards his aunt Emma. Perhaps he was redrawing the phantasy of his own idealised triangulation?[2] What seems sure is the fact that Freud was furious with Dr Dora Teleky whom he viewed as intrusive. This is in stark contrast to his advocacy of Fliess's reckless surgery on this same patient. His anger towards both Teleky and Eckstein is palpable. He projects his own incompetence and intrusiveness onto them. To survive this wrath is difficult for Emma, who I believe always hoped that Freud would one day come back for her. He never did, yet I can't help but think she knew this all along. I believe the dysmenorrhea was one way to communicate the schisms across the body-mind-psyche, the co-ordinates of which mapped out an internal disparity at having to trust the other whom she sensed (even "knew") would be untrustworthy. In so many cases of menstrual irregularities, there is an absent other, a confusion of tongues and/or blurred lines. I imagine that Freud was a disappointment to her and yet I think this was too difficult for her to gather up as a well-judged statement of fact, just as Myrrha could not accept that the blame and the guilt lay at the feet of her father. Adult male figures are absolved from blame. As Irigaray writes:

> It would be too risky to admit that the father might be a seducer, and even that he might want to have a daughter in order to seduce. Or that he might want to become an analyst in order – by means of hypnosis, suggestion, transfer and interpretations that deal with the sexual economy and with the forbidden, proscribed sexual representations – to achieve a lasting seduction of the hysterical woman.
>
> (Irigaray, 1974 cited in Gill, 1985: 38)

As early as 1899, Eckstein had written a paper called "An Important Question of Education" and in it she states:

> a child knows shame only slightly, or not at all, knows no sexual feelings of any kind, and so can only guess that there are other reasons, besides the desire to have children, that would fuel the desire to have sexual intercourse.

Eckstein ends the essay saying that adults "mate when they like each other, in fact, love each other so much that each of them wishes that their child will look like their partner" (Eckstein, 1899–1900: 666–669).

Jeffrey Masson, in his thorough account of the transcripts on Eckstein, links the above ideas to the wording in the minutes from a meeting of the Vienna Psychoanalytic Society on 12 May 1909 in which Freud is quoted as saying of children: "Enlightenment should above all make it clear to them that this is a matter of acts of tenderness, that their parents love each other very much" (Masson, 1992: 244).

It feels to me that Freud the analyst and Eckstein the analysand were like a couple whose relationship was in grave danger and whose union was not one of the love of enlightenment. They parted, the project aborted – symbolised by her severe bleeding. It is as if she sacrificed her own desire and longing for him to fulfil his. She displays parental love towards the young, novice analyst, something that he is unable to match. He is unable to contain her trauma; instead he introjects it, a burden upon his own process, thus proving himself to be ineffective and impotent. The motivation behind the introjection might actually have been caused by rivalrous feelings he had towards her and even the stuff of his own theory on infantile eroticism that emphasises the boy's desire for his mother. He turns this around – it is the girl who desires the penis, believing it will be given over to her by the mother. It is she who desires him. With regards to Emma:

> I shall be able to prove to you that you were right; that her episodes of bleeding were hysterical, were occasioned by longing [*Sensucht*], and probaby occurred at the sexually relevent times [*Sexualterminen*] (the woman, out of resistance has not yet supplied me with the dates).
>
> (Freud, 1896 cited in Bonomi, 2018: 46)

This letter he writes to Fliess 26 on April 1895, and follows it up again in May 1896:

> so far as I know she bled out of longing. She has always been a bleeder, when cutting herself and in similar circumstances; as a child she suffered from severe nosebleeds; during the years when she was not yet menstruating, she had headaches which were interpreted to her as malingering and which in truth had been generated by suggestion ... In the sanatorium, she became restless during the night because of an unconscious wish to entice me to go there... .
>
> (cited in Masson, 1985: 186)

Concluding commentary

> Emma's longing, her eager collaboration in her analysis gave Freud much precious material ... the wish theory of psychosis and dreams; the transferential reconstruction of her early pleasures in menstruation and its prehistory in her battles with her family; fantastic scenes from her inner life, in the no man's land between fantasy and memory, resonating with the sadistic acts and fantasies of an former historical epoch.
>
> (Appignanesi & Forrester, 2005: 137)

I regard Emma Eckstein as the stronger sex and her eventual bleeding created a release of psychic tension and enabled a progression towards recovery. In contrast, Fliess seems unable to do more that simply repress psychic flow and discharge by "unknowingly" leaving the tampon-like gauze in Emma's nose. This blocks the symbolic flow of the unconscious. But the dam was not well thought through in its design, not sufficiently analysed, made of the wrong material and thus buckles and breaks with disastrous consequences. A middle space, a temporary place of respite is provided by Rosanes who freezes the area. Emma bleeds, just as the woman losing a foetus from the womb bleeds. She exonerates Freud and Fliess of all future responsibility. This is a miscarriage ... a miscarriage of justice!

Perhaps Emma aborted the project because she felt the parental couple did not love each other enough to sustain the child; the parental couple being herself and Freud, or Freud and Fliess, and the child being her psychic health.

How Freud contains his own tension, anxiety and stress is via a dream – one of wish fulfilment in which the struggle between men and women, vagina versus penis is momentarily contained to provide the space for some relief and release with no accompanying creative, unwanted procreational burden. It is the best form of contraception. The dream is one of many things, whilst at the same time provides a space for further re-presentation of the Emma episode. Twelve years later after the dream, in 1908, Abraham writes to Freud

> I should like to know whether the interpretation of the paradigm dream in the Interpretation of Dreams is incomplete on purpose (Irma's Injection). I think the trimethylamin leads to the most important part, to sexual allusions, that become more distinct in the last lines.
> (Abraham & Freud 1908 in Falzeder, 1965 [2002]: 19)

Freud replies that in the paradigm dream:

> Sexual megalomania is hidden behind it, the three women Mathilde, Sophie and Anna are the three godmothers of my daughters, and I have them all! There would be one simple therapy for widowhood, of course. All sorts of intimate things, naturally.
> (Abraham & Freud 1908 in Falzeder, 1965 [2002]: 21)

Murray Lionel Wax suggests that Irma is a compound figure made up of different women with the overarching theme being pregnancy in women – Amalia Nathanson Freud (his mother), Anna Hammerschlag-Lichtheim, Martha Freud, Emma Eckstein ("with echoes of yet others"). Wax writes in "Who Are The Irmas? What Are Their Narratives?" (Wax, 1996 [1999]):

> What is peculiarly startling is not the revelation that Freud might have had erotic desires toward his patients, as well as toward women other than his spouse, and that these desires surfaced within a dream, but that he should here have recognized a dual level of meaning of the dream, while elsewhere contending that in interpreting a dream the analyst sought a single motivating wish.
> (Wax, 1996 [1999]: 78)

At that moment of discovering "the flesh one never sees" (Lacan, 1954–1955: 154), Freud is silenced: "This moment of extimacy (rendering what is profoundly intimate in an external representation), produces identification with anxiety, a revelation of human mutability and decay: 'You are this, which is the farthest away from you, which is the most formless'" (Lacan, 1978: 186; Bronfen, 1988: 73).

I think that Emma's body, her dysmenorrhea and her hysteria cleverly contravenes "the prototype of what Lacan named the 'real' i.e., what escapes

both the imaginary and the symbolic registers of meaning" (Bonomi, 2015:
90). She represents the place between the symbolic and the concrete. In
a transcendental state, above and beyond memory, reality and fantasy women
like Emma can prove that transference, notably transference love is indeed
"genuine" and "real" in that it is both concrete, symbolic and all that is in
between. These women are powerful in their vulnerability in that they rise
above the anxieties of mortal men and fear no death. I am highlighting here
that we are observing the evolution of a realm, a middle space as part of an
axis where several states can coexist inter-dependently. Importantly, I would
disagree with Masson (1992), Rush (1977) and others who have been firm in
their criticism of Freud, describing his renouncing of the seduction theory as
him entirely denying his patients the truth of their memories and recollec-
tions in favour of sexual desires and unconscious phantasies in childhood.
Instead, I would support the following:

> Surveying all of Freud's writing when researching their dictionary of psy-
> choanalysis, Laplanche & Pontalis, 1973 [1988]: 404–408) notice that
> even with his evolving framework of autonomous infantile sexuality,
> Freud "continued to assert the existence, prevalence and pathogenic
> forces of scenes of seduction actually experienced by children" ... Des-
> pite Freud's own conceptual uncertainties as he felt he must chose
> between trauma and desire, many other analysts would later suggest that
> there is no essential contradiction between attributing adult symptoms to
> a destructive mix of the two – "real" and fantasized events. Indeed,
> Laplanche (1989) has argued compellingly that all material experiences
> are immediately invested with, and continuously worked and re-worked
> through, psychic fantasy.
>
> (Segal, 1996: 293)

We have seen in earlier chapters case studies of amenorrheic women in analysis who have struggled to distinguish between the illusionary and the real,
struggling to find that all-important middle space. Like Eckstein and Freud
who are linked together through the themes of loyalty and betrayal, the
analysand with SA might wish to be the doll, the transitional object for her
analyst. This might find a resolution to the "either/or" paradigm. Pygmalion,
Higgins and Freud all blow the kiss of life into their "objects" and thus
wishes are transformed from conceptual, hypothetical ideas into a new realm
of reality that resides somewhere between the concrete and symbolic. The
life force of Galatea reconfirms that of Pygmalion, as Eliza's does for Higgins
and Eckstein's does for Freud. These women embody the desires of their
male "creators" and each of these men are in turn reinvented and rejuvenated
with a new lease of life through the mutuality of the project. The women
are the heroes who wake these men up from their slumber. With the gaining
of an identity for each of these women, there comes a process of alienation.
This is what is the most hazardous in the treatment of the amenorrheic

patient for whom transformation, identification and separation are treacherous concepts. The male analyst must not act in the amenorrheic defence against differentiation; and difference must not be disavowed through the integration of the female patient as phallic into the male analyst's narcissistic system.

Freud's understanding of narcissistic love for another as being perceived as subjectively part of the self meant Narcissus' reflection would disappear if he were to leave the pool. The female patient must not become incorporated into the analyst's own narcissism – otherwise what will become of her? An Echo or a Galatea who shows herself capable of malleability in the face of her imagined lover-creator? The only way out is when she finds her voice and when she starts to explore the blame and guilt that lie at the feet of "the father". Often though, these patients first leave and reflect later in self-imposed analytic exile. Wandering, these patients are displaced. They need rehoming. Post treatment, Eckstein worked for several years as a psychoanalyst, but for the last twenty years of her life she spent much of her days in bed rest. Finding it difficult to walk, she confined herself to her sofa: Perhaps the sofa represented the analyst's couch, which she laid upon forever waiting for her fate to be settled. Freud knew, as much as Eckstein did, that the ties between them were formed in such a way that the treatment could never be truly terminated. Freud became defensive, suggesting that the treatment failed because, like a witch who wants the devil, Eckstein was like a child who wished to be possessed by the father. His version of events meant that he and Fliess were mere puppets in her internal theatre of fantasy. But it seems to me that as Eckstein's nose bled, his, like Pinocchio's, grew. In time, Freud will have learnt that you cannot just savagely cut the strings of puppetry, nor discard or mutilate your doll (patient) when she becomes burdensome or when you feel you have outgrown her: Or else be burdened by one's own guilt.

The analyst must trust in and work towards something much deeper than the infatuation or indifference of common souls that the transference will employ defensively as decoys. If Emma did, as Freud believed, renew her bleeding "as an unfailing means of re-arousing my affections", why did he not interpret it in a way that would enable *her* to find meaning in it? Instead, he tries to render her mute and she, in part, absolves his guilt through her mute suffering. At the age of 59, she dies of a stroke. He writes, 13 years later, in "Analysis Terminable and Interminable"

> An analysis lasting three-quarters of a year removed the trouble and restored the patient … her right to a share in life … I cannot remember whether it was twelve or fourteen years after the end of her analysis that, owing to profuse haemorrhages, she was obliged to undergo a gynaecological examination. A myoma was found which made a complete hysterectomy advisable. From the time of this operation, the woman became ill once more. She fell in love with her surgeon, wallowed in masochistic phantasies about the fearful changes in her inside –

phantasies with which she concealed her romance – and proved inaccessible to a further attempt at analysis. She remained abnormal to the end of her life.

(Freud, 1937: 222)

Fascinatingly, Freud never mentions Emma's name in this passage or indeed in any of his publications. Only in Ernest Jones's *Life and Work* is Eckstein's name mentioned, and just once. Notably in another case, the case study of "Little Hans", Freud argues that in an analysis: "a thing which has not been understood inevitably reappears; like an unlaid ghost, it cannot rest until the mystery has been solved and the spell broken" (Freud, 1909, *SE*, X: 122). We cannot help but think of Emma when reading this quote and I would argue that Freud *was* bewitched by her beguiling beauty, her intelligence, her strength and her vulnerability. His experience with her haunted him as he struggled to make sense of the archaic and the new. Despite his determination to render her mute and give her no name (just as Galatea was mute and had no name – she is given one in later texts), and place her in the shadows of his writings they appear to me like two wandering Jews. But she is even more than that in that she represents the motherland. As a maternal object, she is there at his outset, at the place of conception, at the start of Freudian psychoanalysis, a place from which he journeys and relocates time and time again. She is also at the intersectional and she symbolises the transitional, the place of exile. Like Myrrha, she starts out with agency and vigour and later succumbs to a way of being, part alive, part dead, somehow surviving the whole sorry analytic experience, solitary. She is a reminder of his failings but she too is searching for her lost love object and, in this way, his unconscious identification with her torments him. Mistakenly, Freud's harshest critics inadvertently infantilise her, stripping her of the part she played in her participating, witnessing and recalling of events. Does she not in some complicated way collude in the cover-up, burdened by the sign of the times? Of course it is he, as the parental figure in the transference, who should have known better. Significantly though, whilst pitiless to her cause, he does not pity her. Instead, he returns to her over and over again subliminally in his writings. But as the author of the poem "Eishet Chayil" (A Woman of Valour – from Proverbs 31:10) rhetorically asks, "Who Can Find Her?" This poem is famous amongst Jews, sung around the dinner table each Shabbat to honour and thank women in the family. I imagine Freud would have known it well.

Notes

1 Lacan writes "You must start from the text, start by treating it, as Freud does and as he recommends, Holy Writ. The author, the scribe, is only the pen-pusher, and he comes second. The commentaries on the Scriptures were irremediably lost the day when people wanted to get at the psychology of Jeremiah, of Isaiah, of even Jesus Christ. (Similarly, when it comes to our patients, please give more

attention to the text than to the psychology of the author – the entire orientation of my teaching is that" (Lacan, 1954–1955 cited in Miller, 1991: 153).

2 See Lynn, D. (1997) "Sigmund Freud's Psychoanalysis of Albert Hirst", *Bulletin of the History of Medicine*, 71: 69–93.

Bibliography

Alexander, B.K. & Shelton, C.P. (2014) *A History of Psychology in Western Civilisation*. Cambridge: Cambridge University Press.

Anzieu, D. (1975) *L'Auto-analyse De Freud*. Paris: PUF.

Appignanesi, L & Forrester, J. (2005) *Freud's Women*. London: Orion Books Ltd.

Bonaparte, M., Freud, A. & Kris, E. (eds.) (1954) *The Origins of Psychoanalysis. Letters to Wilhelm Fliess, Drafts and Notes: 1887–1902*. trans. E. Mosbacher & J. Strachey. New York: Basic Books.

Bonomi, C. (2013) "Withstanding Trauma: The Significance of Emma Eckstein's Circumcision to Freud's Irma Dream", *Psychoanalytic Quarterly*, 82(3): 689–740.

Bonomi, C. (2015) *The Cut and the Building of Psychoanalysis Vol. 1 – Sigmund Freud and Emma Eckstein*. Hove & New York: Routledge.

Bonomi, C. (2018) *The Cut and the Building of Psychoanalysis: Volume II – Sigmund Freud and Sándor Ferenczi*. London & New York: Routledge.

Bonpart, M., Freud, A. & Kris, E. (eds.), (1950) *Aus Den Anfängen Der Psychoanalyse*. London: Imago.

Bronfen, E. (1988) *The Knotted Subject – Hysteria and Its Discontents*. Princeton, NJ & Chichester: Princeton University Press.

Chasseguet-Smirgel, J. (2005) *The Body and Mirror of the World*. London: Free Association Books.

Daly, C.D. (1943) "The Role of Menstruation in Human Phylogenesis and Ontogenesis", *International Journal of Psychoanalysis*, 24: 151–170.

Dickens, C. (1861). *Great Expectations*. 20th edition. London: Chapman and Hall.

Eckstein, E. (1899–1900) "'Eine Wichtige Erziehungsfrage' (An Important Question of Education)", *Die Neue Zeit, Revue Des Geistigen Und Öffentlichen Lebens*, 18: 666–669.

Erikson, E.H. (1954) "The Dream Specimen of Psychoanalysis", in S. Schlein (ed.), (1995) *Erik H. Erikson – A Way of Looking at Things: Selected Papers from 1930–1980*. New York & London: W.W. Norton Company Inc., 237–279.

Faergeman, P.M. (1955) "Fantasies of Menstruation in Men", *Psychoanalytic Quarterly*, 24(1): 1–19.

Falzeder, E. (ed.), (1965 [2002]) *The Complete Correspondence of Sigmund Freud and Karl Abraham 1907–1925 Completed Edition*. trans. C. Schwarzacher. London & New York: Karnac Books (2002).

Fliess, W. (1897) *Die Beziehungen Zwischen Nase Und Weiblichen Geschlechtsorganen (The Relations between the Nose and the Female Sex Organs)*. Leipzig & Vienna: Franz Deuticke.

Freud, S. (1900) *The Interpretation of Dreams*. trans. J. Crick (1999). Oxford & New York: Oxford University Press.

Freud, S. (1909) *Analysis of a Phobia in a Five Year-Old Boy*. SE, X: 5–149. London: Hogarth Press.

Freud, S. (1915) *Case of Paranoia Running Counter to the Psycho-Analytic Theory*. SE, XIV: 261–272. London: Hogarth Press.

Freud, S. (1925 [1963]). *An Autobiographical Study*. ed. J. Strachey. New York: W.W. Norton & Co.

Freud, S. (1925) *Some Psychical Consequences of the Anatomical Distinction between the Sexes. SE*, XIX: 248–258. London: Hogarth Press.

Freud, S. (1937) "Analysis Terminable and Interminable", *International Journal of Psychoanalysis*, 18: 373–405.

Freud, S. (1985) *The Complete Letters of Sigmund Freud to Wilhelm Fliess, 1887–1904*. ed. J.M. Masson. Cambridge, MA & London: The Belknap Press of Harvard University, 185–186.

Friedman, D.M. (2001) *A Mind of Its Own: A Cultural History of the Penis*. New York & London: The Free Press.

Garrey, M.M., Govan, A.D.T., Hodge, C.H. & Callander, R. (1972) *Gynaecology Illustrated*. Edinburgh, London & New York: Churchill Livingstone.

Gay, P. (1995) *The Freud Reader*. London: Vintage Books.

Gay, P. (2006) *Freud – A Life for Our Time, 2nd Edn*. New York & London: W.W. Norton & Company Ltd.

Geller, J. (2007) *On Freud's Jewish Body: Mitigating Circumcisions*. New York: Fordham University Press.

Graham, P. (1986) *Freud's Self Analysis*. London: Hogarth Press & The Institute of Psychoanalysis.

Grinspoon, L. & Bakalar, J.B. (1976) *Cocaine: A Drug and Its Social Evolution*. New York: Basic Books.

Hartman, F. (1983) "A Reappraisal of the Emma Episode and the Specimen Dream", *Journal of the American Psychoanalytic Association*, 31: 555–586.

Hartman, T. (2007) *Feminism Encounters Traditional Judaism – Resistance and Accommodation*. Lebanon, PA & Waltham, PA: Brandeis University Press.

Hunter, D. (ed.) (1989) *Seduction and Theory: Readings of Gender, Representation and Rhetoric*. Urbana, IL & Chicago, IL: University of Illinois Press.

Irigaray, L. (1974) *Speculum of the Other Woman*. trans. G.C. Gill. New York: Cornell University Press. 1985. Paris: Editions de Minuit.

Jones, E. (1955) *The Life and Work of Sigmund Freud Vol. II*. New York: Basic Books.

Jung, C.G. (1983 [1963]) *Memories, Dreams and Reflections*. London: Flamingo/Fontana.

Knight, C. (1985) "Menstruation as Medicine", *Social Sciences and Medicine*, 21(6): 671–683.

Koestenbaum, W. (1988) "Privileging the Anus: Anna O. And the Collaborative Origin of Psychoanalysis", *Genders*, 3: 57–81.

Lacan, J. (1954–1955) "The Ego in Freud's Theory and in the Technique of Psychoanalysis", in J.-A. Miller (ed.), *The Seminar of Jacques Lacan Book II*. trans. S. Tomaselli (1991). Cambridge & New York: Cambridge University Press.

Laplanche, J. (1989) *New Foundations of Psychoanalysis*. trans. D. Macey. Oxford: Blackwell.

Laplanche, J. & Pontalis, J.B. (1973 [1988]) *The Language of Psychoanalysis*. trans. D. Nicholson-Smith. London: Karnac Books.

Lawrence, M. (2008) *The Anorexic Mind*. London: Karnac Books.

Laws, S. (1990) *Issues of Blood: The Politics of Menstruation*. Hampshire & London: The Macmillan Press Ltd.

Loewenstein, R.M., Newman, L.M., Schur, M. & Solnit, A. (eds.) (1966) *Psychoanalysis – A General Psychology: Essays in Honor of Heinz Hartmann*. New York: International Universities Press.

Lotto, D. (2001) "Freud's Struggle with Misogyny: Homosexuality and Guilt in the Dream of Irma's Injection", *Journal of the American Psychoanalytic Association*, 49(4): 1289–1313.

Masson, J.M. (1985) *The Complete Letters of Sigmund Freud to Wilhelm Fliess 1887–1904*. Cambridge, MA & London: The Belknap Press of Harvard University Press.

Masson, J.M. (1992) *The Assault on Truth*. London: Fontana.

Mattern, S.P. (2008) *Galen and the Rhetoric of Healing*. Baltimore, MD: Johns Hopkins University Press.

Matzner-Bekerman, S. (1984) *The Jewish Child: Halakhic Perspectives*. New York: KTAV Publishing.

Mello, N.K. & Mendelson, J.H. (1997) "Cocaine's Effects on Neuroendocrine Systems: Clinical and Preclinical Studies", *Pharmacology Biochemistry and Behaviour*, 57(3): 571–599.

Nelson Garner, S. (1989) "Freud and Fliess: Homophobia and Seduction", in D. Hunter (ed.), *Seduction and Theory: Readings of Gender, Representation and Rhetoric*. Urbana, IL: University of Illinois Press, 86–109.

Noel Evans, M. (1989) "Hysteria and the Seduction Theory", in D. Hunter (ed.), *Seduction and Theory: Readings of Gender, Representation and Rhetoric*. Urbana, IL & Chicago, IL: University of Illinois Press, 73–85.

Rémy, N. (1585) *Daeonolatria*. Lyons.

Rush, F. (1977) "The Freudian Cover-Up", *Chrysalis*, 1: 31–45.

Schlein, S. (1995) *Erik H. Erikson – A Way of Looking at Things: Selected Papers from 1930–1980*. New York & London: W.W. Norton Company Inc.

Schur, M. (1966) "Some Additional "Day Residues" of the Specimen Dream of Psychoanalysis", in R.M. Loewenstein, L.M. Newman, M. Schur & A. Solnit (eds.), *Psychoanalysis – A General Psychology: Essays in Honor of Heinz Hartmann*. New York: International Universities Press, 45–85.

Segal, L. (1996) "Freud and Feminism: A Century of Contradiction", *Feminism & Psychology*, 6(2): 290–297.

Shaw, G.B. (1916) *Pygmalion*. reprint, ed. D.H. Laurence. London: Penguin Books Ltd. 2003.

Shorter, E. (1992) *From Paralysis to Fatigue: A History of Psychosomatic Illness in the Modern Era*. New York: The Free Press.

Shuttle, P. & Redgrove, P. (1978) *The Wise Wound: Menstruation And Everywoman*. London: Victor Gollancz Ltd.

Sprengnether, M. (1990) "Freud, Fliess and Emma Eckstein", in idem, *The Spectral Mother: Freud, Feminism & Psychoanalysis*. Ithaca, NY: Cornell University Press, 22–38.

Sulloway, F. (1992) *Freud, Biologist of the Mind: Beyond the Psychoanalytic Legend*. Cambridge, MA: Harvard University Press.

Swales, P.J. (1982) "A Fascination with Witches – Medieval Tales of Torture Altered the Course of Psychoanalysis", *The Sciences*, 22(8): 21–25.

Wax, M.L. (1996 [1999]) "Who are the Irmas? What are Their Narratives", in idem, *Western Rationality and the Angel of Dreams: Self, Psyche, Dreaming*. Lanham, MD & Oxford: Rowman & Littlefield Publishers Inc., 69–96.

7   Viewing a female condition through a psychoanalytic (male?) lens

My investigations into why women of menstruating age stop bleeding took me to all parts of the research globe – medical, anthropological, historical, literary, psychoanalytic, etc. – and yet all roads seemed to lead back to the same place: one where the paternal, the patriarchal, the third, the father (however you want to call it) are central to the narratives of many of these women. I came across the most concrete evidence that showed how absent, abusive, intrusive, neglectful, inappropriate male behaviour featured in the traumatic pasts of some women who went on to develop secondary amenorrhea. The cessation of menses acted as a dissociative state, containing a host of feelings and emotions that were repressed and securely embedded in this bodily vacuum. For others, its design was a safe house in a wider context of defeminisation. As written about in the earlier chapters of this book, amenorrhea is a far cry from a "no thing". Sometimes it signifies transcendence, wonder and other worldliness, and other times it represented sorcery, obscurity, strangeness and otherness. It can represent persecution and resistance. It can be a silent protest or a cry for help.

I have tried to present all of the associative narratives together in a coherent way. As my research progressed and took shape, it seemed to me that it was not a clear-cut case of amenorrhea representing what was lacking, passive, or negative. Far from it: indeed, the cessation of menses is courted by women who, rather than running away from the phallocentric model, run towards it, coveting the magic broomstick, the phallic symbol as part of a wider ideology on womanhood. It represents for them a symbol of potency – "I want what you have but I shall make it my own" is the idea. But what happens when menses returns? And what of my own unconscious? Has it penetrated my research so as to create an amenorrheic script that worked for me? These were the questions that needed addressing.

I had set out with the belief that harking back to the Golden Age of psychoanalysis we could show how forward-thinking the amenorrheic woman is. Classical psychoanalytic formulae incorporate the role of the father as being instrumental in separation-individuation. In the beginning with Freudian psychoanalysis, there is the unisex talk of the little girl who, in discovering that she does not have a penis, turns away from her deficient mother and advances towards the father. He has the very thing she wants and the very thing she envies in the masculine. Coming to terms with this lack dominates her journey into the feminine, her psyche having to manage the narcissistic wound of such a castration.

> At this juncture, the girl has attained heterosexuality, but she has yet to attain femininity proper. Until her penis envy is sublimated in the wish to have her father's child, until she embraces the reproductive consequences of vaginal sexuality, an excess of pre-Oedipal masculinity remains (Freud, 1966: 592). Ultimately a woman can obtain feminine gratification only by having a baby to replace the penis she is missing (Freud, 1966: 592: 1990: 312) … Thus, remarks Freud, the vestiges of penis envy never entirely disappear from women's psychic economy (Freud, 1966: 592–593). Women's 'enigmatic' bisexuality is never decisively overcome (Freud, 1966: 595; also see Young-Bruehl, 1990: 12–41).
>
> (Meyers, 1994: 67)

In her failed attempts to become pregnant, when fertilisation has not taken place, the woman is faced with the psychological trauma that comes with each failure to have a child. In each attempt to compensate for the original narcissistic wound, she is in turn castrated – menstruation is castration. Amenorrhea ingeniously overrides nature's pain in its ushering-in the cessation of menses. And in "knowing" that man fears menstruation, as a symbol of castration, the amenorrheic woman aligns herself with the brotherhood more so than with her procreating sisterhood. Man need not fear her. But she is more than his inferior double. After all, the cessation of menses could be seen as the castration of menses, by her own hand. She comes into being, she is her own woman, however the twists and turns of her journey might have played out, through the incorporation of the paternal. The reasons for this have been accounted for in the previous chapters, many of them have themes of trauma, neglect, loss, etc. threading through them. Amenorrhea surmounts these dreads and threats. Many of these women "know" that the acquisition of the phallus in some sense is paramount to their continued living. That she desired this is a complex matter. I find it helpful to think about the issue of desire in terms of the way it threads through the narratives on hysteria, of which the cessation of menses has been a notable feature. Useful in all of this is Lacan's "locating the question at the level of desire" (Lacan, 1966: 129).

In "The Engagement Between Psychoanalysis and Feminism" (1997), Muriel Dimen describes how a woman's desire embodies multiplicity of contradictory states and meanings, "present here and absent there, flaring here, doused there, flickering still elsewhere, its ambiguity, difficulty, and elusiveness the alternate truth of all, of anyone's desire" (Dimen, 1997: 543). I am reminded of the flitting and flirting, the teasing and the game of catch me if you can of the hysteric. What though is behind all of this? I think it's a game of catch me if you can, I'll tell you where I am hiding, don't take too long to find me. Find me! The analyst is required to seek. The father has assigned him this task. In the analytic arena of seduction and reciprocity, hysteria represents the castrating subject whose heart beats desire. She is a "never ending beginning ... She never wants to recover herself in opening, which, when repeated, surfaces like a gaping hole, a cry or a howl" (Webster, 2015).

In *Bonds of Love*, Jessica Benjamin writes of "the desire for recognition, which is an essential component of differentiation and autonomy" (1988: 126). Benjamin argues that a woman does not need the desire of a man to feel fulfilled and she can be the subject of her own desire. But I would ask, which woman truthfully chooses to be self-taught in all of this? As Eliza Doolittle explains to Higgins towards the end of *Pygmalion* "Every girl has a right to be loved" (Shaw, 1916 [2003]: 103). Surely, every child in this world is entitled to be loved?

For Freud and his contemporaries, the analyses of such women who appeared to desire the desire of the other were overwhelming. The first of Freud and his mentor Breuer's hysterics was "Anna O" (Bertha Pappenheim), whose symptoms advanced shortly after her father's untimely death. She was termed as having a "double conscience", which was a split between a "normal" and a "hallucinatory" ontological state. She imagined herself to be pregnant with Breuer's child. In a way, this represented her complete impotence of prediction and her outright omnipotence of thought. Many would come to use Anna O's case as a model of creative expression demonstrating a form of resistance to patriarchal repression. Juliet Mitchell often refers to the creative potential in hysteria, and Jessica Benjamin explains that "Not surprisingly, hysteria was among the first issues explored by feminist criticism, and the idea of the hysteric as an antecedent form of woman's protest against the constraints of the patriarchal family" (Benjamin, 1988: 3).

I wonder to what extent this presentation of hysteria as a protest against the laws of the Father, social and symbolic, masks more than it reveals. What is it that is too hard to bear witness to? The distress, the madness, the insanity that Anna O displayed? That she imagined she could only recover if Breuer did what she asked of him is sometimes too simple a concept for some to grasp. When needs are not met and the psychic conflict is unresolved, aggravated in the therapy even, the patient is, as Nanette Leroux declared, "done for!" All the praise is heaped on the patient for her capacity to sublimate and all the applause for an analysis that perpetuates psychoanalytic theory pales into insignificance if we think of the tragedy that is Anna O. Her wished-for longing in fantasy, not being met in reality, left her suspended in a middle realm, part alive, part dead: another real life Myrrha. Each appearance and disappearance of Breuer left a scar, a fault line in the topography of the patient's mind. In these instances, the analyst is caught between a rock and a hard place and as we know in Anna O's case, Breuer fled. I think we need to talk more truthfully about the reality of such cases and the fallout that comes from a failed analysis.

Understanding hysteria to the order of the unconscious was extremely valuable to Freud, especially as the disordered bodily symptoms could not be explained for in a physiological sense. So too with the any cases of amenorrhea and irregular bleeding for which organic explanations must give way to psychological ones, we have turned to the unconscious for help. But in Freud's early engagement with his patients, so much of the material was left un-interpreted. I think it fell into a gap (which is arguably where the more truthful aspects of the unconscious reside, as Freud said, with those slips and tics, etc.). If the symptoms of hysteria flutter between the psychological and the organic, secondary amenorrhea is at the point of intersection. It fills the gaps. Its presence is that of a black hole that fills the black hole.

What is it that is lacking? It seems to me that what is lacking is affirmation and recognition that every young girl is entitled to – what they did not get first time round from their "real father". What does a young girl do when she can't say for sure what their father is thinking or feeling? With no demonstration of a taking-up followed by a renunciation of longing, love, etc. between father and daughter in neither word nor action, there is no settling-in "period". As Andrew Samuels describes it, what is lacking is the place in which the girl can affirm her own "erotic viability" and make it her own. There is no "erotic playback" (Samuels, 2015: 82). I believed that this vacuum, this non-communicate realm, is one in which amenorrhea will occupy. With no experience of the stabilising other, there is a hole in the symbolic. Amenorrhea is the lack of the lack.

How does she fill this lack in her everyday life in our modern world? She can cleverly take herself out of the shadows of the mothering imagos of "normal" menstruating women and forge a new system for herself and become a mother in unconventional ways. With the revolutionary system of IVF, one can go it alone. But this is not the whole story. Repeated IVF can be an archetypal representation of a mourning ritual that fills an empty space. What is being renegotiated is the original maternal object and in many instances what is being sought after is the actual absent father and together the creation of an intra-psychic coupe is conceptualised as that which can fell an empty space (Barone-Chapman, 2007). How else can she acquire what she needs and incorporate it into her world? She might make a career in a male-dominated profession, or she might embrace a cultural or religious system that advocates traditional patriarchal views. She might turn into a carer, a parental figure and notably in the cases of looking after a sick father, she makes an attempt at self- and other reparation. She might clearly display a "lack" in the father in the way that she identifies herself in relation to gender, or she might contravene the ideas of feminine sexuality as defined by man (but as harried by women) by creating her own ideological framework in which the sanitised, defeminised body rejects an antiquated order. Whichever method chosen, there is in all of them an attempt at reincorporating the shadowy imprints of pain, trauma, loss in a way that the ghosts from the past no longer threaten continued living. She survives, even if she has to play dead.

And amenorrhea, as we have seen in the examples given throughout this book, has often come to represent that which is dead. And in this still life, something new can emerge. Man is afraid of death. He hunts it down. Amenorrhea can hold both the subject's sexual and aggressive drives. She need not project it onto the other like man does. Her unconscious reveals itself through the bodily state of amenorrhea (and if needed, to anorexia) to be unafraid of death. In fact, death becomes her. People understandably react. They think something needs fixing. Fertility must be sought, anorexics must be fed, menses must resume, the hysteric must be rewired. Both men and women make up the cavalry that's come to save her. But doe she want saving? What do these women want?

Freud asked this question in a letter to Marie Bonaparte in 1925, puzzled by woman's resistance to patriarchy. His investigative approach has ignited ceaseless furious debate with many feminists seeking to destroy the patriarchal gunpowder plots that they feel are so dangerous in the hands of trigger-happy men. Whilst Juliet Mitchell explains that "psychoanalysis is not a recommendation *for* a patriarchal society, but an analysis *of* one" (Mitchell, 1974: xiii),many of her feminist compatriots are less generous to Freud. Betty Friedan, Luce Irigaray, Nancy Chodorow, Simone de Beauvoir and Kate Millett amongst others have argued that Freudian psychoanalysis cements patriarchal ideology, constructing feminine sexuality and feminine psychology as passive, disavowing the active and aggressive life-and-death components in the feminine when it comes to matters of procreation, pregnancy and childbirth. This in turn makes a taboo of ambivalence in the feminine, notably maternal ambivalence. De Beauvoir argues against the position that a woman lacking autonomy and choice is at the mercy of masculine subjectivity (De Beauvoir, 1949. Irigaray exposes the erasure of the mother-daughter relationships and the maternal lineages formed along the life cycle of a woman (Irigaray, 1974).

I don't disagree with any of this. Patriarchy does enslave women and many of Freud's ideas, notably that there is only one masculine libido with no feminine one with "its original nature" (De Beauvoir, 1949: 39) is totally outdated. However, when it comes to thinking about the amenorrheic woman whose agency is entangled up with the principles of love and with the masculine ideal, Freudian early concepts on women, particularly in relation to the penis, are very helpful and relevant in our deciphering the meaning behind the amenorrheic narrative. What I have come to term "chase the penis" is concretely and symbolically part of the narrative in some cases – in which case it must be allowed for rather than rejected as subordinate, rudimentary thinking devoid of modern philosophical finesse. Does a girl want the penis? Yes, maybe she does. Is that ok? Yes, absolutely it is! Motivated to remain a child, I can own up to playing my own version of "It" at the age of six or seven. In the playground around the back of the synagogue, whilst the elders were inside praying, I would play "chase the penis". The way I would try to tag the boys and catch them was to touch their trousers in the "private parts". I can remember the perplexed expression on one particular boy's face, a pubertal Persian boy, a few years older and significantly taller than me. I remember he had facial hair. I didn't see the need for privacy. Consciously, this was an attempt at equality: it was in no way a clash of the genders. I turn to Karl Abraham's early paper, "Manifestations of the Female Complex" (1920), in which he presents his evidence to support the view that part of a woman's repressed wishes is that they be male. He includes a vignette of a 2-year-old girl for whom turning into her mother and her sisters, with their long hair and tall, slim figure, is fully acceptable to her but for whom the idea that there will be no penis in the package is far trickier. Abraham writes

> One day as her parents were taking coffee at the table, she went to a box of cigars that stood on a low cabinet near by, opened it, and took out a cigar and brought it to her father. Then she went back and brought one for her mother. Then she took a third cigar and held it in front of the lower part of her body. Her mother put the three cigars back in the box. The child waited a little while and then played the same game over again.
>
> (Abraham, 1920 cited in Strouse, 1974: 111–112)

Abraham continues:

> The fact of the repetition of this game excluded its being due to chance. Its meaning is clear: the child endowed her mother with a male organ like her father's. She represented the possession of the organ not as a privilege of men but of adults in general, and then she could expect to get one herself in the future. A cigar was not only a suitable symbol for her wish on account of its form. She had of course long noticed that only her father smoked cigars and not her mother. Her impulse to put man and woman on an equality is palpably expressed in presenting a cigar to her mother as well.
>
> (Abraham, 1920 cited in Strouse, 1974: 111–112)

In more modern terms we can say that we are not just talking about the actual anatomical differences per se but rather the symbolism of the distraction, how this symbolism develops in the child's mind and how this impacts on her development and her personality. Amenorrhea can often be located at the point of a schism in this process, often around the time of puberty. Freud wrote that part of the young girl's pubertal conflict entailed her attempts to keep her boyish nature which she had up until that point already possessed (Freud, 1914 SE XIV: 88–90).

With Freud in mind, in the role of researcher I asked my teenage daughters (both age 16 at the time) what they thought about penis envy. The youngest replied:

> I don't envy them having a penis but it seems more straight forward to me. Vaginas are complicated. If you just look at them, the actual "thing" itself is such a complicated thing. It can make a girl feel self-conscious about it. I guess it's easier being a man, the glass ceiling and all of that.
>
> (pers. comm. 2017)

I asked her sister, Sarah, the same question: "Boys don't have vaginas and girls do. No one loses out. I have never wanted a penis. Penis and vagina, man and woman – they need one another" (pers. comm. 2017).There are echoes of these statements in Naomi Wolf's 2012 biography *Vagina:*

> An essential paradox of the female condition is that for women to really be free, we have to understand the ways in which nature designed us to be attached to and dependent upon love, connection, intimacy, and the right kind of Eros in the hands of the right kind or man or woman. I believe we should respect the potential for "enslavement" to sexual love in women; to our place with Eros and love. Because only by making room for it, rather that suppressing or mocking it, can we strive to understand it. When a woman is engaged in this struggle with love and need, she is not "subject" to the person in question; she is actually engaged in a struggle with herself, to find a way to reclaim her autonomy, while somehow not shutting herself off from the part of herself that was awakened by the beloved in the longing for connection. A woman struggling with attachment and loss of self is engaged in a struggle for the self as demanding and rigorous as that of any man on any quest narrative. Of course the biological responses I am talking about here have long been identified in psychoanalysis and in literature; only recently has science added new dimensions to and explanations of these mind states elucidated by poets, novelists and students of the psyche.
>
> (Wolf, 2012: 96–97)

As women we don't need to be on the attack nor do we need to play the role of "the everlasting wounded one" (Michelet, 1858 cited in Bonaparte, 1934). Amenorrhea transcends all of this, as the analyses have shown, with the parthenogenetic phantasy of that they can be male and female, mother and father, producing the child alone. Secondary amenorrhea is a woman's attempt to take the masculine and the feminine position: a hybrid. If hysterics idealise the parents as asexual beings (Bollas, 2000: 38), then amenorrhea embodies the ultimate asexual being. I don't think it is submissive of her to seek her autonomy and freedom through her incorporating the father into this image. I think she creatively unites the masculine/feminine pair in a way that allows for her own individuality to emerge out of the process of individuation. She doesn't do it like any other woman; her needs (like theirs) are different and her strategy allows for her coming into being, despite the obstacles she must negotiate along the way. If the real, actual father was lacking, she has found its representation and incorporated it into her own self, with it becoming her own symbol of virility. She is neither wholly passive nor deterministically active, neither submissive nor hostile, neither totally exclusive nor inclusive, inside/outside. She is ahead of her time and whereas the "social processing of biological givens" (Kovel, 1974: 139) is changing, the amenorrheic image has reassuringly been consistent as a powerful tour de force. But this thesis has attempted to not stereotype her as solely aligned to the scripts of Medusa, Lady Macbeth and transcendental beings alone. She can be young, naïve, ripe, curious, lonely, alone and vulnerable, just like the hysteric who Bollas describes as "impishly undermining the ostensible effect of the biological maturation of the self" (Bollas, 2000: 162). If a motivation of some amenorrheics like the hysteric is to remain in a place that avoids maturation and development, standing and waiting and deliberating and then standing and waiting and deliberating some more, then the more it persists the more one has time to craft this dissociative space and then fill it with an "imaginary figure of desire which can serve as a play object for both" (Bollas, 2000: 55).

In one of my last analytic sessions, I recall telling my analyst that in a dream I was at the altar waiting for him to appear and walk down the aisle. Only afterwards did I realise that I had repositioned the genders. Whose story was this? Whose analysis was this? I had changed the Law and now the Law of the "Other" was my Law. But where was he? Good job I left this analyst or I would still be standing at that bloody altar, waiting! As I had described in the earlier chapter on metamorphosis in Shaw's *Pygmalion*, the months after leaving I would often look in the mirror and when I saw my face it appeared to be transforming into a man's face. I was somehow reclaiming and reincorporating the animus back into myself. I was starting over again, and my realignment depended on the masculine – I was to be not the victim of this analysis but the hero, albeit fallen. I was able to eventually give up the ghost and start to replace all that I felt he had stolen from me. I learnt a lot from his mistakes and making sure I never make the same mistakes he did, I have become a much better practitioner than him. I have out-grown him. I have left him behind. No longer melancholic, I have fared well through the mourning process, supported by those analysts who agreed to meet me at significant checkpoints and supported by the commitment of those I love and those who allow themselves to love me.

My amenorrheic years had gone and my menses had returned and onward I marched.

I have written several times about how the return of menses can very often lead to a breakdown in the patient and in the treatment. The grip goes. Freud understood the consequences of this. Around the time of him writing to Ferenczi developing the rules of non partisanship and neutrality on the part of the analyst and eventually underscoring abstinance as a key principle, Freud reflects in his paper "Observations on Transference Love":

> I have already let it be understood that the analytic technique requires of the physician that he should deny to the patient who is craving for love the satisfaction she demands … the patient's need and longing should be allowed to persist in her, in order that they may serve as forces impelling her to do work and make changes, and that we must beware of appeasing those forces by means of surrogates.
>
> (Freud, 1915: 165)

Often it is the case that the analyst finds this too hard to tolerate. Ferenczi for sure buckled under the pressure to heal and assist and rescue the patient, thus acting in. In a letter dated 20 December 1917, Ferenczi wrote that he "gave way to a kiss" with a depressed "very beautiful" woman (Brabant & Falzeder, 1996: xl.) He relates this to a love he felt for his patient Elma which he wrote to Freud about in 1911.A heightened and intolerable shared sense of frustration is illustrated in Freud's early work on hysteria, which uncovered a most enigmatic relationship with both the internalised paternal figure and the externally wished-for father. One way this played out is described by Fink: "In addressing the master, the hysteric demands that he or she produce knowledge, and then goes on to disprove his or her theories" (Fink, 1995: 134). Similarly, "The paradox of the hysteric's desire is that she wants to have a master, the Other, that she herself can control" (Salecl, in Salecl & Žižek, 1996: 186).

Analyst and patient can get stuck in a loop of analytic enquiry with the essence of the relationship being like one of cat and mouse, Tom and Jerry. This can only continue if they have one another. As Salecl says, "The hysteric always deals with the question: 'What will happen to him if he loses me?'" (Salecl, in Salecl & Žižek, 1996: 186).

In all of this madness and mayhem, the amenorrhea signified the lighthouse, steadfast in the seas of change. Patriarchal, phallic symbols matter. In creating a patriarchal social order of their own, patient and analyst appear to be in a relationship but paradoxically this is only achieved through sacrificing the relationship. As Carol Gilligan reads it (1997), the woman searches for the status quo and in doing so overrides conflict by developing hysteria. She becomes anomalous and autonomous, a non-conformist (her lack of menses a present symbol in all of this), yet she is firmly ensconced in the patriarchal establishment.

Many of Freud's female, hysterical patients had been sent by their fathers for treatment. In trying to dissipate the patriarchal mess with which these patients had arrived at his door, Freud overlaid their treatment with another patriarchal system of his own, where his male-centric interpretations mounted their free associations. Irigaray suggests that in describing feminine sexuality, Freud overlooked the fact that each of these women had their own "specificity" (Irigaray, 1974: 69). As we know in psychoanalysis, the words of the patient are determined not just by her own motivations but by what is created and formed between patient and analyst in their "microsociety" (Modell, 1994: 47). Whilst the transference is both "a repeatable occurrence and a unique happening ... [it] is also a uniquely new creation that reflects the patient's response to the personality and technique of the analyst" (Modell, 1994: 48). This is important, as the unconscious pull from the patient for control, resolve, order, fight, etc. (all those virtues so often attributed to man) can knock the analyst off his perch. What results, in Freud's case, is that "The stubborn, independent, unsuggestible hysterics who resisted Freud and were his teachers will give way to 'Freud's women'" (Gilligan, 1997: 156).

It is hoped that this book has, for the reader, located amenorrhea and menstrual irregularities, at the point where things ordinarily give way, at the point of transformation. Within the presentation and symbolisation of menstruation, the amenorrheic form is like the chrysalis that represents the link to the past, present and the future. In many cases, in the past, something has gone wrong and rather than it being verbalised it has been somatised, freeze-framed and drawn onto/into the body. Analysis can be the place for thawing out and it can enable the successful transformative process contained within its own chrysalis. This is precarious. The setting is vital. And indeed in the analysis of all things caught up in menstrual matters, the patient must not be pinned down, studied like a dead butterfly, enamoured by its collector. Beyond the symptoms presented, beyond the images drawn, the stories bound, the dreams told and the conversations had, there are feelings that the analyst must seek to catch, born on the wings of those "butterfly thoughts" (Milner, 1950).

All that is beyond the spoken word – the cry, the call and all that can be transmitted without words resides in the stillness and the peace that is signified by secondary amenorrhea, the silent witness. And yet at the same time, it is hoped that having digested all of the words written in this book, the reader when thinking about amenorrhea need not reach for a single one.

Bibliography

Abelin, E. (1971) "The Role of the Father in the Separation-Individuation Process", in J. McDevitt & C. Settlage (eds.), *Separation-Individuation: Essays in Honour of Margaret S. Mahler*. New York: International Universities Press, 229–252.

Abraham, K. (1920) "Manifestations of the Female Castration Complex", *International Journal of Psychoanalysis*, 3: 1–39 (reprinted in K. Abraham (1927) *Selected Papers of Karl Abraham*, trans. D. Bryan & A. Strachey. London: Hogarth Press and the Institute of Psychoanalysis: 338-369).

Barone-Chapman, M. (2007) "The Hunger to Fill an Empty Space: An Investigation of Primordial Affects and Meaning-Making in the Drive to Conceive through Repeated Use of ART", *Journal of Analytic Psychology*, 52: 479–501.

Benjamin, J. (1988) *Bonds of Love: Psychoanalysis, Feminism and the Problem of Domination*. London: Virago.

Bollas, C. (2000) *Hysteria*. London: Routledge.

Bonaparte, M. (1934) "Passivity, Masochism and Femininity", *International Journal of Psychoanalysis*, 16(3): 325–333.

Brabant, E. & Falzeder, E.Â. (eds.). (1996) *The Correspondence of Sigmund Freud and Sandor Ferenczi*, Vol. 2. 1914–1919. trans. Peter T Hoffer. Cambridge, MA: Harvard University Press.

De Beauvoir, S. (1949) *Le Deuxième Sexe, 2 Vols.* trans. H.M. Parshley (1952) *The Second Sex*. New York: Knopf. Paris: Gallimard.

Dimen, M. (1997) "The Engagement between Psychoanalysis and Feminism", *Contemporary Psychoanalysis*, 33: 527–548.

Fink, B. (1995) *The Lacanian Subject: Between Language and Jouissance*. Princeton, NJ: Princeton University Press.

Freud, S. (1914) *On Narcissism: An Introduction. SE*, XIV. London: Hogarth Press.

Freud, S. (1915). *Observations on Transference-Love. SE*, XII: 157–171. London: Hogarth Press.

Gilligan, C. (1997) "Remembering Iphigenia: Voice, Resonance and the Talking Cure", in E.R. Shapiro (ed.), *The Inner World in the Outer World: Psychoanalytic Perspectives*. New Haven & London: Yale University Press, 143–168.

Irigaray, L. (1974) *Speculum of the Other Woman*. trans. G.C. Gill. (1985) New York: Cornell University Press. Paris: Editions de Minuit.

Kovel, J. (1974) "The Castration Complex Reconsidered", in J. Strouse (ed.), *Women & Analysis – Dialogues on Psychoanalytic Views of Femininity*. New York: Viking Press.

Lacan, J. (1966) *Écrits*. Paris: Éditions du Seuil.

Meyers, D.T. (1994) *Subjection and Subjectivity – Psychoanalytic Feminism and Moral Philosophy*. New York & London: Routledge.

Milner, M. (1950) *On Not Being Able to Paint*. London: Heinemann Educational Books Ltd.

Mitchell, J. (1974) *Psychoanalysis and Feminism – A Radical Reassessment of Freudian Psychoanalysis*. London: Allen Lane.

Modell, A.A. (1994) "The Private Self and Relational Theory", in E.R. Shapiro (ed.), *The Inner World in the Outer World*. New Haven, CT & London: Yale University Press.

Salecl, R. & Žižek, S. (1996) *Gaze and Voice as Love Objects*. Durham, NC & London: Duke University Press.

Samuels, A. (2015) *Passions, Persons, Psychotherapy, Politics*. London & New York: Routledge.

Strouse, J. (1974) *Women and Analysis – Dialogues on Psychoanalytic Views of Femininity*. New York: Viking Press.

Webster, J. (2015) "Being Again: Hysteria as Forgetting, Repetition and Atonement", *European Journal of Psychoanalysis*. online.

Wolf, N. (2012) *Vagina – A New Biography*. London: Virago Press.

Index

234   *Index*

For Product Safety Concerns and Information please contact our EU
representative GPSR@taylorandfrancis.com
Taylor & Francis Verlag GmbH, Kaufingerstraße 24, 80331 München, Germany